Freedom for Capital, Not People

Matthias Schmelzer is an economic historian based in Berlin. He is the author of the award-winning *The Hegemony of Growth* and co-author of *The Future Is Degrowth*.

Freedom for Capital, Not People

The Mont Pèlerin Society and the Origins of the Neoliberal Monetary Order

Matthias Schmelzer

Translated by Joshua Rahtz

VERSO
London • New York

The translation of this book was supported by the
History & Political Economy Project.

This English-language edition first published by Verso 2025
Translation © Joshua Rahtz 2025
First published as *Freiheit für Wechselkurse und Kapital. Die Ursprünge neoliberaler Währungspolitik und die Mont Pèlerin Society*
© Metropolis Verlag 2010

The manufacturer's authorized representative in the EU for product safety (GPSR) is LOGOS EUROPE, 9 rue Nicolas Poussin, 17000, La Rochelle, France contact@logoseurope.eu

All rights reserved

The moral rights of the author and translator have been asserted

1 3 5 7 9 10 8 6 4 2

Verso
UK: 6 Meard Street, London W1F 0EG
US: 207 East 32nd Street, New York, NY 10016
versobooks.com

Verso is the imprint of New Left Books

ISBN-13: 978-1-80429-374-4
ISBN-13: 978-1-80429-375-1 (UK EBK)
ISBN-13: 978-1-80429-376-8 (US EBK)

British Library Cataloguing in Publication Data
A catalogue record for this book is available from the British Library

Library of Congress Cataloging-in-Publication Data
A catalog record for this book is available from the Library of Congress

Typeset in Minion by Hewer Text UK Ltd, Edinburgh
Printed and bound by CPI Group (UK) Ltd, Croydon CR0 4YY

Contents

Preface to the English Edition	vii
Foreword to the 2010 German Edition | Dieter Plehwe	xvii
Acknowledgements	xix
List of Abbreviations	xxi
Introduction	1
1. Contexts of Neoliberal Monetary Policy: The Mont Pèlerin Society and Bretton Woods	14
2. The Origins of Neoliberal Monetary Theory: Internal Debates at the Mont Pèlerin Society Conferences	38
3. Freedom Fighters in Action: The Hegemonisation of Flexible Exchange Rate Theory in the 1960s	97
Conclusion	153
Appendix	161
Biographical Glossary of Important Members of the Mont Pèlerin Society	167
Index	175

Preface to the English Edition

'Make love, not leverage', 'eat the bankers', 'capitalism isn't working'. These were among slogans echoed by protesters at the April 2009 G20 summit in London. With thousands participating in the demonstrations, clashes with the police that left one protestor dead, a thousand-person-strong climate camp opposing carbon trading at Bishopsgate and a Royal Bank of Scotland branch looted, this was one of the most confrontational gatherings in the global wave of unrest sparked by the financial crisis. On 15 September 2008, the financial giant Lehman Brothers had filed for bankruptcy, $613 billion in debt due to overleveraged subprime mortgages, causing the deepest crisis in the global financial system since the Great Depression of the 1930s. The bubble, puffed up by shady Ponzi instruments with obscure names such as credit default swaps (CDS), collateralised debt obligations (CDOs) and mortgage-backed securities (MBS) in reaction to a crisis of capitalist overaccumulation, had finally burst. Millions of people lost their homes, their jobs and their livelihoods, while banks and their assets, deemed 'systemically relevant', were largely bailed out by states and their central banks, shifting the costs onto taxpayers. In the streets, however, many indicated that they would refuse to pay for the crisis detonated by the banks.

Such was the context in which this book was written and first published in German, in 2010. It tries to grasp some of the deeper historical causes of the 2008 crisis, by focusing on the social form money takes and the role of organised neoliberals in transforming the financial order. The book analyses the origins of the contemporary deregulated financial system, driven as it is by speculation, hot money flows, and financialised hyper-globalisation – in other words, the very order that brought the global economy to the brink of collapse. This system – of flexible exchange rates and free capital flows – replaced the relatively stable monetary system of Bretton Woods, which presided over the first two decades after the Second World War. From the Great Depression until well into the 1960s, most economists and policymakers saw free markets for international capital and currency flows as far too destabilising for a robust and well-functioning capitalism. But those neoliberals within and around the Mont Pèlerin Society (MPS) disagreed, and the Bretton Woods order of fixed but adjustable exchange rates and strict capital controls was a major irritant to them. In their eyes, capital and exchange controls counted among the gravest threats not only to the market system but to Western civilisation itself. Zooming in on the debates and activities of this network, I argue that neoliberals deliberately sought to unleash capital against democracy. They set out to use financial deregulation and capital flows to discipline, limit and ultimately frustrate all forms of democratic decision-making at odds with the requirements of markets and profits.

When I wrote *Freedom for Capital, Not People*, I could not have imagined that it might still be of interest a decade and a half on. Yet the issues at the centre of this book are more relevant than ever, even after the zombie-like 'mutant' re-emergence of neoliberal hegemony after the financial meltdown.[1] These include the more general question of the politics of currencies and money, or how the specific social form money takes is politically contested, encapsulates a particular form of rule, and imposes limits on prospects for democracy and social emancipation.[2] Other arguments that have lost little of their relevance today pertain to more specialised areas: neoliberalism as a concerted effort for disciplining democracy through markets; the internal divisions, diversity and collective strategising within

---

1 Philip Mirowski, *Never Let a Serious Crisis Go to Waste: How Neoliberalism Survived the Financial Meltdown*, London: Verso, 2013; William Callison and Zachary Manfredi, eds, *Mutant Neoliberalism: Market Rule and Political Rupture*, New York: Fordham University Press, 2019.

2 For a recent overview of the prehistory of this book, see Stefan Eich, *The Currency of Politics: The Political Theory of Money from Aristotle to Keynes*, Princeton, NJ: Princeton University Press, 2023.

the neoliberal camp; and the influence of neoliberal intellectuals on the transformation of the international monetary and financial system.

Of course, scholarship on these topics, whether archivally based histories or more synthetic social science accounts, has greatly expanded in the intervening years. Major contributions have increased our understanding of the intellectual and social history of the neoliberal movement, and with it the theories, influence, and political economy underpinning the neoliberal 'counter-revolution'.[3]

Three strands of literature are particularly germane to the preoccupations of this book. To begin with, several studies have developed the argument that the *political project* of neoliberalism mainly concerned itself with the 'encasement' of democracy, a project for safeguarding capitalism from mass demands for social justice, economic autonomy and redistribution that has been conceptualised as 'undoing the demos'; others have explored how the original neoliberal efforts aimed at 'de-democratising' the state, economy and society by mobilising market forces, traditional morality and racist ideology, while new attention has been directed to the links between these developments and the more recent rise of authoritarian and reactionary forms of neoliberal family values, social conservativism and right-wing populism.[4]

---

3   See, for example, Quinn Slobodian, *Globalists: The End of Empire and the Birth of Neoliberalism*, Cambridge, MA: Harvard University Press, 2018; Daniel Stedman Jones, *Masters of the Universe: Hayek, Friedman, and the Birth of Neoliberal Politics*, Princeton, NJ: Princeton University Press, 2012; Angus Burgin, *The Great Persuasion: Reinventing Free Markets since the Depression*, Cambridge, MA: Harvard University Press, 2012; Wolfgang Streeck, *Buying Time: The Delayed Crisis of Democratic Capitalism*, New York: Verso, 2014; Melinda Cooper, *Counterrevolution: Extravagance and Austerity in Public Finance*, New York: Zone Books, 2024; Quinn Slobodian, *Crack-Up Capitalism: Market Radicals and the Dream of a World without Democracy*, New York: Metropolitan Books, 2023; Gary Gerstle, *The Rise and Fall of the Neoliberal Order: America and the World in the Free Market Era*, New York: Oxford University Press, 2023; Mirowski, *Never Let a Serious Crisis Go to Waste*; George Monbiot and Peter Hutchison, *The Invisible Doctrine: The Secret History of Neoliberalism*, London: Allen Lane, 2024.

4   Slobodian, *Globalists*; Wendy Brown, *Undoing the Demos: Neoliberalism's Stealth Revolution*, New York: Zone Books, 2015; Wendy Brown, *In the Ruins of Neoliberalism: The Rise of Antidemocratic Politics in the West*, New York: Columbia University Press, 2019; Melinda Cooper, *Family Values: Between Neoliberalism and the New Social Conservatism*, New York: Zone Books, 2019; Callison and Manfredi, *Mutant Neoliberalism*; Clara E. Mattei, *The Capital Order: How Economists Invented Austerity and Paved the Way to Fascism*, Chicago: University of Chicago Press, 2022. For a diverging account, see Gerstle, *The Rise and Fall of the Neoliberal Order*.

A second set of contributions have reinforced the importance of the neoliberal intellectuals at the heart of this study in the evolution of the monetary and financial system since the 1970s. Special emphasis has been given to the academic debates launched by Milton Friedman and other MPS members' advocacy for floating exchange rates.[5] This literature has rendered in higher resolution the networking efforts undertaken at international conferences, which during the 1960s and 1970s aimed both at forging a scholarly consensus and influencing expert debates and policymaking processes.[6] More evidence has surfaced for the political influence of the networks around 'Shultz, Friedman, and all that bunch' (as stated by Nixon in 1973, according to newly examined secret tapes) in preparing the move to floating exchange rates, or what has become known as the 'Nixon shock.'[7] One result has been to illuminate the broader impact of this globalist framework in promoting floating exchange rates and free capital movements as a lever for the neoliberal restructuring of economies around the world, pursued under the guise of deregulation, liberalisation and privatisation.[8]

---

5 Sebastian Edwards, 'Milton Friedman and Exchange Rates: History and Controversies', *History of Political Economy* 55, no. 5 (1 October 2023): 831–67; Sebastian Edwards, 'One Hundred Years of Exchange Rate Economics at The University of Chicago: 1892–1992', *Journal of the History of Economic Thought*, 25 (April 2024): 1–23; Youn Ki and Yongwoo Jeung, 'Ideas, Interests, and the Transition to a Floating Exchange System', *Journal of Policy History* 32, no. 2 (1 April 2020): 151–82; Youn Ki, 'Intellectual Entrepreneurs and U.S. International Monetary Policy Change in the Early 1970s', *Policy Studies* 44, no. 3 (4 May 2023): 356–76; Maurice Obstfeld and Douglas A. Irwin, *Floating Exchange Rates at Fifty*, Peterson Institute for International Economics, 2024; Naomi R. Lamoreaux and Ian Shapiro, *The Bretton Woods Agreements*, New Haven, CT: Yale University Press, 2019. See also, for Friedman's later advocacy, Sebastian Edwards and Leonidas Montes, 'Milton Friedman in Chile: Shock Therapy, Economic Freedom, and Exchange Rates', *Journal of the History of Economic Thought* 42, no. 1 (March 2020): 105–32. For a different perspective, see Christoffer J. P. Zoeller, 'Closing the Gold Window: The End of Bretton Woods as a Contingency Plan', *Politics and Society* 47, no. 1 (March 2019): 3–22.

6 Carol M. Connell, *Reforming the World Monetary System: Fritz Machlup and the Bellagio Group*, London: Taylor & Francis, 2012; Carol M. Connell and Joseph Salerno, eds, *Monetary Reform and the Bellagio Group: Selected Letters and Papers of Fritz Machlup, Robert Triffin and William Fellner*, five vols, London: Taylor & Francis, 2014; Forrest Capie, 'Reforming the World Monetary System: Fritz Machlup and the Bellagio Group', *Business History*, 4 July 2014.

7 James L. Butkiewicz and Scott Ohlmacher, 'Ending Bretton Woods: Evidence from the Nixon Tapes', *Economic History Review* 74, no. 4 (2021): 220.

8 Eric Helleiner, 'The Life and Times of Embedded Liberalism: Legacies and Innovations since Bretton Woods', *Review of International Political Economy* (2

Preface to the English Edition

Neoliberalism, in this book, is understood neither as a coherent doctrine nor as a discrete economic epoch, but rather in terms of the collective intellectual project of an organised group of academics, businessmen and policy entrepreneurs who elaborated and circulated ideas within a common normative and intellectual framework. In this vein, a number of studies have further highlighted the significance of the MPS, the plurality of the neoliberal thought collective and the importance of their internal debates and strategies for coalition-building.[9] Despite this bevy of new scholarship, however, the basic arguments of this book and the specific case study at its core remain as timely as ever.

The period since we rallied against financial capitalism in London has been taken by some to mark the 'end of neoliberalism' or of the advent of 'post-neoliberalism'; others describe it as a 'mutant', 'zombie' iteration of a neoliberalism that is in effect 'half-dead, half-alive'.[10] In an era of rising protectionism, right-wing ideology and deglobalisation, neoliberal ideologies have certainly experienced a backlash. But they have also rearticulated themselves by forging new alliances and taking on novel forms.[11] Yet, independently of how one defines these developments, the effects of ending Bretton Woods, introducing floating exchange rates within liberalised markets, and thereby unleashing capital against democracy continue to be observed. Three dimensions of the current conjuncture are worth highlighting.

Today, as in the 1960s, there is an immense interest in the form that money takes as a central factor in politics and social life. Monetary

---

November 2019); Dieter Plehwe, Quinn Slobodian and Philip Mirowski, *Nine Lives of Neoliberalism*, New York: Verso, 2020; Obstfeld and Irwin, *Floating Exchange Rates at Fifty*; Barry Eichengreen, *Exorbitant Privilege: The Rise and Fall of the Dollar*, New York: Oxford University Press, 2011; Douglas A. Irwin, 'The Nixon Shock after Forty Years: The Import Surcharge Revisited', *World Trade Review* 12, no. 1 (January 2013): 29–56; Luke A. Nichter, *Richard Nixon and Europe: The Reshaping of the Postwar Atlantic World*, Cambridge: Cambridge University Press, 2017.

9   See, for example, Plehwe, Slobodian and Mirowski, *Nine Lives of Neoliberalism*; Quinn Slobodian and Dieter Plehwe, *Market Civilizations: Neoliberals East and South*, New York: Zone Books, 2022; Cornel Ban, *Ruling Ideas: How Global Neoliberalism Goes Local*, New York: Oxford University Press, 2016.

10   Callison and Manfredi, *Mutant Neoliberalism*; George Monbiot, *How Did We Get Into This Mess?: Politics, Equality, Nature*, London: Verso, 2016; Mirowski, *Never Let a Serious Crisis Go to Waste*; Aditya Chakrabortty, 'You're Witnessing the Death of Neoliberalism – from Within', *Guardian*, 31 May 2016.

11   See, for example, Slobodian, *Crack-Up Capitalism*.

policy is more than ever a political question of direct concern to people otherwise uninterested in its arcana. There is reason to think that the global system of money and finance is approaching a disruptive threshold of historic significance, with the potential to change how societies invest, insure and trade. Of course, the form of money – essentially the socially and politically constructed 'promise to pay' – has always fluctuated.[12] What is distinctive about the transformation of money in the early twenty-first century is, first of all, the proliferation of digital currencies and tokens, which evoke the regimes of monetary policy discussed in the book in new and complex ways. Operating in the shadows of hegemonic monetary systems, these cannot simply be seen as tools for bottom-up emancipation pitted against authoritarian central banks and austerity-inducing monetary politics, as is sometimes claimed by their boosters. Rather, non-fungible tokens (NFTs), Web3, blockchain technology, crypto and decentralised autonomous organisations (DAOs) are at the forefront of a financial revolution driven increasingly by transnational platforms and central banks themselves. In the name of flexibility and efficiency they prefigure the end of physical cash, thereby jeopardising privacy and further undermining democracy.[13] Such developments signal the exhaustion of the quantitative easing regime since 2019. Although they are far too complex to be analysed in any detail here, they may be seen as a coda to the history discussed in the present book. They represent one prospectus for the so-called post-neoliberal order, whose features cannot be understood as progressive, promising in some instances to surrender still more authority to the lords of finance themselves, potentially directly by administrative means.

The terms in which this new monetary architecture is discussed recall the earlier debates canvassed in what follows. In the field of digital currencies, for example, the highly restricted, limited and market-disciplining logic of Bitcoin bears comparison to the built-in scarcity of gold – and if introduced more broadly, could reproduce the logic of the gold standard – while the seemingly endless

---

12 David Graeber, *Debt: The First 5,000 Years*, New York: Melville House, 2014; Geoffrey Ingham, *The Nature of Money*, Cambridge: Polity, 2004.
13 Rachel O'Dwyer, *Tokens: The Future of Money in the Age of the Platform*, 1st ed., New York: Verso, 2023; Eswar S. Prasad, *The Future of Money: How the Digital Revolution Is Transforming Currencies and Finance*, Cambridge, MA: Harvard University Press, 2023.

proliferation of absurdly branded private money over the decade of quantitative easing (QE) resembles the wild speculation enabled by free-floating exchange rates. To this familiar opposition, a third pole may be added: central bank digital currency, issued either formally by central banks themselves or – what is functionally equivalent – by the largest private banks. This novel form of money is distinct in that it introduces the prospect of directly imposing socio-political conditions on transactions or penalising savers through very low interest rates. It is perhaps for this reason that the more principled neoliberals themselves have joined in to sound the alarm when it comes to some of these innovations. As the historian Adam Tooze has suggested, paraphrasing Antonio Gramsci, 'crypto is the morbid symptom of an interregnum, an interregnum in which the gold standard is dead but a fully political money that dares to speak its name has not yet been born'.[14]

Another live issue in contemporary discussions is the status of the dollar as the world reserve currency, an 'exorbitant privilege' ratified by the shift to floating exchange rates described in this book. The effects of this fateful decision, as a volume published on its fiftieth anniversary records, 'went far beyond the international monetary system and have had momentous geopolitical and political as well as economic and financial implications'.[15] Today, if dollar hegemony remains intact, ever more voices question its permanence, and with it, the ability of the US to maintain its unrivaled geopolitical position. In this regard, the present moment likewise echoes that of the 1970s, when monetary policy reflected the jostling between world powers and management of the relations among allies. With the introduction of the BRICS basket of currencies and the prospect of de-dollarisation it suggests, in the aftermath of Brexit and the eurozone crisis, forecasts of re-regionalisation often turn on monetary policy. Still, amid chatter of deglobalisation and evidence of a fall in capital flows, the share of transactions conducted in dollars has remained relatively stable over the last decades. Nonetheless, the US 'dollar creditocracy' is threatened by the internal contradictions of QE, and the US current account and budget deficits continue to exert

---

14 Adam Tooze, 'Crypto and the Politics of Money', Chartbook #74, adamtooze.substack.com, 22 January 2022.
15 Obstfeld and Irwin, *Floating Exchange Rates at Fifty*, 9.

downward pressure on the dollar, exacerbating resentment of US unilateralism.[16]

Finally, the liberalisation of capital movements in the 1970s must be seen as one side of the exhaustion of economic growth across the advanced industrialised countries; both are effects of overaccumulation, declining productivity growth and have taken the form of secular stagnation. The subsequent period has seen a tremendous explosion of fictitious capital, or financial assets that are in essence claims on future production and profit. The financialisation of the post-Fordist era has produced a lopsided economy, where such claims exceed by significant measure the size of the underlying real economy. Its logic is that of a growthless casino, based on transfer and appropriation largely decoupled from real-world use values. Such a top-heavy dynamic was exactly what produced the over-leveraging responsible for the 2008 meltdown. Pledges to re-regulate and curb the power of finance aside, the metastasis of fictitious capital has continued apace. While the use of some assets – those complex instruments at the heart of the housing and financial crisis, such as CDOs – did indeed decline, the overall quantity of fictitious capital has in fact continued to increase. This dynamic, evident in the outsized importance of the finance, insurance and real estate (FIRE) sector and the run-up in prices of housing and art objects as financialised assets, touches on the central thesis of this book. Trading in global foreign exchange markets – the marketplace that determines the exchange rate for global currencies and that originates in its modern form from abolishing the Bretton Woods system – soared from negligible levels in the 1970s to a nominal value of $620 billion in 1989 and $4.5 trillion in 2008; by 2022 it stood at $7.5 trillion.[17] Such massive flows of money, buoying a 'technofeudal' rentier class, pose a potentially systemic problem given the attendant pressure to seek their realisation in the real economy.[18] In the age of climate overshoot, secular stagnation

---

[16] Radhika Desai and Michael Hudson, 'Beyond Dollar Creditocracy: A Geopolitical Economy', *Real World Economics Review* 97 (2021); Robert Greene, 'The Difficult Realities of the BRICS' Dedollarization Efforts – and the Renminbi's Role', Carnegie Endowment for International Peace, 2023, carnegieendowment.org.

[17] Cédric Durand, *Fictitious Capital: How Finance Is Appropriating Our Future*, London: Verso, 2017.

[18] Cédric Durand, *How Silicon Valley Unleashed Techno-Feudalism: The Making of the Digital Economy*, London: Verso, 2024.

Preface to the English Edition

and polycrisis, these claims on future production – now far greater than global GDP – create a fundamental dilemma.[19] Given mounting evidence that calls into question the ambition of greening economic growth, efforts to realise future profits of fictitious capital will lead to either unsustainable growth that dangerously destabilises planetary life or an alternative post-growth scenario, in which societies regain democratic control and turn fictious capital into stranded assets.[20]

Set against this horizon, the financial turmoil of the early 1970s, which brought down the Bretton Woods system, seems relatively insignificant. That crisis was exploited by the neoliberals at the centre of this book to push through a programme decades in the making, with the goal of constraining democracy to liberate capital. This history argues that the political economy of global finance results from the interaction between intellectual currents struggling for hegemony under objective circumstances, constrained by social forces that shape them in turn in a historical process punctuated by crises. The interplay of all these factors determines the form money takes and the monetary policy of states – yet these seemingly arcane issues fundamentally govern and constrict our lives, our democracies and our futures. Some of the most consequential developments of the last century are covered from this viewpoint in the present book. Their effects are still being felt today, even if their origins have been obscured.

---

19 Wim Carton and Andreas Malm, *Overshoot: How the World Surrendered to Climate Breakdown*, London: Verso, 2024; Michael Lawrence, Thomas Homer-Dixon, Scott Janzwood, Johan Rockstöm, Ortwin Renn and Jonathan F. Donges, 'Global Polycrisis: The Causal Mechanisms of Crisis Entanglement', *Global Sustainability* 7 (January 2024): e6.

20 Matthias Schmelzer, Andrea Vetter and Aaron Vansintjan, *The Future Is Degrowth: A Guide to a World Beyond Capitalism*, London: Verso, 2022.

Foreword to the 2010 German Edition

Dieter Plehwe

In *States and the Reemergence of Global Finance*, the political scientist Eric Helleiner devoted several footnotes to the importance of the Mont Pèlerin Society's debates on international monetary policy and the role of many of its members in the political transition to a regime of flexible exchange rates. He declined a suggestion that he look more closely into the wider circle of academic experts in finance, of central and private bankers, because his research interests had led him into other areas. But as so often in life, an opportunity missed opened up another to be seized.

Such was the case for the author of the present book, a groundbreaking study of how a highly successful epistemic community in favour of flexible exchange rates emerged within the neoliberal thought collective. Matthias Schmelzer has carefully reconstructed the controversy that pitted older neoliberal proponents of a return to the gold standard (Ludwig von Mises, Michael Heilperin, Jacques Rueff) against a younger generation who advocated for free-floating exchange rates in conjunction with comprehensive capital mobility (among them Fritz Machlup, Milton Friedman, Gottfried Haberler, William Fellner, Friedrich Lutz). Schmelzer documents the fascinating conceptual transformation that took place over the course of the 1950s and 1960s, not without serious friction, initially, within the neoliberal camp. Prior to the '60s, flexible exchange rates were considered a downright criminal path towards instability, unworthy of serious consideration by the 'government economists' concerned about the future of the Bretton Woods system. Rebels in the neoliberal camp showed a certain audacity when they formed an international group of 'non-governmental economists' in 1963 – it took another thirty years for academia to recognise the importance of such 'private authorities' in international relations as a major research topic. In the second part of his work, Schmelzer describes how the MPS economists around Machlup moved beyond academic analysis to develop and market strategically calibrated proposals for reform. Neoliberal think tanks and international conferences (held in such locales as the scenic Bellagio and the no less beautiful Bürgenstock) played a central part in this enterprise.

Looking back, the Chicago economist Harry Johnson drew a distinction between two types of conferences, analogous to the production of capital and consumer goods: one serves to generate new knowledge, the other to persuade. The mechanisms of persuasion, first in academia and then among central and private bankers on an international scale, are revealed here in an exemplary manner. Schmelzer provides a precise explanation of the often merely asserted ideological foundations of epistemic communities (their norms and fundamental convictions), and he broaches the question of their conditions of possibility, the infrastructure and social technologies to disseminate new political orientations and projects.

Acknowledgements

Scholarly work is not done in a small, secluded room, segregated from its particular social and research setting. The extent to which this applies to the Mont Pèlerin Society members' contributions to economic and monetary policy is one of the central topics of this book. The same can of course be said of this work itself, and I would therefore like to express my sincere thanks to the people who made it possible. I am particularly grateful to Hartmut Kaelble, Gabriele Metzler and the research colloquium at the Chair of Economic and Social History at Humboldt University Berlin for all their support. I owe a very special debt of gratitude to Dieter Plehwe, who advised this research from the outset. Many important insights for this work emerged from discussions in our working group on the Mont Pèlerin Society at the Wissenschaftszentrum Berlin (WZB) – so a big thank you also goes to Lea Hartung. I would also like to offer my special thanks to Alexander Nützenadel and his colloquium and to Rüdiger Graf, Andrea Vetter, Sarah Goldschmidt, Max Kölling, Julia Roßhart and Lea Hagen for critical discussions and valuable advice. I owe my interest in the Mont Pèlerin Society to Gillian Hart of the University of California, Berkeley. For their help with archival research, I would like to kindly thank the great staff at the Liberaal Archief in Ghent, Belgium. It is a great honour that this book is finally published also in English. It would not have been possible without the excellent work of translation, fact-checking, and improving the prose, content and argument by Joshua Rahtz. I am also grateful to the entire team at Verso, in particular Grey Anderson, Jeanne Tao and Conor O'Brien. And I want to thank the History and Political Economy Project for providing the funding for the translation, and to Quinn Slobodian for the initiative that sparked this endeavour.

List of Abbreviations

ABA	American Bankers Association
ACF	Advocacy Coalition Framework
AEI	American Enterprise Institute
AFA	American Finance Association
AFL-CIO	American Federation of Labor and Congress of Industrial Organizations
BIS	Bank for International Settlements
CEA	Council of Economic Advisers
CED	Committee for Economic Development
CMRE	Committee for Monetary Research and Education
ENCMP	Economists' National Committee on Monetary Policy
FEE	Foundation for Economic Education
ICC	International Chamber of Commerce
IEA	Institute of Economic Affairs
IMF	International Monetary Fund
LA	Liberaal Archief, Ghent, Belgium
MPS	Mont Pèlerin Society
NBER	National Bureau of Economic Research
NICB	National Industrial Conference Board
NYT	*New York Times*
NZZ	*Neue Zürcher Zeitung*
OECD	Organisation for Economic Co-operation and Development

UNCTAD	United Nations Conference on Trade and Development
WEI	Walter Eucken Institut
WP	*Washington Post*
WSJ	*Wall Street Journal*

Introduction

Capitalism is mired in its deepest crisis since the 1930s. The collapse of the financial markets in 2007 has since expanded into a global crisis of the entire world economy; the neoliberal monetary and financial order has failed spectacularly. Its core characteristics are the internationalisation of trade and currency competition, the increasing power of transnational corporations, and the simultaneous concentration of capital and increase in global poverty. This book concerns itself with the theoretical roots of the contemporary monetary system at the heart of this crisis, characterised by liberalised capital movements and floating exchange rates. It traces how these demands were first conceived of and then propagated by organised neoliberals throughout the post–Second World War period.[1]

The widespread idea that the liberalisation of international financial markets since the 1970s was the inevitable consequence of technological and economic developments has been refuted decisively by the historian

---

1 In the following I will use 'flexible', 'free' and 'floating' exchange rates interchangeably. I understand the terms in the broadest sense to mean exchange rates that are not stabilised in a fixed relation to a commodity (e.g., gold) or another currency by government interventions, but which arise through primarily private transactions on foreign exchange markets (see Ronald MacDonald, *Floating Exchange Rates: Theories and Evidence*, New York: Routledge, 1988; Milton Friedman, 'The Case for Flexible Exchange Rates', in *Essays in Positive Economics*, Chicago: University of Chicago Press, 1953).

Eric Helleiner. The establishment of the current open financial order of free capital movements and floating exchange rates not only was made possible by 'the support and blessing of states' but was also based on a fundamental transformation in thinking around economic and monetary policy.[2] It was by no means self-evident at the turn of the 1970s that flexible exchange rates and liberalised capital markets should be regarded as a feasible and, at least in US government circles, desirable monetary order: at the time, the Bretton Woods system (1944–71) still stipulated a regime of fixed rates and controls on international capital movements. Indeed, until the second half of the 1960s, flexible exchange rates were regarded by both economists and especially political and business leaders as 'a species of lawbreaking behaviour', to be 'scornfully dismissed or even ignored', and there was widespread rejection of liberalised capital markets.[3] However, this marginalised, minority position (it is estimated that in the early 1950s less than 5 per cent of economists worldwide advocated for floating exchange rates) would experience a most remarkable upswing: by the end of the 1960s, not only had a clear majority of economists come around to floating exchange rates or at least become convinced of their theoretical validity (estimates put the figure as high as 90 per cent), but government officials likewise began to take the theory seriously. Influential American bankers called for greater flexibility, and within the administration of US president Richard Nixon, high-ranking advisers (among them Marina Whitman) and members of the government called for floating rates and the free movement of capital.[4]

The end of the Bretton Woods monetary system, triggered by Nixon's decision in August 1971 to suspend the dollar's convertibility into gold,

---

2 Eric Helleiner, *States and the Reemergence of Global Finance: From Bretton Woods to the 1990s*, Ithaca, NY: Cornell University Press, 1994, vii.

3 Robert Leeson, *Ideology and the International Economy: The Decline and Fall of Bretton Woods*, New York: Palgrave, 2003, 9; Robert Triffin, 'The Impact of the Bellagio Group on International Reform', in Jacob S. Dreyer, ed., *Breadth and Depth in Economics: Fritz Machlup – The Man and His Ideas*, Lexington: Lexington Books, 1978, 146. See also Robert Solomon, *The International Monetary System, 1945–1976: An Outsider's View*, New York: Harper and Row, 1977, 60.

4 This work is almost exclusively about men – mainly due to the patriarchal structure of the Mont Pèlerin Society, which is at the centre of the present work, but also because nearly all economists who took part in these debates were men. Whitman, an exception, was a member of the CEA under Nixon and the first woman in this position.

Introduction

marked an exceptionally far-reaching change in global history: contemporaries like the German central banker Otmar Emminger perceived it as a kind of 'Copernican revolution' that would come to be regarded as a 'decisive point of departure for the neoliberal project of a deregulated world market'.[5] Floating exchange rates gained global acceptance in the 1970s, although this was soon followed by a growing movement towards the reintroduction of fixed exchange rates in specific areas, as in the eurozone.[6]

Various studies have shown that the collapse of Bretton Woods was due in large part to the ascendancy of neoliberal monetary theory and their proponents' influence within the Nixon administration. On this view, only the academic prestige and concerted advocacy for floating exchange rates and liberalised capital markets can fully explain why the Bretton Woods order was not reformed and essentially preserved at the beginning of the 1970s – despite many efforts – but instead replaced by a less cooperative, competition-orientated system of floating exchange rates and liberalised foreign exchange and capital markets.[7]

In what follows, I show how this fundamental and far-reaching change in economic and monetary thinking came about. The focus here is on the transnationally organised neoliberal economists and monetary

---

5 Otmar Emminger, *On the Way to a New International Monetary Order*, Washington, DC: American Enterprise Institute, 1976, 13; Christoph Scherrer, *Globalisierung wider Willen: Die Durchsetzung liberaler Außenwirtschaftspolitik in den USA*, Berlin: Edition Sigma, 1999, 323. On the latter thesis, see also Jörg Huffschmid, *Politische Ökonomie der Finanzmärkte*, Hamburg: VSA Verlag, 2001, 106–32.

6 On the worldwide implementation of floating exchange rates from the mid-1970s onwards, see Barry Eichengreen, *Globalizing Capital: A History of the International Monetary System*, Princeton, NJ: Princeton University Press, 1996, 126–91; Peter Isard, *Globalization and the International Financial System: What's Wrong and What Can Be Done*, Cambridge: Cambridge University Press, 2005; MacDonald, *Floating Exchange Rates*; Maurice Obstfeld and Alan Taylor, *Global Capital Markets: Integration, Crisis, and Growth*, Cambridge: Cambridge University Press, 2004. Kathleen McNamara has shown that fixed exchange rates could prevail in the EEC only after a neoliberal consensus on a stable, anti-inflationary monetary policy had been established within the European states and once European monetary policy was harmonised (following the example of Germany, a hard-currency country). See Kathleen McNamara, *The Currency of Ideas: Monetary Politics in the European Union*, Ithaca, NY: Cornell University Press, 1999.

7 The most important studies are Leeson, *Ideology and the International Economy*; John S. Odell, *U.S. International Monetary Policy: Markets, Power, and Ideas as Sources of Change*, Princeton, NJ: Princeton University Press, 1982; and Helleiner, *States and the Reemergence of Global Finance*.

experts who promoted flexible exchange rates and liberalised capital markets in the US and Europe, and who helped to popularise these concepts at a succession of international conferences and panel discussions, across publications and in their roles as government advisers. Guided by the observation that knowledge is always embedded in social and political contexts, in networks and organised relationships, I argue that the scholarly development and socio-political hegemonisation of the theory of floating exchange rates was due above all to the activism of the Mont Pèlerin Society (MPS), the most consequential transnational network of an emerging neoliberalism.[8] This connection, hitherto never examined in detail in historical scholarship, is the subject of this study.

The MPS was founded in 1947 by the liberal-conservative economist Friedrich von Hayek as a coterie of market-liberal economists, intellectuals, publicists and businessmen. Its mission was to renew liberalism through multi-generational, interdisciplinary and transnational collaboration. MPS members made it their task not only to counter Keynesian and socialist theories, which they portrayed as 'totalitarian', but also to disseminate their own ideas tirelessly. Hayek described this motivation succinctly in a memo on the eve of the first MPS conference: 'We must raise and train an army of fighters for freedom. If, despite overwhelming public opinion against us, we work to shape and lead this opinion, our case is by no means hopeless.'[9] In the now considerable literature on this topic, the MPS is regarded as the most significant outpost of the international neoliberal movement; its emergence in the immediate postwar period inaugurated neoliberalism's march across the globe towards certain triumph, which from the beginning of the 1980s appeared undeniable.[10]

---

   8   With regard to membership of the MPS, I draw on lists of participants in the MPS conferences at the Liberaal Archief in Ghent, as well as a very comprehensive but incomplete list based on research by Bernhard Walpen and Dieter Plehwe (the list includes 815 members whose membership could be proven with certainty).
   9   Quoted in Alan Ebenstein, *Friedrich Hayek: A Biography*, New York: Palgrave Macmillan, 2001, 143.
   10   On the evaluation and classification of the MPS, see the landmark work Bernhard Walpen, *Die offenen Feinde und ihre Gesellschaft: Eine hegemonietheoretische Studie zur Mont Pèlerin Society*, Hamburg: VSA Verlag, 2004. See also the contributions in Philip Mirowski and Dieter Plehwe, eds, *The Road from Mont Pèlerin: The Making of the Neoliberal Thought Collective*, Cambridge, MA: Harvard University Press, 2009.

Introduction

Along with analysis of the role of the MPS's 'freedom fighters' in debates over monetary policy, the present work aims to contribute to the historiography of early neoliberalism. It therefore not only tracks the emergence of monetary policy positions that have remained dominant to this day, but also maps the most important internal controversy within the neoliberal camp. For the theory backing flexible exchange rates was hardly uncontested at the time.

At the start of the 1950s, a clear majority of MPS members backed the reintroduction of the classical gold standard – then an extreme minority position within the discipline of economics. These advocates for a return to the gold standard understood floating exchange rates to be in direct contradiction with the precepts of liberal economic order, at best an impractical theoretical gimmick, at worst a capitulation to Keynesian state-interventionists. Nevertheless, the concept of flexible exchange rates was first developed as a neoliberal reform, almost exclusively by a small number of MPS members, who attempted to persuade their colleagues over the course of intensive and contentious in-house discussions. Throughout the 1950s and 1960s, no issue gave rise to more disagreement at the roughly biennial MPS conferences than did the correct neoliberal strategy for reforming the Bretton Woods system.

This dispute was exceptionally vexed, and it contributed to deepening rifts within the MPS, sometimes ruining friendships. But the efforts of those advocating floating exchange rates were not in vain: although by no means all MPS members were convinced by the end of the 1960s, the pro-flexibalisation contingent grew significantly over this period, eventually establishing their theory at MPS conferences as the dominant, albeit still contested, concept of neoliberal reform. This ascendancy was paralleled in economics writ large, thanks in no small part to MPS members, with a notable impact on the academic discipline and policy alike.

The 2008 world economic crisis intensified criticism of the neoliberal monetary order and attendant economic theories. The assumption that market forces and currency speculation would most efficiently determine correct exchange rates has been discredited for some time.[11]

---

11 UNCTAD partly summarises the criticism succinctly: 'Currency speculation drives exchange rates systematically away from the fundamentals and tends to lead to

In the aftermath of the Great Financial Crisis, the United Nations Conference on Trade and Development (UNCTAD) 2009 report followed numerous well-known economists in calling for an increased use of international capital controls so as to reduce the risk of future crises.[12] The MPS, however, remained intransigent: at the March 2009 global conference held in New York, Greg Lindsay once again emphasised the importance of floating exchange rates, calling them 'probably the most important market reform of the last 25 years'.[13]

Methodologically, this book traverses the disciplines of intellectual, economic, political and contemporary history. It aims to build upon recent research on the force of ideas and, in particular, economic ideas, with special attention to the organisational and substantive connections between independent yet networked experts and their influence on the production and distribution of knowledge. The classical history of ideas, which deals with immanent developments of a scholarly literature, is complemented here by network-theoretical, sociological and cultural-historical approaches, especially with regard to the socio-political contextualisation of academic debates, their organisational and institutional anchoring. Whereas a commonplace view holds that the 'best' theories and methods prevail in economics as a science through objective criteria – a perspective from which the emergence and dissemination of these ideas is a 'non-subject' – the present work takes seriously the importance of how scientific knowledge is diffused, popularised and applied.[14]

For the research programme driving this study, which focuses on the contexts of production and distribution of economic knowledge, certain

---

overvaluation and current-account deficits.' See its *Trade and Development Report 2009: Responding to the Crisis – Climate Change Mitigation and Development*, Geneva: UNCTAD, 2009, xii.

12 Ibid., 118–20; Carmen M. Reinhart and Kenneth Rogoff, 'Is the 2007 US Sub-prime Crisis So Different? An International Historical Comparison', *American Economic Review* 98, no. 2 (2008).

13 Greg Lindsay, economist at the neoliberal think tanks Centre for Independent Studies, Sydney, in his lecture 'Tales from the South Pacific', available at montpelerin.org.

14 According to David C. Colander and A. W. Coats, this is one of the main reasons why so little research has been done on the dissemination of economic ideas. (Colander and Coats, eds, *The Spread of Economic Ideas*, Cambridge: Cambridge University Press, 1989, 1).

traditional notions are discarded in favour of newer approaches that examine the narrative and rhetorical structure of economic theories, paradigms and schools.[15] Ideas can exercise a powerful, even decisive influence on states as well as private actors – especially amid the general 'scientification' of societies, increasingly complex economic conditions, and the resulting influence of economic experts.[16] Science and expertise constitute highly complex processes characterised by openings and closures, wherein different theories, paradigms, individuals and traditions struggle for recognition and dominance. However influential, the MPS has never exerted the sort of comprehensive control imagined by conspiracy theorists.[17]

Chapters 3 and 4 of the present work are based on an interactivist model of popularisation, which is distinct from older, diffusionist research. The latter understood the transfer of knowledge as hierarchical, a one-way street: knowledge is produced in a neutral manner by a narrow, homogeneous circle of experts and subsequently disseminated in simplified form to laypeople. By contrast, this work – following developments in intellectual history – focuses on interconnections and reciprocal influence among scholars, popularisers and their publics.[18]

---

15 See especially the work of Deirdre McCloskey, who – herself an economist trained in Chicago – has dealt extensively with the narrative and rhetorical structures of economic knowledge (see Deirdre N. McCloskey, *The Rhetoric of Economics*, Madison: University of Wisconsin Press, 1998).

16 On the 'scientisation of the social' and the concomitant 'politicisation of science' – a process which, starting in the nineteenth century, has intensified especially since the 1950s – see the introduction in Peter Weingart, 'Verwissenschaftlichung der Gesellschaft – Politisierung der Wissenschaft', in *Zeitschrift für Soziologie* 12 (1983); on the relationship of economic experts to politics, see Peter Weingart, *Die Stunde der Wahrheit? Vom Verhältnis der Wissenschaft zu Politik, Wirtschaft und Medien in der Wissensgesellschaft*, Weilerswist: Velbrück Wissenschaft, 2001, esp. chapter 5; on the expansion and professionalisation of the 'knowledge elites', see Peter M. Haas, 'Introduction: Epistemic Communities and International Policy Coordination', in *International Organization* 46, no. 1 (1992), esp. 7–16.

17 On the critique of conspiracy theory as related to the MPS, see Walpen, *Die offenen Feinde und ihre Gesellschaft*, 27–30. On the enterprise of science, see Colander and Coats, *The Spread of Economic Ideas*.

18 On the concept of popularisation, see Carsten Kretschmann, 'Einleitung: Wissenspopularisierung – ein altes, neues Forschungsfeld', in Carsten Kretschmann, ed., *Wissenspopularisierung: Konzepte der Wissensverbreitung im Wandel*, Berlin: Akademie Verlag, 2003; and on the history of entanglement – *histoire croisée* – see Michael Werner and Bénédicte Zimmermann, 'Beyond Comparison: *Histoire croisée* and the Challenge of Reflexivity', *History and Theory* 45 (February 2006): 30–50.

Scholars were far from the only parties involved in the production and discussion of theories and concepts within the MPS network, and sociopolitical circumstances as well as the 'audience' to be convinced also played a central role. Knowledge production within the MPS must be understood in terms of the wider academic, economic and political environment, which has influenced the discussions from the very start, and which is in turn subject to influence.

The MPS is best understood as an interdisciplinary network or thought collective of economists, politicians, intellectuals and businesspeople. It was organised transnationally from its inception and acted accordingly.[19] Within this thought collective, partisans of floating exchange rates represented a multinational epistemic community of experts (the term here is a critical reference to Peter Haas).[20] The concept 'epistemic communities' is borrowed from political science; it was developed in the 1990s in an effort to analyse the role of knowledge and experts themselves as they were implicated in transnational political events. To neglect the history of their conditions of formation and organisational context is to risk taking for granted naive accounts of their existence as collectives comprising people who share common core beliefs and act collectively as a 'community'.[21] Here, the focus is instead on the real organised cooperation of MPS experts and their debates, as conducted at Society conferences, which provided very material foundations of collaboration.

---

19 On network theories, see Silke Adam and Hanspeter Kriesi, 'The Network Approach', in Paul A. Sabatier, ed., *Theories of the Policy Process*, Boulder, CO: Westview Press, 2007; and for a focus on transnational networks in Europe, see Karen Heard-Lauréote, 'Transnational Networks: Informal Governance in the European Political Space', in Wolfram Kaiser and Peter Starie, eds, *Transnational European Union: Toward a Political Space*, London: Routledge, 2005. Similar approaches are taken in Maarten Hajer, 'Discourse Coalitions and the Institutionalisation of Practice: The Case of Acid Rain in Great Britain', in Frank Fischer and John Forester, eds, *The Argumentative Turn in Policy Analysis and Planning*, Durham, NC: Duke University Press, 1993, as related to 'discourse coalitions'; in relation to 'transnational advocacy networks', see Margaret E. Keck and Kathryn Sikkink, 'Transnational Advocacy Networks in International and Regional Politics', *International Social Science Journal* 51, no. 159 (1999): 89–101.

20 Haas, 'Introduction: Epistemic Communities and International Policy Coordination', 3.

21 This argument is advanced by the founders of the Advocacy Coalition Framework (ACF), Paul Sabatier and Hank Jenkins-Smith, who criticise both Peter Haas and early work on the ACF approach. See Paul A. Sabatier and Hank C. Jenkins-Smith, 'The Advocacy Coalition Framework', in Sabatier, *Theories of the Policy Process*, 138.

The historiography of Bretton Woods generally has paid remarkably little attention to the theories and influence of monetary experts and academic economists.[22] Yet in the few works that do pursue the topic, contributions of individual members of the MPS are indeed featured prominently. In the sole study to date on post-war monetary theories, the Australian economic historian Anthony Endres concentrates on the output of fourteen renowned economists, those who are in his view among the most significant thinkers regarding monetary questions in the Bretton Woods era, of whom nine were members of the MPS (Endres refers to them as the 'great architects of international finance', the title of his book).[23] In his archive-based study of the role of ideology in the collapse of Bretton Woods and the implementation of floating exchange rate theory, the historian Robert Leeson holds Milton Friedman primarily responsible, but the other central advocates of flexible exchange rates inside the MPS – namely, Gottfried Haberler, Fritz Machlup and George Stigler – are also featured prominently.[24] Helleiner's work, for its part, argues that the emergence of the current financial order can be understood only through an analysis of the role of transnationally networked neoliberal intellectuals, and he duly highlights the contributions of MPS members Hayek, Wilhelm Röpke, Friedman, Haberler, Machlup and William Simon.[25] John Odell's pathbreaking book maps the incidence of different Bretton Woods–era ideas inside American monetary policy

22   Thus, as Robert Leeson complains, justifiably, Friedman's highly important role in the collapse of Bretton Woods is not mentioned at all in the official history of the IMF. See Leeson, *Ideology and the International Economy*, 15. See also J. Keith Horsefield and Margaret de Vries, *The International Monetary Fund 1945–1965: Twenty Years of International Monetary Cooperation*, vol. 2, *Analysis*, Washington, DC: International Monetary Fund, 1969; and Joanne Gowa, *Closing the Gold Window: Domestic Politics and the End of Bretton Woods*, Ithaca, NY: Cornell University Press, 1983; among others.

23   Members of the Chicago School (Milton Friedman and Harry Johnson) and the Austrian School (Friedrich von Hayek and Ludwig von Mises, along with Wilhelm Röpke and Mises's student Michael Heilperin), as well as the market-liberal economists Jacques Rueff, Charles Rist and Frank Graham, were all themselves members of the MPS. See Anthony M. Endres, *Great Architects of International Finance: The Bretton Woods Era*, London: Routledge, 2005, 209.

24   Leeson, *Ideology and the International Economy*.

25   Helleiner, *States and the Reemergence of Global Finance*, 66, 115. Also mentioned: Hayek, Röpke, Heilperin, Robbins, Erhard, Einaudi, Stigler, Rueff, Rüstow, Lutz (ibid., 66, 71). Helleiner, however, fails to cover internal controversies within neoliberalism when he argues that the American neoliberals around Friedman and Haberler relied on Hayek and Röpke in their popularisation of floating exchange rates (115f.).

circles; those of Friedman, Haberler, Machlup, William Fellner and Paul McCracken are given particular prominence.[26]

In studies of the Bretton Woods monetary system and monographs dealing with individual protagonists, MPS proselytisers for floating exchange rates frequently appear though most often only in passing – in connection with the spread of the theory.[27] Yet intellectuals are mostly analysed in these works as individual, atomised researchers whose respective positions are understood to be shaped mainly by biography, related personal political-ideological viewpoints or their position within universities and other institutions. Such a limited and frankly myopic perspective conceals the integration of many of the central economists involved into transnational networks as they traversed different schools of academic economics. Only in the studies by Helleiner and Leeson is the organisational connection of the various scholars in the context of the MPS touched upon, though it is not examined in any great depth.[28]

---

26   Odell, *U.S. International Monetary Policy*, esp. 92f, 254f, 306–42.

27   On Friedman: besides Leeson, *Ideology and the International Economy*, Odell, *U.S. International Monetary Policy*, esp. 309; Paul Volcker and Toyoo Gyohten, *Changing Fortunes: The World's Money and the Threat to American Leadership*, New York: Times Books, 1992, 46; Francis J. Gavin, 'Ideas, Power, and the Politics of America's International Monetary Policy during the 1960s', in Jonathan Kirshner, ed., *Monetary Orders: Ambiguous Economics, Ubiquitous Politics*, Ithaca, NY: Cornell University Press, 2002, 199f. On Machlup, see Dreyer, *Breadth and Depth in Economics*, especially Robert Triffin's contribution, 'The Impact of the Bellagio Group on International Reform'. On Haberler, see Harold James and Michael Bordo, 'Haberler versus Nurkse: The Case for Floating Exchange Rates as an Alternative to Bretton Woods?', discussion paper no. 2001-08 at University of St. Gallen, 2001; Anthony Y. Koo, introduction to Gottfried Haberler, *The Liberal Economic Order*, vol. 1, *Essays on International Economics*, Brookfield, VT: Edward Elgar Publishing House, 1993; Volcker and Gyohten, *Changing Fortunes*, 151; Robert Solomon, *International Monetary System, 1945–76: An Outsider's View*, New York: Joanna Cotler Books, 1977, 169. On Fellner, see James N. Marshall, *William J. Fellner: A Bio-Bibliography*, Westport, CT: Greenwood Press, 1992. On Sohmen, see Charles Kindleberger, 'Egon Sohmen', in John Eatwell, Murray Milgate and Peter Newman, eds, *The New Palgrave Dictionary*, vol. 4, London: Macmillan, 1987, 220. On Lutz, see Verena Veit-Bachmann, 'Friedrich A. Lutz: Leben und Werk', in Viktor Vanberg, ed., *Währungsordnung und Inflation. Zum Gedenken an Friedrich A. Lutz (1901–1975)*, Tübingen: Mohr-Siebeck, 2003, esp. 36f. On the 'German neoliberals', especially Lutz and Meyer, see Peter Bernholz, *Geldwertstabilität und Währungsordnung*, Tübingen: Mohr, 1989; and on Graham, see Anthony M. Endres, 'Frank Graham's Case for Flexible Exchange Rates: A Doctrinal Perspective', *History of Political Economy* 40, no. 1 (2008): 133–62.

28   Helleiner also refers to the MPS at one point (and in two footnotes) but fails to provide a more extensive analysis of the specific role of the MPS – many of the

Introduction

It is otherwise with the growing body of research on MPS, which has been gathering momentum in recent years. Although neoliberal monetary policy has not yet been analysed specifically in this historiography, these studies form an important point of reference for the present undertaking. Critical engagement with the MPS network can be traced back to the touchstone 'hegemonic-theoretical' and neo-Gramscian *Die offenen Feinden und ihre Gesellschaft* by Bernhard Walpen. Other landmark studies by authors such as Dieter Plehwe, Phil Mirowski, François Denord, Lea Hartung, Jürgen Nordmann and Ralf Ptak, treating more specialised topics, have appeared in two edited volumes. More recent contributions are discussed in the preface above.[29]

Notably, the academic study done by the members of the MPS itself provides a good example of the working methods of this neoliberal network. In 2008, Philip Plickert published a history of the MPS, *Wandlungen des Neoliberalismus* in the Aktionsgemeinschaft Soziale Marktwirtschaft (ASM) series; the book was lavished with praise in a number of reviews by neoliberal authors, and celebrated as the defining study of the network. Plickert dismisses the existing literature in sweeping terms as 'leftist' and biased, before proceeding to offer an uncritical, credulous account of the MPS that cannot match those that he rejects. Yet as a participant in MPS conferences, Plickert is himself part of this very network.[30] His doctoral supervisor Joachim Starbatty, professor

---

intellectuals and political advisers he sees as considerably influential are MPS members, yet this connection is not clearly rendered in the text. See Helleiner, *States and the Reemergence of Global Finance*, 66, 115. See also Leeson, *Ideology and the International Economy*, 42, 46, 104, 150.

29 Walpen, *Die offenen Feinde und ihre Gesellschaft*; Dieter Plehwe, Bernhard Walpen, Gisela Neunhöffer, eds, *Neoliberal Hegemony: A Global Critique*, New York: Routledge, 2006; Mirowski and Plehwe, *The Road from Mont Pèlerin*. Also important is the study on the origins of the MPS in 'Red Vienna' by Jürgen Nordmann, *Der lange Marsch zum Neoliberalismus. Vom Roten Wien zum freien Markt – Popper und Hayek im Diskurs*, Hamburg: VSA Verlag, 2005; on ordoliberalism in the FRG see Ralf Ptak, *Vom Ordoliberalismus zur Sozialen Marktwirtschaft: Stationen des Neoliberalismus in Deutschland*, Opladen: Leske und Budrich, 2004.

30 Plickert reported, for example, on the MPS regional meeting in Hamburg in 2004 in an article in the ultra-liberal magazine *Eigentümlich-frei* (no. 42, pp. 26–7), which, according to the editor André Lichtschlag, is 'on the side of the libertarian resistance' and fights against the 'neo-socialist expropriation' of current federal policy under the motto *'eigentümlich frei – mehr netto'* (peculiarly free – more net profit). Plickert presented his book at its Hayek conference in 2007.

emeritus of economics at the University of Tübingen, earned his doctorate and habilitation under the supervision of MPS member Alfred Müller-Armack and is currently chairman of the ASM. The book's second reader, the professor Josef Molsberger, is co-editor of the journal *Ordo: Jahrbuch für die Ordnung von Wirtschaft und Gesellschaft*, which is decisively influenced by members of the MPS.

A note about the structure of the present book: while chapter 1 discusses both the MPS and the Bretton Woods monetary system by way of introduction, chapter 2 uses MPS conference debates over monetary policy to illustrate how flexible exchange rates gained ground over the 1950s and 1960s as a neoliberal concept of reform, in opposition to the classical liberal solution of the gold standard. The network that emerged from these debates was instrumental in popularising flexible exchange rates within economics, familiarising central bankers with the idea and propagating it within the Nixon administration, as chapter 3 argues. Finally, the conclusion briefly summarises the findings. For clarity, distilled biographical information covering the most important MPS members is compiled in an appended glossary at the end of the volume.[31]

This is a source-based historical work drawing on a combination of unpublished and published material. Chapter 2 relies on unpublished documents from the MPS conferences, held at the Liberaal Archief (LA) in Ghent, Belgium.[32] These consist in the (unfortunately incomplete) written papers of the speakers, as they were distributed to those in attendance.[33] Regrettably, the discussions that took place between the delivery of these papers, and the private conversations which may have occurred during other breaks – one of the main motivations for such international meetings – cannot be reconstructed verbatim. Still, the available texts give a good picture of what topics were discussed informally, and the respective positions of the participants. The 1961 MPS conference in Turin is a good example, as audio recordings of the event

31 The glossary makes no claim to be exhaustive. Due to the focus of the work, only MPS members are mentioned, with the density of biographical information varying according to the importance of the subject in the context of this work.

32 The unpublished documents from the Liberaal Archief (LA) are cited as follows: [name], [title, where available], LA [year], [page number].

33 The papers are donations from two members: Christian Gandil, a Danish economist, MPS member since 1949 and vice-president of the MPS; and Jacques Van Offelen, former minister in Belgium, main organiser of the 1962 MPS meeting in Knokke, Belgium, and vice-president of the MPS.

are well preserved. Although more participants engaged in the verbal debates, and although these contributions tended to be more concise and even cursory, they emphasised internal differences starkly and were directed at those present at the conference; a comparison indicates that the arguments advanced in oral contributions and the themes discussed on this occasion track the written essays rather closely.[34] In addition to this corpus, reference is made to the few reports on MPS conferences in the *Neue Zürcher Zeitung* (*NZZ*), as well as to a large number of publications by prominent MPS members.

Chapter 3 draws on the official publications of conference panel discussions, lectures, statements, reports and anthologies, along with the published output of MPS members. These are supplemented by articles from American newspapers and, where available, participant accounts. The chapter also discusses an article by the co-organiser of the Bellagio conferences Robert Triffin on their impact, found in a 1978 anthology published in honour of Fritz Machlup. Certain key MPS members, however, left no autobiographical or first-person writings (Machlup, Haberler, Lutz, Fellner); in the cases of Friedman, Johnson and Stigler, who did, there is regrettably hardly any usable information to be found in them.

34 See audio recordings of the MPS conference in Turin in 1961, available at 'Conferenza: 1961 Mt. Pelerin Society – Risorse Audio', Rediscovering Bruno Leoni, brunoleoni.it. A comparison of the articles published on MPS conferences in the *NZZ* and the conference documents also shows that the essays provide a good insight into the topics discussed.

1
Contexts of Neoliberal Monetary Policy

The Mont Pèlerin Society and Bretton Woods

To frame the question at hand, to give an overview of the field of inquiry and to present a more rounded portrait of the historical actors, two distinct contexts for neoliberal monetary policy must be treated at the outset. First is that of ideas: among members of the Mont Pèlerin Society, there was a widespread conviction of their potency. A survey of the specific ideas circulating within the Society from its inception will help situate debates over international financial regulation and the motives of the participants. A second context is institutional. An outline of the Bretton Woods monetary system, the object of MPS criticism, along with the prevailing opinion of economists at the time, is therefore also necessary.

The Mont Pèlerin Society: A transnational neoliberal network and the power of ideas

With the onset of the Great Depression and, consequently, the adoption of Keynesian and more broadly state-interventionist ideas, there also emerged a wider criticism of laissez-faire liberalism. Many contemporaries interpreted the latter as among the main contributing causes of the Depression and the rise of fascism. In response to these developments, a group of European liberals began to organise themselves transnationally, with the aim of renewing liberalism.[1] In 1938 the French philosopher Louis Rougier invited twenty-six hitherto only superficially linked intellectuals and economists from across the US and Europe to Paris to discuss Walter Lippmann's *The Good Society*.[2] Participants in this Colloque Walter Lippmann (CWL) agreed to refer to the new approach under development – which would set itself apart from classical liberalism – as 'neoliberalism'.[3] Thwarted prematurely by the Second World War, it was only in the post-war period that these efforts would be renewed.[4] The economist Friedrich von Hayek, already quite influential at the time, together with the Swiss businessman Albert Hunold organised a meeting from 1 to 10 April 1947 at the Hotel du Parc in Mont Pèlerin, a small town near Lake Geneva.[5] The conference was attended by thirty-eight intellectuals, publicists, politicians and economists from various countries in Europe and the US, including fifteen of the twenty-six participants of the CWL.[6] Considered by those attending to be a great success, this meeting gave rise to a permanent society, a 'club', which – since the men could not agree on another name – was to be called simply the Mont Pèlerin Society.[7] Hayek, who dominated the first decades of the MPS intellectually as well as organisationally, opened

---

1 For this interpretation of liberalism, see the paradigmatic Karl Polanyi, *The Great Transformation: The Political and Economic Origins of Our Time*, Boston: Beacon Press, 1957 (1944).

2 Lippmann (1889–1974), an influential American journalist, had in 1937 written *The Good Society*, a book which shaped the then-emerging neoliberalism.

3 See François Denord, 'Aux origines du néo-libéralisme en France. Louis Rougier et le Colloque Walter Lippmann de 1938', *Le Mouvement Social* 195 (2001); Bernhard Walpen, *Die offenen Feinde und ihre Gesellschaft: Eine hegemonietheoretische Studie zur Mont Pèlerin Society*, Hamburg: VSA Verlag, 2004, 45–83; Dieter Plehwe, introduction to Philip Mirowski and Dieter Plehwe, eds, *The Road from Mont Pèlerin: The Making of the Neoliberal Thought Collective*, Cambridge, MA: Harvard University Press, 2009, 10–26.

4 On the role played by certain MPS members in German fascism, see Walpen, *Die offenen Feinde und ihre Gesellschaft*, 93–8.

5 On the founding of the MPS, see Richard Cockett, *Thinking the Unthinkable: Think-Tanks and the Economic Counter-revolution 1931–1983*, London: Harper Collins, 1995, 105–9; Alan Ebenstein, *Friedrich Hayek: A Biography*, New York: Palgrave Macmillan, 2001, 140–6; Walpen, *Die offenen Feinde und ihre Gesellschaft*, 84–117.

6 A full list of the participants is published in Walpen, *Die offenen Feinde und ihre Gesellschaft*, 391f.

7 Ibid., 101; Ronald Max Hartwell, *A History of the Mont Pelerin Society*, Indianapolis: Liberty Fund, 1995, 25.

his inaugural speech at its first meeting with an explanation of his motivation for the project:

> If the ideals in which I believe unite us ... are to have a chance of revival, a great intellectual task is in the first instance required before we can successfully meet the errors which govern the world today. This task involves both purging traditional liberal theory of certain accidental accretions which have become attached to it in the course of time, and facing up to certain real problems which an over-simplified liberalism has shirked or which have become apparent only since it had become a somewhat stationary and rigid creed.[8]

Hayek's goal, as well as that of many of the MPS members, was twofold: at a theoretical level, he sought first to renew a conservative laissez-faire liberalism, which had fallen into disrepute in the wake of the Depression; second, he aimed to roll back theoretically and practically the advances of collectivism (by which Hayek meant not only socialism but Keynesianism and Roosevelt's New Deal policies), on the basis of expressly neoliberal theories. The most important task was to link the different, scattered and isolated liberals transnationally, thus strengthening and concentrating their work – the MPS was, as Friedman put it, a 'rallying point' for outnumbered troops.[9] In a 'Statement of Aims', its founding members agreed on six basic principles that should underpin the future work of the MPS. One of these objectives was to address 'the problem of the creation of an international order conducive to the safeguarding of peace and liberty and permitting the establishment of harmonious international economic relations'.[10] Just how MPS members

---

8 Friedrich von Hayek, 'Opening Address to Mont Pelerin Conference', Liberaal Archief in Ghent (hereafter, LA), 1947, 2.

9 Quoted in George H. Nash, *The Conservative Intellectual Movement in America since 1945*, New York: Basic Books, 1976, 26.

10 'Statement of Aims', LA, 2. The work of the MPS was also to focus on the following areas:
1. The analysis and exploration of the nature of the present crisis so as to bring home to others its essential moral and economic origins.
2. The redefinition of the functions of the state so as to distinguish more clearly between the totalitarian and the liberal order.
3. Methods of re-establishing the rule of law and of assuring its development in such manner that individuals and groups are not in a position to encroach

sought to heed this command at the Society's conferences over the 1950s and 1960s is the subject of the present study.

From its inception, members of the MPS, backed by industry and sympathetic institutions, have convened on a near annual basis, whether at biennial worldwide meetings or at interim regional get-togethers. Like the CWL, the MPS was deliberately transnational from the outset, and sought to gather academics across disciplines alongside businessmen, publicists, intellectuals and politicians; but membership has always been disproportionately populated by American and European economists.[11] To this day, its members are almost exclusively white men.[12] As late as the 1970s, Friedman saw no advantage in having a woman serve on the Society's membership-selection committee. In 1975, twenty-eight years after the founding of the MPS, James Buchanan wrote to its secretary, Ralph Harris, to ask whether Tom Sowell could attend a meeting: 'This would be a "first" for the Mont Pelerin, since Sowell is, as you perhaps know, a black.'[13]

The MPS is organised as a 'closed society' of like-minded people, mainly a men's club, with new members accepted only by invitation.[14]

---

upon the freedom of others and private rights are not allowed to become a basis of predatory power.
4. The possibility of establishing minimum standards by means not inimical to initiative and functioning of the market.
5. Methods of combating the misuse of history for the furtherance of creeds hostile to liberty.

For the full statement of aims, see montpelerin.org.

11 The total of over 1,100 members of the MPS (including all deceased members) come from over fifty countries, with a quite uneven distribution: 39.4 per cent US, 8.6 per cent Germany, 8.4 per cent UK, 6.2 per cent France, 3.7 per cent Japan; Latin America total 9.5 per cent, Asia 5.4 per cent, Africa 2 per cent (see the lists compiled by Walpen, *Die offenen Feinde und ihre Gesellschaft*, 393-7, and in Dieter Plehwe and Bernhard Walpen, 'Between Network and Complex Organization: The Making of Neoliberal Knowledge and Hegemony', in Dieter Plehwe, Bernhard Walpen and Gisela Neunhöffer, eds, *Neoliberal Hegemony: A Global Critique*, New York: Routledge, 2006, 35).

12 See Plehwe and Walpen, 'Between Network and Complex Organization', 34, and Walpen, *Die offenen Feinde und ihre Gesellschaft*, 387.

13 Quoted in Rick Tilman, *Ideology and Utopia in the Social Philosophy of the Libertarian Economists*, Westport, CT: Greenwood, 2001, 100.

14 Women were entirely absent in its early years, and its membership was historically overwhelmingly made up of men. An examination of the MPS and neoliberal intellectuals from the perspective of critical gender studies is still pending. On the exclusion of women from 'men's organisations' (such as Freemasons) using the British example,

Hayek made this clear in his opening speech: 'It must remain a closed society not open to all and sundry, but only to people who share with us certain common convictions.'[15] The press was likewise decidedly excluded and the conferences were to be regarded – according to Hayek– 'as private meetings' with 'everything said here in discussion "off the record", as the Americans say'.[16] The MPS did not take political positions in public, and this facilitated contentious internal debates, while ensuring that scrutiny fall on individual members' achievements rather than on the institutional and collaborative origins of many of their views.[17] A strength of the MPS was that its network linked various economic schools – in addition to the primarily European members of the Austrian School and the German Freiburg School of Ordoliberalism, a number of economists from the emerging Chicago School.[18] MPS conferences had a number of functions, such as the production, internal discussion and international diffusion of neoliberal ideas, to be outlined briefly in chapter 2. The membership grew from about 200 in the 1950s to over 300 in the 1960s.[19] Among the political figures who joined its ranks were German Chancellor Ludwig Erhard, Italian President Luigi Einaudi, Czech President Václav Klaus and EU Commissioner Frits Bolkestein. Eight members of the MPS have been awarded the so-called Nobel Prize in Economic Sciences, which has significantly advanced the reputation of neoliberal theories.[20]

The MPS is generally regarded as the most significant association of an emerging post-war neoliberalism. The term 'neoliberalism' is used here in a broad sense that includes its historical roots – it refers to 'a

---

see Barbara Rogers, *Men Only: An Investigation into Men's Organisations*, London: Pandora, 1988.

15   Hayek, 'Opening Address to Mont Pelerin Conference', 22, and similarly 2.
16   Ibid., 12.
17   See Plehwe and Walpen, 'Between Network and Complex Organization', 34.
18   For details on the different schools in the MPS, see Mark Skousen, *Vienna and Chicago, Friends or Foes? A Tale of Two Schools of Free-Market Economics*, Washington, DC: Capital Press, 2005. Skousen is himself a member of the MPS. See also Walpen, *Die offenen Feinde und ihre Gesellschaft*, 62–73, 101–11.
19   The number of members grew relatively quickly. As early as 1951 there were 172, in 1961 there were 258, in 1966, 323, and by 1975, 381. The number of members was later limited to 500.
20   Friedrich von Hayek 1974, Milton Friedman 1976, George Stigler 1982, James Buchanan 1986, Maurice Allais 1988, Ronald Coase 1991, Gary Becker 1992 and Vernon L. Smith 2002.

spectrum *of positions that have emerged historically in different places in Europe and the US and share the common denominator of opting for the price mechanism and the market*.[21] Since there is no neoliberal programme, but rather several neoliberalisms, much room exists for internal contradictions and corresponding 'disputes and struggles'.[22] According to Hayek, the content of liberalism – and neoliberalism – can be understood as:

> A policy which deliberately adopts competition, markets and prices as its ordering principles and uses the legal framework enforced by the state in order to make competition as effective and beneficial as possible – and to supplement it where, and only where, it cannot be made effective.[23]

In the scholarly literature, the MPS has variously been described as a 'transnational worldview community', 'international elite network', 'comprehensive transnational discourse community', 'think tank' and 'neoliberal thought collective'.[24] Set in context, the period from the late

---

21 Walpen, *Die offenen Feinde und ihre Gesellschaft*, 64, and 62–5. Since many members of the MPS also describe themselves as 'liberal' in addition to 'neoliberal', this term will be used in the following to refer to positions and persons discussed in the MPS (in contrast to the Anglo-American use of 'liberal').

22 Ibid., 64.

23 Quoted in Cockett, *Thinking the Unthinkable*, 113; see also Friedrich Lutz, 'Bemerkungen zum Monopolproblem', *Ordo* 8 (1956), 19. On the history and implementation of neoliberalism, see David Harvey, *A Brief History of Neoliberalism*, Oxford: Oxford University Press. 2005; Monica Prasad, *The Politics of Free Markets: The Rise of Neoliberal Economic Policies in Britain, France, Germany, and the United States*, Chicago: University of Chicago Press, 2006; Susanne Soederberg, Georg Menz and Philip G. Cerny, eds, *Internalizing Globalization: The Rise of Neoliberalism and the Decline of National Varieties of Capitalism*, Basingstoke: Palgrave Macmillan, 2005.

24 Dieter Plehwe and Katja Walther, 'Im Schatten von Hayek und Friedman: Die Vielflieger im Kreise der Mont Pèlerin Society. Quantitative Analyse als Explorationsinstrument der historisch-sozialen Netzwerkforschung', in Berthold Unfried et al., eds, *Transnationale Netzwerke im 20. Jahrhundert: Historische Erkundungen zu Ideen und Praktiken, Individuen und Organisationen*, Leipzig: Akademische Verlagsanstalt, 239; Dieter Plehwe and Bernhard Walpen, 'Wissenschaftliche und wissenschaftspolitische Produktionsweisen im Neoliberalismus Beiträge der Mont Pèlerin Society', *PROKLA. Zeitschrift für kritische Sozialwissenschaft* 115, no. 2 (1999), 205; Dieter Plehwe, 'The Making of a Comprehensive Transnational Discourse Community', in Marie-Laure Djelic and Sigrid Quack, eds, *Transnational Communities*

1970s – specifically from arrival in power of Margaret Thatcher (1979) and Ronald Reagan (1980) – is usually interpreted as the moment when the practical effect of the ideas developed in the MPS was first felt.[25] But with respect to the hegemony of liberalised capital markets and flexible exchange rates, members of the MPS network had exercised considerable influence over monetary policy debates and key decision-makers since the 1960s.

Basing himself on the lectures he delivered at the first MPS conference, Hayek developed a series of social-philosophical reflections on the effective enforcement of ideas that were subsequently widely accepted within the MPS. Dieter Plehwe and Bernhard Walpen have described Hayek's reflections as components of a Gramscian 'hegemonic' strategy.[26] On this point, Plehwe and Walpen focus primarily on Hayek's 1949 article 'The Intellectuals and Socialism', in which questions of hegemony are addressed in a decidedly compact manner. In what follows, I will show that Hayek had discussed the power of ideas starting in the 1930s, especially in relation to monetary questions.[27] Hayek assumed that the spread of Keynesian ideas, popularised above all by particularly active intellectuals, was the main cause of the collapse of the classical liberal monetary system represented by the gold standard: 'the abandonment of the gold standard in England [can rightly] be described

---

and the Regulation of Business, Cambridge: Hartung, 2010; Mirowski and Plehwe, *The Road from Mont Pèlerin*.

25 See Walpen, *Die offenen Feinde und ihre Gesellschaft*, 196–225; Harvey, *A Brief History of Neoliberalism*, 22f. For example, twenty-two of Reagan's seventy-six economic advisers were MPS members, many of whom held high government posts (see Hartwell, *A History of the Mont Pelerin Society*, 213).

26 Plehwe and Walpen, 'Wissenschaftliche und wissenschaftspolitische Produktionsweisen', 206–11.

27 Hayek had first discussed the power of ideas in 1932 and then in 1937 in studies on the gold standard and on 'monetary nationalism', where he already elaborated its central elements. See Friedrich A. von Hayek, 'Was der Goldwährung geschehen ist', in *Was der Goldwährung geschehen ist. Ein Bericht aus dem Jahre 1932 mit zwei Ergänzungen* (Walter Eucken Institut: Vorträge und Aufsätze 12), Tübingen: J.C.B. Mohr, 1965 [1932], 7, 25; Friedrich A. von Hayek, *Monetary Nationalism and International Stability* (Institut Universitaire de Hautes Études Internationales, Genève), London: Longmans, Green and Co, 1937, xii, 94. What came later was the application of this theory – which was developed by observing the effectiveness of the Keynesian ideas he opposed – to the neoliberal ideas that Hayek advanced in the context of the MPS; that is, the transformation of theory into strategy.

as, "the economic consequences of Mr. Keynes'", he wrote in 1932.[28] Hayek here alluded Keynes's 1925 paper entitled 'The Economic Consequences of Mr. Churchill', in which Keynes discussed the 'rules of the game' of the gold standard. Hayek continues:

> The fact that the otherwise so conservative heads of the central banks deviated relatively lightly from the traditional rules of monetary policy can be attributed to the influence of new, scientifically propagated monetary policy ideas that became widespread in the post-war years.[29]

Hayek did not limit himself to historical observations, but rather sought to generalise them: already in his 1937 study on the gold standard, he had stressed that abstract and principled 'academic discussion . . . in the long run forms public opinion and . . . in consequence decides what will be practical politics some time hence'.[30] In 1949 he put forward a succinct formulation:

> Experience suggests that . . . it is merely a question of time until the views now held by the intellectuals become the governing force of politics . . . What to the contemporary observer appears as the battle of conflicting interests has indeed often been decided long before in a clash of ideas confined to narrow circles.[31]

The creation of the MPS was motivated in large part by Hayek's belief that the dissemination of ideas requires institutional mediation by networks and organisations.[32] This initiative was one component of an effort to harness 'the clash of ideas in narrow circles' to ensure the

---

28 Hayek, 'Was der Goldwährung geschehen ist', 25.
29 Ibid., 7.
30 Hayek, *Monetary Nationalism and International Stability*, xii.
31 See, from 1949, Friedrich A. von Hayek, 'The Intellectuals and Socialism', in *The Collected Works of F. A. Hayek*, vol. 10, *Socialism and War: Essays, Documents, Reviews*, ed. Bruce Caldwell, London: Routledge, 1997, 221–37, 222. Hayek clearly took the cue from his antagonist John Maynard Keynes, *The General Theory of Employment, Interest and Money*, London: Macmillan, 2007 [1936], 283.
32 Plehwe and Walpen, 'Wissenschaftliche und wissenschaftspolitische Produktionsweisen', 209.

application and institutionalisation of neoliberal thought.[33] A long-term vision was required, as ideas were understood to become hegemonic only over the course of 'two or three generations'.[34] Strategically, Hayek stressed the need to overcome the paralysis and weakness then afflicting the neoliberal camp and stepped-up efforts at the 'effective refutation' of adversaries' errors, while elaborating a utopian programme to raise politics above the merely quotidian. It was not a question of making 'practical, sensible and realistic' proposals; as Hayek formulated it, 'What we lack is a liberal utopia.'[35] Hayek's 'original thinkers' were to develop this utopian, strategic and forward-looking framework, but he also considered the 'second-hand dealers in ideas' to be necessary for gaining influence at a mass level.[36]

The MPS debates analysed here may be understood as an attempt to redeem Hayek's claim that 'much must be done in the realm of ideas before we can hope to achieve the basis of a stable international system'.[37] The present study attempts to take Hayek's hegemonic strategy seriously in the very area in which he discussed it most frequently: that is, in relation to the international monetary order. To what extent did the MPS, by elaborating an alternative 'utopia' and propagating it among monetary policy experts and economists, succeed in effectively discrediting its opponents' positions?

The Bretton Woods monetary system: Autonomous monetary policy, fixed exchange rates and capital controls

In July 1944, forty-four countries led by the US (with its chief negotiator Harry Dexter White) and UK (represented by Keynes) adopted the Bretton Woods Monetary Agreement at the eponymous winter resort in New Hampshire. The system it established encompassed the majority of

---

33 Hayek, 'Monetary Nationalism and International Stability', xii; Hayek, 'The Intellectuals and Socialism', 222.
34 Hayek, 'The Intellectuals and Socialism', 228.
35 Ibid., 233, 237.
36 The term was used by Hayek to describe institutions and think tanks such as the Institute for Economic Affairs in London, which he founded, and which organised the popularisation of neoliberal ideas and theories, refined them, disseminated them so as to influence the wider society, which he understood in this regard to be passive. Ibid., 221.
37 Hayek, 'Monetary Nationalism and International Stability', xiii.

the non-communist world from the late 1940s to the early 1970s. Widely analysed across numerous studies,[38] Bretton Woods was central to the unique post-war constellation of reforms that John Ruggie has aptly termed 'embedded liberalism'.[39]

Robert Gilpin has characterised the dynamic particular of Bretton Woods as 'Keynes at home and Smith abroad'.[40] On the one hand, the monetary agreement set up an open and liberal international *trade* order (but also included extensive *capital account* controls): this was its 'Smith abroad' component. On the other hand, in accordance with the prevailing consensus of the time, Keynesian demand management was permitted, with the aim of stabilising the crisis-prone economy and guaranteeing a certain level of social security, growth and full employment: this was Keynes at home.[41] Theoretically, such a constellation was informed by economic theories then generally referred to as Keynesian, which held that an economy left to the play of market forces produces stagnation and crises given a systemic tendency to generate insufficient demand. The problem, according to the then developing consensus among economists, could be remedied only by way of state investment policy and economic regulation with the goal of full employment.[42]

At the heart of the Bretton Woods Agreement, as it developed historically, was a system of fixed but adjustable exchange rates, backed by

38 Among the best historical accounts are Barry Eichengreen, *Globalizing Capital: A History of the International Monetary System*, Princeton, NJ: Princeton University Press, esp. chapter 4; J. Keith Horsefield and Margaret Garritsen de Vries, *The International Monetary Fund 1945-1965: Twenty Years of International Monetary Cooperation*, Washington, DC: International Monetary Fund, 1969; Harold James, *International Monetary Cooperation since Bretton Woods*, Washington, DC: International Monetary Fund, 1996.

39 John Gerard Ruggie, 'International Regimes, Transactions, and Change: Embedded Liberalism in the Postwar Economic Order', *International Organization* 36, no. 2 (1982). The concept of 'embeddedness' can be traced back to Karl Polanyi, *The Great Transformation: The Political and Economic Origins of Our Time*, Boston: Beacon Press, 1944. Keynes's and White's plans were published in Horsefield and de Vries, *The International Monetary Fund 1945-1965*, vol. 3, 3-36 and 37-96.

40 Robert Gilpin, *The Political Economy of International Relations*, Princeton, NJ: Princeton University Press, 1987, 355.

41 See Ruggie 'International Regimes, Transactions, and Change'; Eric Helleiner, *States and the Reemergence of Global Finance: From Bretton Woods to the 1990s*, Ithaca, NY: Cornell University Press, 1994, 25-50.

42 On Keynes's theories and the corresponding historical literature, see, besides Keynes's *General Theory* (1936), above all Peter Hall, ed., *The Political Power of Economic Ideas: Keynesianism across Borders*, Princeton: Princeton University Press, 1989.

international capital controls, with the US dollar playing a prominent role as reserve currency. All currencies were pegged to the dollar, which in turn was pegged to gold, with the US guaranteeing the exchange of each national currency into gold at the fixed rate (one troy ounce of gold was equivalent to thirty-five US dollars).[43] In order to be able to combine fixed exchange rates – then seen as a necessary precondition of a liberal trade order – with an autonomous Keynesian monetary policy, far-reaching international capital movements and exchange controls had to be introduced.[44]

Bretton Woods thus departed decidedly from both the classical gold standard and free exchange rate regimes – precisely those two proposed reforms which would be discussed and championed inside the MPS. Here, a widely accepted theorem of international macroeconomics, namely the so-called impossibility theorem or basic policy trilemma, is particularly well suited for the historical analysis of various monetary regimes.[45] The policy trilemma holds that a government is only ever able to realise two of the following three objectives simultaneously: first, fixed exchange rates; second, an autonomous monetary policy directed towards internal goals such as stability, full employment or growth; and third, the internationally free movement of capital.

The three main historical exchange rate regimes – the gold standard (1871 to 1914), Bretton Woods (1944 to 1971) and flexible exchange rates (1973 to the present) – have each solved the trilemma differently; each was compelled to sacrifice one of the three objectives in the name of the other two, in accordance with the socio-economic context and prevailing economic theories (see figure 1).[46]

---

43 See Helleiner, *States and the Reemergence of Global Finance*, 25–50; Ruggie, 'International Regimes, Transactions, and Change'; Peter Isard, *Globalization and the International Financial System: What's Wrong and What Can Be Done*, Cambridge: Cambridge University Press, 2005; James, *International Monetary Cooperation*.

44 See Helleiner, *States and the Reemergence of Global Finance*, 25–50.

45 This trilemma was developed formally in the early 1960s by economists Fleming and Robert Mundell. Contemporary historical applications of this theorem are to be found in Isard, *Globalization and the International Financial System*; James, *International Monetary Cooperation*; Kathleen McNamara, *The Currency of Ideas: Monetary Politics in the European Union*, Ithaca, NY: Cornell University Press, 1999; Maurice Obstfeld and Alan Taylor, *Global Capital Markets: Integration, Crisis, and Growth*, Cambridge: Cambridge University Press, 2004.

46 On the periodisation of currency regimes, see Obstfeld and Taylor, *Global Capital Markets*; Eichengreen, *Globalizing Capital*.

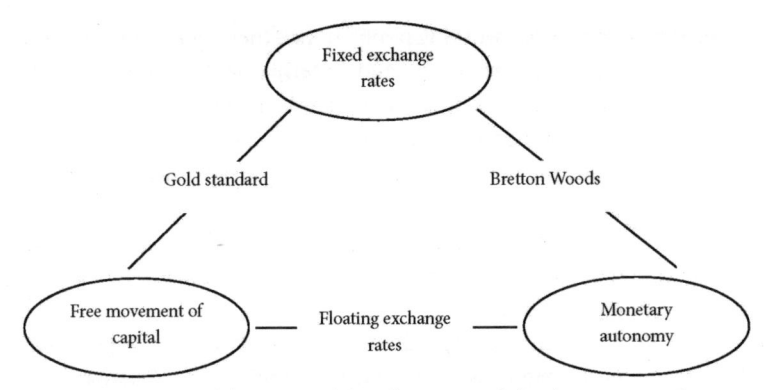

Figure 1. Diagram of the impossibility theorem and the three principal monetary systems

The classical gold standard prevailed in a period during which most industrialised countries followed the Bank of England and established collateral requirements for redeeming gold in their respective currencies (Europe 1871, United States and Japan 1879). This created an internationally accepted monetary system based on a set of unwritten rules.[47] The gold standard combined fixed exchange rates with high capital mobility – international capital movements around 1900 were at about the level of the 1990s (proportional to the gross national product of leading countries).[48]

In order to enable free capital movements at fixed exchange rates in this first phase of globalisation, domestic monetary policy had to be guided exclusively by external considerations, meaning the stabilisation of exchange rates.[49] Karl Polanyi described in striking terms what this

---

[47] This gold standard was based on three fundamental principles: establishment of a gold parity (e.g., 1 troy ounce of gold equals 20.67 US dollars – to create fixed exchange rates between the currencies); gold backing regulations with regard to the amount of cash in circulation; a gold redemption obligation of the central banks vis-à-vis private customers and other central banks. See Rolf Caspers, *Zahlungsbilanz und Wechselkurse*, Munich: R. Oldenbourg Verlag, 2002, 159f., and also Mark Skousen, *The Structure of Production*, New York: New York University Press, 1990, esp. 226f. On the historical gold standard, see Barry Eichengreen, *Golden Fetters: The Gold Standard and the Great Depression, 1919–1939*, New York: Oxford University Press, 1995.

[48] Isard, *Globalization and the International Financial System*, 57.

[49] On the mechanism of the gold standard, which was systematised as early as 1752 by David Hume as the so-called price-specie flow mechanism, see Eichengreen, *Globalizing Capital*, 25–30.

meant concretely for the working population: if the balance of payments, stabilisation of exchange rates and international capital markets demanded it, falling wages or rising unemployment had to be accepted.[50] The gold standard ensured that the control and regulation of money remained beyond the sphere of everyday democratic politics, despite the increasing politicisation of economic policy.[51] For, as a standard textbook summarises it, the 'stability of exchange rates [was] based on the subjection of national economic policy to the dictates of the balance of payments equilibrium'.[52]

Barry Eichengreen has argued convincingly in *Globalizing Capital* that a monetary system like the gold standard (fixed exchange rates combined with the absence of capital controls) is profoundly anti-democratic and therefore became increasingly dysfunctional from the 1920s onwards. Under democratic conditions, with strong labour movements and Keynesian approaches gaining international acceptance, no government remained in a position to base monetary policy solely on the quantity of gold and the maintenance of fixed exchange rates; internal considerations such as full employment and growth instead gained importance.[53]

The gold standard collapsed during the First World War, and the attempt to establish a gold currency standard at the Genoa Economic and Financial conference of 1922 failed by the 1930s due to central banks' unwillingness to cooperate, extremely high levels of capital controls and the fact that under pressure from the trade unions, the

---

50 The classical gold standard had already ceased to function entirely automatically at the beginning of the twentieth century due to its self-destructive tendencies. Instead, the central banks tried to cushion the disastrous consequences of a possibly necessary deflation by using evermore unbacked paper money (see Polanyi, *The Great Transformation*, 210–17).
51 Eichengreen, *Golden Fetters*, esp. 30.
52 Caspers, *Zahlungsbilanz und Wechselkurse*, 161. Polanyi also presented this in detail in 1944.
53 Eichengreen, *Globalizing Capital*, 30f. Eichengreen describes the main reasons for the functioning of the gold standard as the restriction of the right to vote to (propertied) men, weak labour parties and unions, and the high flexibility of wages and prices, as well as the willingness to accept high unemployment. James describes the difficulties of French politicians in the 1930s in deciding between capital controls and devaluation – a discussion that illustrates vividly the political pressures generating the trilemma. See Harold James, *The End of Globalization: Lessons from the Great Depression*, Cambridge, MA: Harvard University Press, 2001, 189–97.

rules of the game applying to the gold standard were increasingly violated on domestic economic grounds.[54] The attempts to re-establish a gold standard after the First World War were also attempts to curb the political power of labour and the voting population; their failure was an expression of a new balance of power and the unwillingness of working people to accommodate downward adjustments on their wages.[55] The subsequent short phases of strongly fluctuating flexible exchange rates in the 1920s led on the one hand to competitive devaluations – in order to secure competitive advantages in international trade, various countries undervalued their currencies and thus set in motion a catastrophic downward spiral (the so-called beggar-thy-neighbour policy). On the other hand, currency speculation and speculative, short-term international capital flows (so-called hot money) triggered sometimes quite dramatic exchange rate fluctuations. The period prior to the establishment of the Bretton Woods system was characterised by national isolation, a high level of capital controls, destabilising speculation, wildly fluctuating exchange rates, continuous devaluations and a general absence of a functioning monetary order.[56]

Return to the free trade regime of the gold standard was rejected at Bretton Woods, as it would have subordinated domestic and welfare state–oriented monetary policy to the rationality of international capital markets and thus would have precluded an autonomous monetary policy aimed at full employment. Instead, the role of the state was to be strengthened significantly vis-à-vis the market.[57] In US Treasury Secretary Hans Morgenthau's representative formulation, the new financial order was to be an 'instrumentality of sovereign governments and not of private financial interests'; governments were to 'drive ... the usurious money lenders from the temple of

---

54 Caspers, *Zahlungsbilanz und Wechselkurse*, 164; Obstfeld and Taylor, *Global Capital Markets*, 37.
55 Matt Hampton, 'Hegemony, Class Struggle and the Radical Historiography of Global Monetary Standards', *Capital and Class* 89 (2006).
56 Eichengreen, *Golden Fetters*; Eichengreen, *Globalizing Capital*, 45–91.
57 Keynes had already shown the weaknesses of the gold standard in his 1923 *Tract on Monetary Reform* and, according to a biographer of Keynes, 'within a decade Keynes's position had won the allegiance of at least half the world'. R. F. Harrod, *The Life of John Maynard Keynes*, London: Macmillan, 1966, 339.

international finance'.[58] Instead of a principle of convertibility – the orientation of domestic economic policy according to the requirements of international payments and capital movements – full employment became the main goal, to which international monetary policy would be subordinated.[59] To achieve this, it was neither an automatic mechanism nor the observation of general rules to discipline policy that prevailed, but rather enlargement of the scope for decision-making by governments and monetary authorities.[60] Faith in the natural balancing effect of market forces and avoidance of state intervention in the movement of goods and capital was now considered outdated. Harry Dexter White, the chief American negotiator, argued:

> The theoretical bases for the belief still so widely held that interference with trade and with capital and gold movements etc., are harmful, are hangovers from a Nineteenth Century economic creed, which held that international economic adjustments, if left alone, would work themselves out toward an 'equilibrium' with a minimum of harm to world trade and prosperity.[61]

The prevailing ambition, aptly described by Ragnar Nurkse in an influential League of Nations publication, was 'to make international monetary policy conform to domestic social and economic policy and not the other way round'.[62]

---

58 Quoted in Richard N. Gardner, *Sterling-Dollar Diplomacy: The Origins and the Prospects of Our International Economic Order*, New York: McGraw-Hill, 1969 [1956], 76.
59 See Anthony M. Endres, *Great Architects of International Finance: The Bretton Woods Era*, London: Routledge, 2005, 23.
60 James, *International Monetary Cooperation*, 37.
61 Quoted in J. Keith Horsefield and Margaret Garritsen de Vries, *The International Monetary Fund 1945–1965*, vol. 3, Washington, DC: International Monetary Fund, 1969, 64.
62 Ragnar Nurkse, *International Currency Experience: Lessons from the Inter-war Period*, Geneva: League of Nations, 1944, 230. The work of Nurkse (1907–1959) was exemplary of the Bretton Woods consensus. 'That book distilled a series of lessons from the interwar experience that expresses in the form of a historical analysis the philosophy underlying the Bretton Woods solution.' Harold James and Michael Bordo, 'Haberler versus Nurkse: The Case for Floating Exchange Rates as an Alternative to Bretton Woods?', discussion paper no. 2001-08 of University of St. Gallen, 2001, 7.

But the system of flexible exchange rates was just as firmly rejected at Bretton Woods, especially because the brief experience with free exchange rates in the 1920s was understood as disastrous and linked to the Great Depression.[63] Economists' arguments were directed specifically against the dangers of competitive devaluation and speculative, destabilising capital movements. Nurkse summed up the zeitgeist as follows: 'If there is anything that the inter-war experience has clearly demonstrated, it is that paper currency exchanges cannot be left free to fluctuate.' He continued: It 'would almost certainly result in chaos'. Nurkse, for his part, argued that exchange rates should be altered as infrequently as possible, and that when they were, such changes should be undertaken only in coordination with the international community and with the aid of capital controls to prevent speculation.[64]

Under the Bretton Woods regime, the stability of the international monetary order and international free trade could be guaranteed only with the help of fixed exchange rates. These were to be supported by the central banks through intervention in foreign exchange markets, undertaken to ensure that parities did not fluctuate by more than 1 per cent. The International Monetary Fund (IMF) was founded to cushion balance-of-payments deficits, to 'promote exchange rate stability, to maintain orderly exchange arrangements among members, and to avoid competitive exchange depreciation'.[65] Only in exceptional situations, cases of fundamental disequilibrium, were changes in exchange rates permissible – in consultation with the IMF and with the aid of capital controls. For various reasons, but above all so as not to endanger the prestige of a national currencies – and under pressure from the industries involved in foreign trade and in order to avoid

---

63 Nurkse, *International Currency Experience*, 210. Both Keynes and White rejected floating, market-determined exchange rates. Anthony M. Endres, 'Frank Graham's Case for Flexible Exchange Rates: A Doctrinal Perspective', *History of Political Economy* 40, no. 1 (2008), 133–62, 150.

64 Nurkse, *International Currency Experience*, 118, 128, 225. In general, the financial turmoil of the inter-war period is explained by speculative short-term capital flows. James, *International Monetary Cooperation*, 37; Eichengreen, *Globalizing Capital*, 88–91. See also the critique of destabilising capital flows in Hayek, *Monetary Nationalism and International Stability*, 72.

65 Article 1 of the IMF's founding Articles of Agreement, quoted in James, *International Monetary Cooperation*, 50.

currency speculation – adjustments of exchange rates were intended to be exceedingly rare, even if the possibility was in principle kept in reserve.[66]

For all these reasons, the Bretton Woods system simultaneously enabled autonomous, democratic monetary policy and enshrined a stable international trade order through fixed exchange rates. In accordance with the aforementioned trilemma, the free movement of capital was restricted drastically. According to the historian Harold James, 'almost every analyst' considered 'control on capital movements for an unlimited time' to be a necessary precondition for international trade.[67] Capital movements would serve solely to facilitate the payments necessary for commerce across national borders. States were explicitly granted the right to control all capital movements and were even encouraged to use controls in cases of destabilising capital flows. In the same vein, article VI of the IMF's Articles of Agreement stated that all member countries may 'exercise such controls as are necessary to regulate international capital movements', as long as these controls do not 'restrict payments for current transactions', which would restrict free trade.[68] Eric Helleiner has described in detail the extent to which both cooperative capital controls and national exchange controls were institutionalised in the Bretton Woods agreements. He summarises the arrangement as follows: 'The overriding principle, however, was restriction: states were given the explicit right to control *all* capital movements.'[69] Accordingly, the post-war decades witnessed 'densest restrictions on capital sales in the history of international capitalism to date'.[70]

Yet the Bretton Woods compromise was marked by failure from the outset, as inherent contradictions spoiled its ability to function. Even where the rejection of floating exchange rates and the promotion of capital controls did have stabilising effects on the global economy,

---

66   Eichengreen, *Globalizing Capital*, 94, 122.
67   James, *International Monetary Cooperation*, 38. See also Eichengreen, *Globalizing Capital*, 93–135.
68   IMF, Articles of Agreement of the International Monetary Fund, 1944, available at imf.org.
69   Helleiner, *States and the Reemergence of Global Finance*, 49.
70   Jörg Huffschmid, *Politische Ökonomie der Finanzmärkte*, Hamburg: VSA Verlag, 2001, 117. See also Obstfeld and Taylor, *Global Capital Markets*.

Bretton Woods itself was structured in such a way that it was bound to be torn apart by crises. This was mainly due to the fact that, firstly, effective mechanisms were lacking to remedy imbalances in trade and payments; and secondly, the US dollar's function as reserve currency was unsustainable. Keynes had addressed these two points in his original plans, which he drafted on behalf of the British government in the early 1940s. But he was unable to push his preferred solutions through in negotiations, since their multilateral orientation and focus on the international balance above all were too far-reaching for the US, the emergent hegemonic power.[71]

Keynes's planned International Clearing Union included a world currency (Keynes called it 'bancor'), rendering superfluous any given hegemonic reserve for the clearing of interstate balances, and he was particularly concerned with effective means for reducing such imbalances; sanctions for surpluses in current accounts were of special importance.[72] Keynes's ideas regarding the international monetary system are still highly pertinent, and they have been the subject of extensive discussion since the 1990s, especially with respect to global imbalances.[73]

Despite these defects, the Bretton Woods monetary system did function with relative stability for two decades. After a series of minor crises in which new parities were set, the full convertibility of currencies was finally achieved by the end of 1958 in Europe, followed by Japan in 1964.[74] With the exception of Canada, which floated its dollar from 1950 to 1962, the regime functioned with stable fixed exchange rates from 1949 to 1967 and experienced only two changes to the parity of

---

71   On the negotiations, see Elke Muchlinski, 'Kontroversen in der internationalen Währungspolitik: Retrospektive zu Keynes-White-Boughton und IMF', *Interventionen. Zeitschrift für Ökonomie* 2, no. 1 (2005), and Raymond F. Mikesell, *The Bretton Woods Debates: A Memoir*, Princeton, NJ: Princeton University Press.

72   Keynes amended and revised his plans several times between 1941 and 1944 at the insistence of the British Treasury and the Bank of England – especially with regard to sanctions against surplus countries. The various drafts and versions are printed in John Maynard Keynes, 'Activities 1940–1944. Shaping the Post-war World: The Clearing Union', in *The Collected Writings of John Maynard Keynes*, vol. 25, London/Cambridge: Macmillan/Cambridge University Press, 1980.

73   See Paul Davidson, *Financial Markets, Money and the Real World*, Cheltenham: Edward Elgar Publishing, 2002, esp. 231–52.

74   Huffschmid, *Politische Ökonomie der Finanzmärkte*, 116.

major currencies.[75] Key to the functioning of the system was the political and economic strength of the US, which had initially dispensed with capital controls after the war and, as the country with the leading currency and 'banker of the world', provided the liquidity necessary to meet high demand across the war-ravaged European economies.[76] The worldwide dollar glut of the 1960s was caused mainly by the twin factors of expansionary American monetary and fiscal policy (especially Lyndon B. Johnson's Great Society programme of the second half of the 1960s) and the inflationary financing of the American war in Vietnam. Its effects were ambiguous. Although the dollar began to serve more comprehensively as the basis for the monetary system *in toto*, allowing the industrialised countries to pursue their respective domestic growth and full-employment objectives without overly rigid monetary discipline,[77] greater demand for foreign dollar reserves, combined with the expansive monetary policy of the global hegemon itself, undermined confidence in the value of the dollar – just as the so-called Triffin dilemma had predicted from the early 1960s.[78]

75   These were the devaluation of the French franc in 1958 and the joint revaluation of the West German mark and the Dutch guilder in 1961. See Peter Isard, *Exchange Rate Economics*, Cambridge: Cambridge University Press, 1995, 190.

76   This aspect is emphasised above all by Robert Gilpin, *The Political Economy of International Relations*, Princeton, NJ: Princeton University Press, 1987, 131–42, here 133.

77   McNamara, *The Currency of Ideas*, 82–93, covers one of the characteristics of Bretton Woods: nation-states were able to follow quite different paths of economic development. The national economic policies of the industrialised nations are described in detail in the respective country studies in the anthology on Keynesianism edited by Hall in 1989.

78   On the Triffin dilemma, see Robert Triffin, *Gold and the Dollar Crisis: The Future of Convertibility*, New Haven, CT: Yale University Press, 1960. Robert Triffin (1911–1993), Belgian economist and professor at Yale, was one of the most important theorists on currency issues and an influential policy adviser in the 1960s. The so-called Triffin dilemma held that in a monetary system based for international liquidity on a national reserve currency such as the US dollar, a scarcity of liquid assets arises (were the US to balance its budget), or alternatively, when confidence in the international reserve currency (in this case, the dollar) is undermined, the system is threatened in the long run by collapse. On Triffin, see Albert Steinherr, 'Robert Triffin', in Albert Steinherr and Daniel Weiserbs, eds, *Evolution of the International and Regional Monetary Systems: Essays in Honour of Robert Triffin*, London: Macmillan, 1991; Endres, *Great Architects of International Finance*, 102–22; John S. Odell, *U.S. International Monetary Policy: Markets, Power, and Ideas as Sources of Change*, Princeton, NJ: Princeton University Press, 1982, 89–164.

Consequently, gold reserves in the US shrank, while foreign dollar reserves, in principle covered by this gold, rose rapidly. By the end of the 1960s, their official value had grown to 40 billion (after the Second World War, they were only 6 billion), against only 12 billion dollars' worth of gold (after the Second World War, they were 20 billion).[79] In August 1971, foreign dollar reserves amounted to more than three times the value of American gold reserves at the prevailing rate of thirty-five US dollars per ounce.[80] This prompted private speculators and governments alike to follow the example of de Gaulle's France, which in the second half of the 1960s redeemed large quantities of dollars for gold from the US Federal Reserve, further weakening the dollar.[81]

Since central bankers and politicians clung to the foundations of Bretton Woods and were guided above all by Triffin's postulates, the reform efforts of the 1960s focused on international cooperation and the expansion of liquidity. In addition to agreements on mutual support within the IMF and the establishment of the so-called General Arrangements to Borrow, initiatives from the mid-1960s onwards were primarily directed at creating sufficient international liquidity. After long negotiations, the creation of an artificial currency not backed by gold, the so-called special drawing rights (SDRs), was decided upon in 1967, but it was hardly sufficient to resolve these structural problems.[82]

The fundamental deficiencies of the monetary order attained special virulence when international capital flows surged in the late 1960s, along with the rapid growth of international banking. From 1957

---

79   George P. Shultz and Kenneth W. Dam, *Economic Policy beyond the Headlines*, New York: Norton, 1977, 114.

80   Paul A. Volcker and Toyoo Gyohten, *Changing Fortunes: The World's Money and the Threat to American Leadership*, New York: Times Books, 1992, 12; Gardner, *Sterling-Dollar Diplomacy*, li, Shultz and Dam, *Economic Policy beyond the Headlines*, 114.

81   From 1965 onwards, de Gaulle not only sharply criticised the expansive monetary policy of the US and its 'exorbitant privilege' while calling for the reintroduction of the gold standard, but also exploited the weakness of the dollar for geopolitical reasons, in an attempt to build a less asymmetrical monetary order. See also Odell, *U.S. International Monetary Policy*, 120; Christopher S. Chivvis, 'Charles de Gaulle, Jacques Rueff and French International Monetary Policy under Bretton Woods', *Journal of Contemporary History* 41, no. 4 (2006), 701–20.

82   The historian John Odell has convincingly shown that the reform focus on the creation of the SDR was mainly due to the influence of the studies of the economist Robert Triffin. See Odell, *U.S. International Monetary Policy*, esp. 130.

onwards, the London Eurodollar market, a forerunner of today's offshore financial markets, offered the bankers' dream: a means to circumvent government regulations, standards (such as reserve requirements and caps on interest rates) and taxes; unrestricted foreign exchange and credit trading; and the creation of a Eurobond market for bonds and securities denominated in foreign currencies.[83] Not only did growing international private capital movements force governments to intervene ever more heavily in foreign exchange markets, but major industrialised countries, unable to tame capital flows in any other way, introduced additional and more stringent controls from the mid-1960s onwards. This was especially so for American governments under John F. Kennedy and Johnson.[84]

However, neither restrictive financial market and foreign exchange policies nor extensive reform and cooperation efforts could prevent a dramatic currency crisis from erupting in the autumn of 1968, to be followed by a series of exchange rate readjustments – which until then had remained quite stable — accompanied by ever-increasing quantities of speculative capital.[85] In order to curb the drastic outflow of gold from the US, in 1968 an official gold market, stabilised by government arrangements at thirty-five dollars per ounce of gold, was hived off from the private gold market, where the price fluctuated freely and instantly shot up.[86] The crisis intensified sharply in the early 1970s, as the Nixon administration pursued a decidedly passive foreign exchange policy (of so-called benign neglect) while at the same time the outflow of gold from the US grew. Finally, in August 1971, Nixon closed the gold window – the US abolished the convertibility of the dollar unilaterally,

---

83 Helleiner, *States and the Reemergence of Global Finance*, 81–91; Gary Burn, *The Re-emergence of Global Finance*, London: Palgrave Macmillan, 2006, 95; Heather Gibson, *The Eurocurrency Markets, Domestic Financial Policy and International Instability*, London: Macmillan, 1989, 3–29; Catherine R. Schenk, 'The Origins of the Eurodollar Market in London: 1955–1963', *Explorations in Economic History* 35, no. 2 (1998), 221.

84 Horsefield and de Vries, *The International Monetary Fund 1945–1965*, vol. 3, 296, 375f.

85 On the chronology of the final phase of Bretton Woods, see especially Peter M. Garber, 'The Collapse of the Bretton Woods Fixed Exchange Rate System', in Michael D. Bordo and Barry Eichengreen, eds, *A Retrospective of the Bretton Woods System*, Chicago: University of Chicago Press, 2006, 465f. See also Eichengreen, *Globalizing Capital*, 128–32; McNamara, *The Currency of Ideas*, 93–7.

86 Odell, *U.S. International Monetary Policy*, 178.

without consultation with the IMF, effectively ending the Bretton Woods system.[87]

To grasp the significance of the debates on international monetary arrangements within the MPS, it is essential first to understand the intellectual climate of the 1950s and 1960s on this subject. The majority of economists were generally satisfied with the structure of Bretton Woods, and most reform proposals even into the 1960s were directed towards improvements of its basic terms.[88] Apart from broad scepticism concerning market mechanisms and the price system, and the widespread rejection of liberalised and deregulated capital markets in the Keynesian-dominated field, most economists rejected both the gold standard and flexible exchange rates until well into the 1960s.[89] The gold standard was regarded as an anachronistic relic of the past, supported by an extremely small minority (some estimates put the figure at less than 1 per cent). One of these, MPS member Murray Rothbard, lamented in 1962 that the gold standard 'now is considered an absurd anachronism, a relic of a tribal fetish'.[90]

Floating exchange rates, too, were almost universally rejected and ignored; by one estimate, only 5 per cent of economists supported them

---

87 Joanne Gowa, *Closing the Gold Window: Domestic Politics and the End of Bretton Woods*, Ithaca, NY: Cornell University Press, 1983.

88 See for example the statement by American economists in 'Economists Back Bretton Program', *NYT*, 19 February 1945, 10. A good overview of the general reform proposals is provided in the edited anthologies by Seymour Harris, ed., *The Dollar in Crisis*, New York: Harcourt, Brace and World, 1961, and Herbert G. Grubel, ed., *World Monetary Reform: Plans and Issues*, Stanford, CA: Stanford University Press, 1963; and the report of the Brookings Institution, *The United States Balance of Payments in 1968*, Washington, DC: Brookings Institution, 1963.

89 Fixed exchange rates and a fixed gold price were considered the 'Newtonian foundations' of Bretton Woods. Leeson, *Ideology and the International Economy*, 20; Volcker and Gyohten, *Changing Fortunes*, 7.

90 Murray N. Rothbard, 'The Case for a Genuine Gold Dollar', in Leland Yeager, ed., *In Search of a Monetary Constitution*, Cambridge, MA: Harvard University Press, 1962, 94. While in the 1920s about 10 per cent of economists still described themselves as 'Austrians' (and therefore mainly advocated the gold standard), between 1950 and the beginning of the revival of the Austrian School in the US (after the Nobel Prize was awarded to Friedrich von Hayek in 1974) this proportion was far below 1 per cent. See Richard Vedder and Lowell Gallaway, 'The Austrian Market Share in the Marketplace of Ideas, 1871–2025', *Quarterly Journal of Austrian Economics* 3, no. 1 (2000), 33.

in the early 1950s.[91] Opposition from governments and the private sector was even more widespread than among economists. 'Until the 1960s, it was widely accepted both by academic and IMF economists that floating exchange rates were a species of law-breaking behaviour', one historical account states.[92] And one of the most important economists of the time, Robert Triffin, wrote about the 1950s and 1960s: 'Even though adopted in despair some twenty years later, this simple prescription [of flexible exchange rates] was then scornfully dismissed or even ignored by most academic and virtually all government experts.'[93] The gold standard – the other neoliberal option – was not seriously considered within government circles, with the exception of de Gaulle's France, and floating exchange rates were overlooked entirely in the 1950s, with the exception of Canada.[94] But while advocates of a classical gold standard remained in a minority position until the end of the 1960s, by then a clear majority of economists – some estimates put the figure at 90 per cent – had become convinced of a theory arguing for floating exchange rates, backed an extension of exchange rate flexibility.[95] Moreover,

---

91 See Milton Gilbert's commentary in Milton Friedman, 'The Lessons of U.S. Monetary History and Their Bearing on Current Policy: Memorandum Prepared for Consultant's Meeting, Board of Governors, Federal Reserve System, October 7, 1965', reprinted in Milton Friedman, *Dollars and Deficits: Inflation, Monetary Policy and the Balance of Payments*, Englewood Cliffs, NJ: Prentice-Hall, 1965, 183f.; Michael Heilperin, 'International Monetary Problems: Return to the Gold Standard?', LA 1965; Milton Friedman and Robert Roosa, *The Balance of Payments: Free Versus Fixed Exchange Rates*, Washington, DC: American Enterprise Institute, 1967, 133f. Richard N. Cooper ('Exchange Rate Choices', Conference Series, Federal Reserve Bank of Boston, June, 1999, 99–136, here 103) writes: 'Initially Friedman was nearly alone in his views. Most contemporary economists favoured fixed exchange rates and feared the instabilities that flexible exchange rates might bring, or reveal.'

92 Endres, *Great Architects of International Finance*, 9.

93 See Robert Triffin, 'The Impact of the Bellagio Group on International Reform', in Jacob S. Dreyer, ed., *Breadth and Depth in Economics*, Lexington: Lexington Books, 1978, 146. See also Solomon, *International Monetary System, 1945–76*, 60.

94 See Eugene N. White, Michael D. Bordo and Dominique Simard, 'An Overplayed Hand: France and the Bretton Woods International Monetary System', Departmental Working Papers, Rutgers University, Department of Economics, 1996; Chivvis, 'Charles de Gaulle, Jacques Rueff and French International Monetary Policy under Bretton Woods'; Michael D. Bordo, Ali Dib, Lawrence Shembri, 'Canada's Pioneering Experience with a Flexible Exchange Rate in the 1950s: (Hard) Lessons Learned for Monetary Policy in a Small Open Economy', NBER Working Paper no. 13605, 2007.

95 Friedman and Roosa, *The Balance of Payments*, 133–4. Here, Friedman estimated an increase from 5 to 75 per cent from 1953 to 1967. Others assumed that by the

governments also had come to terms with these arguments, and influential private bankers along with various members of the Nixon administration demanded flexibilisation. In what follows, the neoliberal MPS network's role in this development will be discussed in greater detail.[96]

---

end of the 1960s at least 90 per cent accepted or supported the theory of flexible exchange rates as theoretically conclusive. See Egon Sohmen, *Flexible Exchange Rates: Theory and Controversy*, Chicago: University of Chicago Press, 1961, xi; Friedman and Roosa, *The Balance of Payments*, 177.

96   Because there were also some Keynesian-oriented economists in the 1950s and 1960s who advocated floating exchange rates or managed changes in parities, it must be emphasised that the present study has a special focus on neoliberal economists. See chapter 2. The Keynesian work of greatest significance is James Meade, *The Balance of Payments* (vol. 1 of *The Theory of International Economic Policy*), Oxford: Oxford University Press, 1951, 218–31.

2

The Origins of Neoliberal Monetary Theory

Internal Debates at the Mont Pèlerin Society Conferences

This chapter maps the activities of the core advocates of floating exchange rates operating inside the MPS. The normative, principled and explanatory convictions of those who proved particularly influential are presented here in some detail. These intellectual progenitors can be tracked through a close analysis of contemporary debates on the MPS conference circuit, then among the most significant venues for the transnational neoliberal drive to flexibilisation.

When capitalism's blood congeals: Monetary policy as a key problem for emerging neoliberalism

The issue of currency gave rise to the most ubiquitous, elaborate and controversial debates that took place within the nascent post-war neoliberal thought collective. Flexible exchange rates were 'the most continuously debated topic' at MPS meetings, according to Friedman,[1] and as late as 1984, the American journalist John Davenport, one of the participants of that year's MPS conference, 'elicited a laugh by observing that the original Pelerinians could agree on everything save the subjects

---

1 Quoted in George H. Nash, *The Conservative Intellectual Movement in America since 1945,* New York: Basic Books, 1976, 419, fn. 197.

of God and gold'.[2] On many other points, a high degree of conformity among MPS members prevailed, but finding consensus across the neoliberal spectrum proved particularly difficult when it came to currency reform. In his insider's history of the MPS, Ronald Hartwell writes that 'the only two items that consistently produced disagreement ... were the gold standard versus other means of producing a monetary order, and the interrelated issue of fixed versus flexible exchange rates'.[3] This most enduring and vexed dispute illustrates that neoliberalism is no *pensée unique* (to use Ignacio Ramonet's term), but rather a mode of thought best conceptualised as a plurality.[4]

Why were monetary questions so central to an emerging organised neoliberalism? Apart from the obvious fact that the MPS was compelled to face the topic so as to clarify and coordinate its programme, the politics of currency featured among the central global economic concerns of the latter half of the 1950s, and it only grew more prominent over the following decade. International trade and payment imbalances increasingly threatened the harmonious growth of the industrialised countries, and currency crises leading to a repetition of the economic crisis of the 1930s were perceived as fundamental threats to world peace. For international organisations, politicians and economists devoted to matters of economic policy, monetary questions were of greatest relevance. Neoliberal economists therefore sought answers to the problems encountered in managing exchange rates, and the theory of floating rates gained traction in response to the urgent need for new conceptual and political models to deal with monetary policy.[5]

It is notable that MPS members placed a premium on the substantive

---

2 Greg Kaza, 'The Mont Pelerin Society's 50th Anniversary', *Freeman* 47, no. 6 (1997), available at fee.org.

3 Ronald Max Hartwell, *A History of the Mont Pelerin Society*, Indianapolis: Liberty Fund, 1995, xvii; 114, 119; George Stigler, *Memoirs of an Unregulated Economist*, Chicago: University of Chicago Press, 1988, 145.

4 The concept *pensée unique* was coined by the editor of *Le Monde Diplomatique* Ramonet. See *Le Monde Diplomatique* (January 1995), 1; on the 'plurality' of neoliberalism, see Bernhard Walpen, *Die offenen Feinde und ihre Gesellschaft. Eine hegemonietheoretische Studie zur Mont Pèlerin Society*, Hamburg: VSA Verlag, 2004, 62–83.

5 Barry Eichengreen, *Globalizing Capital: A History of the International Monetary System*, Princeton, NJ: Princeton University Press, 1996; Harold James, *International Monetary Cooperation since Bretton Woods*, Washington, DC: International Monetary Fund, 1996; John S. Odell, *U.S. International Monetary Policy: Markets, Power, and Ideas as Sources of Change*, Princeton, NJ: Princeton University Press, 1982.

questions of how to organise an international monetary system. Not only was Bretton Woods understood as inimical to the interests of the MPS, but in the view of some within the Society, it represented nothing less than the greatest threat to liberal economic order itself. Two points in particular anchored this outlook, articulated by the advocates of both flexible exchange rates and the gold standard, which may be regarded as the fundamental maxims of neoliberal monetary thought. First, the MPS rejected currency and capital controls; and second, it sought to prevent or counteract Keynesian and democratically determined economic policy by means of an automatic market mechanism.

In order to reconcile international free trade and monetary autonomy with fixed exchange rates, Bretton Woods had found a compromise (along the lines of the aforementioned impossibility theorem of macroeconomics) in controls on the international movement of capital and foreign exchange. It is hardly surprising that this option was sharply rejected by all members of the MPS.[6] In the Society's internal discussions – and especially in debates on monetary policy – the rhetoric of freedom and associated hostility to capital controls are both quite pronounced. Yet each term must be historicised, given the Cold War context of systemic ideological competition, in which backing the 'free world' was paramount. Nevertheless, it was a characteristic of the MPS that out of all forms of state intervention in the economy, controls on international foreign exchange transactions should have been feared and scorned with such vehemence. Friedman, for example, declared in his bestseller *Capitalism and Freedom* that 'there is much experience to suggest that the most effective way to convert a market economy into an authoritarian economic society is to start by imposing direct controls on foreign exchange'. He detected the threat of an authoritarian economy looming specifically over the US of the late 1960s. Here he invoked socialist economies along with the welfare state, as the latter was, in his view, a precursor of the former. In Friedman's view, 'the most serious short-run threat to economic freedom in the United States today' emanated from the controls introduced in the name of the balance of payments.[7]

---

6 See also Helmut Schoeck, 'Der Stand des liberalen Denkens', *NZZ*, 16 September 1957, 10.

7 Milton Friedman, *Capitalism and Freedom*, Chicago: University of Chicago Press, 1962, 57.

Controls on foreign exchange and financial markets, according to Friedman and Gottfried Haberler were 'congealing the blood of capitalism'[8] and, as per Machlup, such measures could lead to the 'abolition of the market system' as a whole;[9] for Mises, they might even precipitate the 'decline of Western civilisation'.[10] But it was not enough that all these dangers should emanate from state regulation of trade. In the most influential statement of neoliberalism, appearing in 1944, *The Road to Serfdom*, Hayek had already assigned a prominent role to exchange controls and declared that they were exemplary of his central argument: state regulation of the economy leads to unfreedom. State regulation of foreign exchange is 'the decisive advance on the path to totalitarianism and the suppression of individual liberty' and, Hayek continued, 'the complete delivery of the individual to the tyranny of the state, the final suppression of all means of escape'.[11] It is particularly revealing of neoliberalism's conceptualisation of freedom that, from its point of view, the greatest danger to individual liberty stems from the regulation of capital mobility – from state interventions, in other words, carried out in the name of international stability and national welfare, that scarcely infringe on the vast majority of the population that does not live by exploiting global capital movements. For the members of the emerging neoliberal thought collective, however, such controls were to be considered a central problem. MPS discussions therefore inevitably revolved around the question of which monetary system renders exchange and capital controls superfluous or even impossible.

In addition to the establishment of extensive capital controls, Bretton Woods also provided the international framework for the widespread application of Keynesian economic policies in the 1950s and 1960s.

---

8   Milton Friedman and Robert Roosa, *The Balance of Payments: Free versus Fixed Exchange Rates*, Washington, DC: American Enterprise Institute, 1967, 183.

9   Fritz Machlup, *International Payments, Debts, and Gold: Collected Essays by Fritz Machlup*, New York: Scribner, 76. The quotation is from Machlup's paper 'Three Concepts of the Balance of Payments and the So-Called Dollar Shortage', which appeared in *The Economic Journal* in March 1950.

10 Ludwig von Mises, *The Theory of Money and Credit*, New Haven, CT: Yale University Press, 1954, 434.

11 Friedrich A. von Hayek, *The Road to Serfdom*, London: Routledge, 1944, 92; see also Friedrich A. von Hayek, *Monetary Nationalism and International Stability* (Institut Universitaire de Hautes Études Internationales, Genève), London: Longmans, Green and Co., 1937, 71f.

Bretton Woods was, one might say, the international institutionalisation of what Hayek had criticised in the 1930s as 'monetary nationalism', the idea that democratic monetary policy made sense within a nation-state framework.[12] Keynesianism and monetary nationalism had been 'built into the post-war international organisation of monetary affairs', he observed in his only publication on monetary issues during the existence of Bretton Woods.[13]

For Hayek and many of his MPS colleagues, the post-war settlement forced countries to adopt an inflationary monetary policy that in turn led to the expansion of the state apparatus, germ of further collectivist and totalitarian leanings. Already at the founding meeting of the MPS in 1947, Hayek emphasised in his opening speech that one of the most important issues of the newly founded society should be the fight against inflationary Keynesian economic policy: 'The inflationary high-pressure economy which, as has been justly observed by more than one member, is at the moment the main tool by which a collectivist development is forced on the majority of countries, including even the United States.'[14] Ideologically, the MPS therefore attempted to reverse the assumed chain of effects and to search for an international financial architecture through which societies would be guided towards liberal-market policies. Monetary questions were discussed within the MPS from the beginning in relation to this perspective, and the core problem, posed as a question by an unnamed member in an article covering the 1950 MPS conference, was how to design an international monetary system that could 'counterbalance inflationary pressures and the arbitrary expansion of government spending with an effective and, as far as possible, automatically functioning counterweight'.[15] Hayek had made it clear at the MPS's founding that the

---

12 Hayek, *Monetary Nationalism*.
13 Friedrich A. von Hayek, 'Bemerkungen über die Funktion von Währungsreserven und den Begriff der internationalen Liquidität', in *Was mit der Goldwährung geschehen ist. Ein Bericht aus dem Jahre 1932 mit zwei Ergänzungen* (Walter Eucken Institut: Vorträge und Aufsätze 12), Tübingen: J.C.B. Mohr, 1965, 33. Cf. Mises, *The Theory of Money and Credit*, 434.
14 See Friedrich A. von Hayek, 'Opening Address to Mont Pèlerin Conference', LA 1947, 13. Inflation was treated as one of the most serious problems at MPS conferences; the threat it posed to the wealthy was of particular concern. See Schoeck, 'Der Stand des liberalen Denkens'.
15 'Freiheit, Gleichheit, und Gerechtigkeit. Zur Konferenz der Mont Pèlerin Society in Bloemendaal (Holland)', *NZZ*, 23 September 1950, 6.

answer would mean restricting democratic say over economic policy. His formulation of the essential question was: 'How can monetary policy be automatic, and outside the range of politics?'[16]

Indeed, the reasoning of many MPS members was frankly antidemocratic. Hayek and Rueff, as neoliberal conservatives, were highly critical of mass democracy on the grounds that it could not resist the seduction of Keynesianism, and consequentially inflation.[17] This understanding drove the search for a monetary system capable of blocking democratically determined economic policy through *automatic* mechanisms, at once *apolitical* and *market-driven*, thereby insulating decision-makers from majorities calling for a demand-oriented policy aimed at full employment.

These twin priorities – of a neoliberal monetary policy that could at once guarantee the free movement of capital and preempt inflationary pressures – dominated the MPS debates of the 1950s and 1960s. What must not be overlooked, however, is that such requirements reflected not merely the preferences of academic economists but ideas propagated since the 1940s by influential banking circles, especially in New York, albeit with only limited success. While bankers reconciled themselves for a time with the restrictive elements of Bretton Woods, even as they held on to the conviction that an open, liberal financial order was incompatible with both fixed exchange rates and international free trade, MPS neoliberals sought to institutionalise free capital movements and automatic, anti-inflationary adjustments.[18]

The traditional market-liberal solution to these two demands was the gold standard, which in the nineteenth century had facilitated the expansion of liberal trade relations, orthodox national monetary policy and globalised capital linkages without capital controls.[19] Accordingly,

---

16   Quoted in Hartwell, *History of the Mont Pelerin Society*, 37.

17   See Jacques Rueff, *L'Ordre Social*, Paris: Recueil Sirey, 1945, 489–640; Hayek, *The Road to Serfdom*; Mises, *The Theory of Money and Credit*, esp. 416–38; Otto Veit, 'A New Stage in International Monetary Policy', LA 1960.

18   Eric Helleiner, *States and the Reemergence of Global Finance: From Bretton Woods to the 1990s*, Ithaca, NY: Cornell University Press, 1994, 40–50, 76f.; James, *International Monetary Cooperation*, 64; 'Economists Back Bretton Program', *NYT*, 19 February 1945, 10; John Gerard Ruggie, 'International Regimes, Transactions, and Change: Embedded Liberalism in the Postwar Economic Order', *International Organization* 36, no. 2 (1982), 393.

19   See, for greater detail, Eric Helleiner, 'Denationalizing Money: Economic Liberalism and the "National Question" in Currency Affairs', in Emily Gilbert and Eric

from the founding of the MPS through to the early 1950s, almost all members were in favour of a return to the classical gold standard in principle, even if, given the force of socio-political circumstances, compromises such as the commodity reserve standard retained some support.[20] In the course of the subsequent decade, however, an ever larger group within the MPS abandoned any hope of returning to the classical gold standard and instead pushed for a system of floating exchange rates, to be traded on liberalised foreign exchange markets.

Protagonists of both camps agreed on political ends, at least. They hoped that the reforms they counselled, presented before the MPS with characteristic urgency when it came to monetary policy, would rescue the world from the totalitarianism presaged by a fully planned economy. The alternatives facing the Society were either the gold standard or floating exchange rates, each promised to secure a world of liberalised and globalised trade in goods and capital markets. But the two fractions saw only obstacles to their common aims in each other's reforms. Two examples illustrate the dynamic at play. Ludwig von Mises ended his major work on monetary and credit theory with the plaintive remark that the gold standard was the necessary precondition for preventing the 'utopia of totalitarian all-encompassing planning'.[21] For his part, Friedman wrote in a 22 January 1953 letter to John Davenport, the editor of *Fortune* and fellow MPS member:

> The problem has recently become again highly topical and I feel more strongly than ever that the single most urgent step in international affairs is the establishment of a system of flexible exchange rates; that if this was done, the result on an international level would be nearly as striking as the results on a national level for the German monetary reform; that if it is not done, there is no chance at all for the real liberalization of trade, economic integration in Europe, or any of the other

---

Helleiner, eds, *Nation-States and Money: The Past, Present and Future of National Currencies*, London: Routledge, 1999.

20 Most MPS members followed the early Hayek and his teacher Ludwig von Mises. Cf. Friedrich A. von Hayek, 'Was der Goldwährung geschehen ist', in *Was der Goldwährung geschehen ist. Ein Bericht aus dem Jahre 1932 mit zwei Ergänzungen* (Walter Eucken Institut: Vorträge und Aufsätze 12), Tübingen: J.C.B. Mohr, 1965 [1932]; Hayek, *Monetary Nationalism and International Stability*; Mises, *The Theory of Money and Credit*, first published in 1924; 'Freiheit, Gleichheit, und Gerechtigkeit'.

21 Mises, *The Theory of Money and Credit*, 457.

noble objectives towards which our external policy has supposedly been directed.[22]

Two camps of freedom fighters: Understanding the controversy

What developed subsequently within the MPS was a fundamental and distinctly acute conflict that ran implicitly or explicitly through all debates on the currency question at the Society's conferences of the 1950s and especially the 1960s. The controversy represented a struggle between schools of neoliberal thought, as articulated by Mark Skousen, who writes that 'anyone who has ever attended a Mont Pèlerin Society meeting will quickly attest that this international group of freedom-fighters are divided into two camps: followers of the Austrian school and followers of the Chicago school'.[23] While Mises and his students favoured the gold standard, Friedman's Chicago School pressed for free-floating exchange rates of noncallable paper money, where the money supply would be continuously and uniformly expanded within a national framework according to a fixed rule.[24] In other words, these factions held diametrically opposed views regarding the central tenets of neoliberal monetary policy.[25]

---

22 Quoted in Robert Leeson, *Ideology and the International Economy: The Decline and Fall of Bretton Woods*, New York: Palgrave Macmillan, 2003, 45. See also Milton Friedman, 'The Case for Flexible Exchange Rates', in *Essays in Positive Economics*, Chicago: University of Chicago Press, 1953, 203.

23 Mark Skousen, *Vienna and Chicago, Friends or Foes? A Tale of Two Schools of Free-Market Economics*, Washington, DC: Capital Press, 2005. The Austrian School, founded by Carl Menger in Vienna at the end of the nineteenth century, saw its central theories developed by his students Mises and Hayek. The Chicago School, for its part, emerged from the work of Frank H. Knight, Henry Simons and Jacob Viner, then based in the Economics Department at the University of Chicago; its second generation's most prominent figures, Milton Friedman and George Stigler, carried its traditions forward.

24 On the Austrian School, see Skousen, *Vienna and Chicago, Friends or Foes?* On the Chicago School, Robert Van Horn and Philip Mirowski, 'The Rise of the Chicago School of Economics and the Birth of Neoliberalism', in Philip Mirowski and Dieter Plehwe, eds, *The Road from Mont Pèlerin: The Making of the Neoliberal Thought Collective*, Cambridge, MA: Harvard University Press, 2009; Melvin W. Reder, 'Chicago Economics: Permanence and Change', *Journal of Economic Literature* 20, no. 1 (1982).

25 Interestingly, during the 1950s there were also two camps with regard to the neoliberal position on trade unions. See Yves Steiner, 'The Neoliberals Confront the Trade Unions', in Mirowski and Plehwe, *The Road from Mont Pèlerin*.

Because some of the most important participants in the MPS debates cannot be clearly assigned to one or another of these schools, or indeed may have changed their positions over time, the classical 'church history' account is inadequate. Some of Mises's most prominent students – namely, Machlup and Haberler – defected to the floating exchange rate camp over the course of the 1950s. And the German ordoliberals of the Freiburg School founded by Walter Eucken and Franz Böhm originally supported the gold standard, but its well-known younger representatives like Friedrich Lutz and Fritz Meyer promoted free exchange rates from the 1950s and early 1960s onwards.[26]

If the history of the conflict as a dispute between schools of thought is insufficient, one alternative approach is to focus on the geographical origin, place of residence and national or regional outlook of the economists involved. Although such explanations may clarify the choice of the preferred monetary system in individual cases and, above all, the focus on certain lines of argument, they describe only rather vague tendencies. It is notable, for example, that floating exchange rates were promoted aggressively in the US and Germany.[27] However, an analysis that interprets the differences in opinion as a conflict of generations – or, more precisely, age cohorts – reveals far more.[28]

The gold standard was championed above all by those who were born before the turn of the twentieth century and who had therefore experienced the disastrous events associated with floating currencies during the early 1920s. This cohort was educated in the pre-Keynesian era.[29] A

---

26 On ordoliberalism, see Ralf Ptak, *Vom Ordoliberalismus zur Sozialen Marktwirtschaft: Stationen des Neoliberalismus in Deutschland*, Opladen: Leske und Budrich, 2004; Henry M. Oliver Jr, 'German Neoliberalism', *Quarterly Journal of Economics* 74, no. 1 (1960).

27 For example, the argument of imported inflation played a role above all for economists from the hard currency country of Germany, while various US-Americans, concerned about the negative balance of payments of the US, were concerned primarily with the possibility of unilaterally abandoning the gold exchange guarantee.

28 The term 'age cohort' is more correct than 'generation' in this context, as it only refers to a specific social grouping (economists), it is transnational and the age gaps are relatively small. For an introduction to generational research, see Ulrike Jureit, *Generationenforschung*, Göttingen: Vandenhoeck & Ruprecht, 2006, 131.

29 Ludwig von Mises (born 1881), Henry Hazlitt (1894), Philip Cortney (1895), Jacques Rueff (1896), Otto Veit (1898), Wilhelm Röpke (1899), Friedrich von Hayek (1899), William Hutt (1899), Arthur Burns (1904). I am referring here not only to the people who participated in the MPS conferences but also to other prominent MPS members.

particularly important group of economists, born in the first decade of the twentieth century, backed the gold standard until the 1950s or early 1960s but thereafter promoted floating rates.[30] Finally, economists born after 1910 were almost uniformly in favour of floating exchange rates.[31] The fact that this was a conflict between different generations was self-evident to MPS members.[32] Michael Heilperin noted in 1965 that he was insisting on the 'classical' equalisation mechanisms of the gold standard, 'however old-fashioned they may appear to the younger economists'.[33]

This distinction may be explained through the varying experiences and processes of academic socialisation. Older economists had first-hand memories of a time when national monetary policy was guided exclusively by the dictates of the financial markets and exchange rates, but this appeared to their younger colleagues to be an outmoded remnant of classical liberalism out of step with reality. And while the older generation still remembered vividly the disastrous era of floating exchange rates of the early 1920s, associated with rampant inflation and the abandonment of the discipline imposed by the gold standard, younger members interpreted these events differently; above all they questioned the extensive capital controls and restrictions on foreign exchange of the 1940s, and were more willing to accept contemporary social and political realities (strong trade unions, national monetary policy, economic planning) as unchangeable in the short term. They

30   Among them were some of its most influential advocates within the MPS: Gottfried Haberler (born 1900), Friedrich Lutz (1901), Fritz Machlup (1902), William Fellner (1905), Fritz Meyer (1907).

31   George Stigler (born 1911), Milton Friedman (1912), Enoch Powell (1912), Paul McCracken (1915), Herbert Stein (1916), Herbert Giersch (1921), Harry Johnson (1923), Leland B. Yeager (1923), Arnold Harberger (1924), Egon Sohmen (1930). Michael Heilperin (1909) advocated the gold standard only after the experience with floating exchange rates in the 1920s, thus representing a special case (see also Michael Heilperin, 'Monetary Reform in an Atlantic Setting', LA 1965, 3). Albert Hahn (1889) is an exception if only because he was a Keynesian until the 1940s (cf. Jan-Otmar Hesse, 'Some Relationships between a Scholar's and an Entrepreneur's Life: The Biography of L. Albert Hahn', *History of Political Economy* 39 [2007]). Other exceptions are the American Arthur Kemp (1916), as well as Mises's student Hans Sennholz (1922), who emigrated from Germany to the US, both younger advocates of the gold standard.

32   See Stigler, *Memoirs of an Unregulated Economist*, 145. There, Stigler recalls that 'the gold standard was the cherished goal of the older members, but not of the younger economists'.

33   Michael Heilperin, 'International Monetary Problems: Return to the Gold Standard?', LA 1965, 2.

thus set out in search of new neoliberal monetary reforms. The flexibalisation of exchange rates, by contrast, was still seen by many of their elders as an instrument of Keynesian policy and social planning, whereas fixed rates were understood as the epitome of liberalism. But the younger economists were less biased in their pursuit of realistic answers to these novel problems. The fundamental rejection of flexibalisation by many of the early MPS members – Hayek described floating exchange rates as a central element of 'monetary nationalism' – makes these heated debates in the MPS legible to contemporary readers.[34]

Of networks, disciples and the faith in freedom: The functions of the MPS conferences

The most important functions of the MPS conferences in the formation and dissemination of floating exchange rate theory and the emergence of a corresponding international neoliberal advocacy network can be enumerated as follows:

1. Production of neoliberal knowledge
2. Production and discussion of strategies of neoliberal (knowledge) politics
3. Internal and sometimes antagonistic debate
4. Transnational distribution and networking
5. Broadening and strengthening of the possibilities of influence
6. Social-psychological encouragement in a community of co-thinkers.[35]

---

34 On the importance of fixed exchange rates for the classical liberal monetary order, see Mises, *The Theory of Money and Credit*, 396ff.; Hartwell, *History of the Mont Pelerin Society*, xvii, 114, 119; Eichengreen, *Globalizing Capital*, 50. Paradigmatic for this is the most important study of monetary systems by the founder of the MPS, Friedrich von Hayek, which had influenced many MPS members. In it, Hayek focused on criticising flexible exchange rates as one of the worst consequences of 'monetary nationalism' (i.e., widespread Keynesian-oriented national monetary policy) and propagated 'absolute fixedness of exchange rates' (Hayek, *Monetary Nationalism and International Stability*, 73, 84).

35 These points are roughly based on a 1970 circular by Friedman, then president of the MPS, in which he retrospectively described the three main functions of the MPS, cited in Hartwell, *History of the Mont Pelerin Society*, 162–4, 222.

The intensive internal discussions firstly contributed to the preservation, production and expansion of neoliberal thought concerning currency regimes and to the further development of the theory of floating exchange rates. Key arguments were presented at MPS conferences to be evaluated by colleagues before they appeared in print. At the same time, the MPS constituted a space in which strategies for hegemonisation and popularisation could be articulated and refined. Society conferences offered the opportunity to discuss theories in a 'sympathetic environment', an 'atmosphere of intimacy and of common goodwill'.[36] This was particularly important given the antagonism between those who favoured a return to the gold standard and those who favoured flexibalisation; a dispute of such intensity could only be had out under such conditions.

MPS members organised through various networks, some of them embedded in universities and think tanks, prioritising cross-fertilisation of ideas so as to take on the 'hinge functions' of issue- and agenda-setting.[37] Back-and-forth at MPS conferences led a number of economists from diverse geographical and organisational contexts to back flexible exchange rates on the strength of compatible but apparently independent arguments. The conferences also encouraged the broadening and strengthening of members' capacities of influence. Hartwell distinguishes between the 'innovators' of new ideas and 'followers', 'who depend on the meetings of the Society to strengthen and refurbish their ideas'.[38] Granted, this distinction reflects the problematic and rather elitist model of knowledge production and distribution fundamental to the MPS worldview (it is similar to Hayek's distinction between 'original thinkers' and 'second-hand dealers in ideas'), but it was a notable feature in the promulgation of flexible exchange rate theory and the ascendancy of its proponents within the MPS.[39] Others were to accept their role of merely repeating, formalising or adapting such views. For this, think tanks were central.

The MPS assumed the fundamental social purpose for its membership, though it is resistant to analysis, of 'encouraging isolated

---

36 Friedman, quoted in Hartwell, *History of the Mont Pelerin Society*, 162, 164.
37 Walpen, *Die offenen Feinde und ihre Gesellschaft*, 110.
38 Hartwell, *History of the Mont Pelerin Society*, 202f.
39 Friedrich A. von Hayek, 'The Intellectuals and Socialism', in *The Collected Works of F. A. Hayek*, vol. 10, *Socialism and War: Essays, Documents, Reviews*, ed. Bruce Caldwell, London: Routledge, 1997, 222. The essay is from 1949.

defenders of freedom and renewing their belief that they are not alone.'[40] Bernhard Walpen has described the MPS in this context as a 'secularised sect' bound together by sinews of transnational sociability.[41] Of particular importance were the personal contacts, friendships and 'camaraderie' repeatedly invoked by R. M. Hartwell, born out of the lengthy social gatherings that unfolded between substantive debates, along with the nearly spiritual exaltation of a community of like-minded thinkers convened as an esoteric club of the chosen.[42] Machlup described this function of the MPS as follows:

> Its only functions are to organize meetings to debate issues of public and international concern, and thus to afford its members, through exchange of ideas with like-minded students of and believers in liberty, opportunities for recharging their moral batteries: these batteries are likely to run down or even go dead if their owners lack intellectual contacts with other analysts of the free society and are constantly exposed to the judgements of collectivists and socialists of all parties.[43]

Friedman, for his part, characterised the Society this way:

> The Mont Pelerin Society has veritably been a spiritual fountain of youth, to which we could all repair once a year or so to renew our spirits and faith among a growing company of fellow believers; the one time a year when a generally beleaguered minority could stop looking over their shoulders and let themselves go in a thoroughly supportive environment.[44]

It must have been rather encouraging for advocates of flexible exchange rates, who were extremely marginal in 1950s academia, to meet and exchange ideas with confederates from different countries and to advance their theory not in isolation but as members of a

---

40 Friedman, quoted in Hartwell, *History of the Mont Pelerin Society*, 162.
41 Walpen, *Die offenen Feinde und ihre Gesellschaft*, 108ff.
42 Hartwell, *History of the Mont Pelerin Society*, 216.
43 Fritz Machlup, foreword to Fritz Machlup, ed., *Essays on Hayek*, London: Routledge & Kegan Paul, 1977, xii.
44 Milton Friedman, introduction to ibid., xxif.

self-conscious network.[45] MPS members described themselves and their colleagues repeatedly as 'believers' in flexible exchange rates, as 'gold worshippers', or as 'convinced believer[s] in the international gold standard'.[46] The economist Charles Kindleberger, who during the 1960s was himself intensively involved in these matters, observed only half-jokingly that some economists worshipped flexible exchange rates as a 'god'. Kindleberger reserved the title of 'Archbishop of Canterbury' for MPS member Harry Gordon Johnson, de facto leader of a religious cult.[47]

Before exploring the aforementioned factors any further, we must first turn to the chronology of the MPS discussions, with an eye to the strategy, internal dynamics and international diffusion of floating exchange rate theory.[48] Society debates over Bretton Woods fall into two phases: the period dating from the founders' meeting in 1947 to the end of the 1950s, when, although the majority of MPS members remained wedded to the gold standard, flexible exchange rates came to figure prominently; and a second phase that runs from 1961, the year of the longest-running debate to date, where for the first time the opposing positions divided participants equally, to the last relevant discussion on

---

45   MPS member Hartwell writes in his history of the MPS that one of the most important functions of MPS conferences was to 'strengthen their beliefs and resolve' of isolated liberals through 'information, reassurance, security, and camaraderie'. See Hartwell, *History of the Mont Pelerin Society*, 202.

46   For example, Fritz Machlup, 'On Terms, Concepts, Theories, and Strategies in the Discussion of Greater Flexibility of Exchange Rates', in George N. Halm, ed., *Approaches to Greater Flexibility of Exchange Rates: The Bürgenstock Papers*, Princeton, NJ: Princeton University Press, 1970, 45. Machlup described the advocates of the gold standard as 'gold worshippers'. Fritz Machlup, 'International Monetary Systems and the Free Market Economy', in *International Payments Problems: A Symposium Sponsored by the American Enterprise Institute for Public Policy Research*, Washington, DC: American Enterprise Institute, 1966, 172. And Hayek wrote in 1937: 'I am a convinced believer in the international gold standard.' See Hayek, *Monetary Nationalism and International Stability*, xiii.

47   Charles Kindleberger, 'The Exchange-Stability Issue at Rambouillet and Jamaica', in Edward M. Bernstein et al., eds, *Reflections on Jamaica (Essays in International Finance)*, Princeton, NJ: Princeton University Press, 1976, 29. It is clear from the context that he was referring primarily to Friedman and Egon Sohmen.

48   The role of the MPS conferences and personal meetings with 'fellow believers' in encouraging and confirming the advocates of flexible exchange rates can be discussed only in passing. Camaraderie, personal friendship and exchange are emphasised repeatedly by participants and scholars. See, for example, Friedman, introduction to Machlup, *Essays on Hayek*, xxi, and Walpen, *Die offenen Feinde und ihre Gesellschaft*, 108f.

the topic before Nixon's decision to close the gold window in 1971. Over this latter period, champions of the gold standard found themselves increasingly on the defensive.[49]

It is striking that some partisans of flexible exchange rates, especially Friedman, Haberler and Hahn, participated much more frequently at MPS conferences than others, that advocates of flexible exchange rates presented far more papers and that proponents of the gold standard took part disproportionately in the two most contentious gatherings, in 1961 and 1965 (see table 2, p. 162).[50]

The 1950s

At the first MPS conference in 1947, nearly all participants were convinced that fixed exchange rates, liberalised capital markets and, ideally, the reintroduction of the classical gold standard constituted the monetary system most consistent with the Society's principles. But this outlook changed dramatically over the course of the 1950s. Alongside Friedman, two German economists, Friedrich Lutz and Albert Hahn, advanced the flexible exchange rate model to significant effect. Theoretically, the idea of flexible exchange rates was thereby sanctified within the MPS as at least a potential neoliberal reform project, to which an increasing number of economists subsequently 'converted'. Already by the 1961 conference, it could be presented as an equally viable alternative to the gold standard. While the theory was initially put forward as a clear minority position inside the MPS (without encountering much opposition), it fed a controversy which slowly gathered steam in the late 1950s. By the following decade, it was at the centre of the most

---

49   The turn of the 1960s also marked a certain break in the broader academic debates on currency, in the transition from the international 'dollar gap' to the 'dollar glut', in part triggered by the publication of Triffin's 1960 study on the so-called Triffin dilemma, which shifted scholarly attention (see chapter 1).

50   Friedman and Haberler each presented papers on the topic at five conferences; others who participated in the debate more than once were the advocates of floating exchange rates Lutz (three papers) and Machlup (two papers), and the gold standard advocates Heilperin (three papers), Rueff (three papers) and Veit (two papers). Of a total of thirty-four contributions, twenty-two were presented by advocates of floating exchange rates, twelve by advocates of the gold standard – and of these again seven were presented at the MPS conferences in 1961 and 1965.

significant dispute within the organisation. To understand the popularisation of flexible exchange rates during the 1960s, a closer look at the arguments tabled on their behalf is in order.

From the debut of the MPS, the classical liberal proposal to reintroduce the 'good old gold standard' was accompanied by debate over alternative market-liberal currency orders. Stigler noted in his opening comment: 'Any automatic features of the gold standard have disappeared. Also, our problem is much more one of deflation, on which the gold standard has very little to say.'[51] The renowned Princeton economist Frank Graham dominated debates on monetary policy at the inaugural conference, where he argued for a commodity reserve standard, or a currency system linked to a commodity index, as an alternative to the classical gold standard. The basis of value in Graham's proposed system would no longer be a metal, such as gold, but a fixed basket of goods, which was thought to reduce dependence on any one commodity and its attendant fluctuations. Such a standard might be combined with both fixed exchange rates and a 'perfectly free foreign exchange market' – one of Graham's significant innovations.[52] Graham died in 1949, but as a prominent established critic of the classical gold standard, his Depression-era work revolutionised international trade and equilibrium theory.[53] He is still regarded as one of the first to make a liberal case for flexible exchange rates. As early as 1947, then, the idea of a flexible exchange rate as a neoliberal alternative to Bretton Woods had already been introduced – as the opinion of a singular, influential economist who presented it as an extension of the commodity standard.

Friedman later recalled that his 'active involvement in the political process', particularly forceful in the context of his theory of flexible exchange rates, began with the MPS's founding meeting.[54] Whether Friedman was inspired by Graham remains an open question, but it is

---

51 This quote is from a summary of the discussion of the first MPS conference, 'Contra-Cyclical Measures, Full Employment, and Monetary Reform', based on the notes of Mrs Hahn, LA 1947, 180–91.

52 Ibid., 182. Graham opened after Stigler's introduction.

53 Anthony M. Endres, 'Frank Graham's Case for Flexible Exchange Rates: A Doctrinal Perspective', *History of Political Economy* 40, no. 1 (2008).

54 Milton Friedman and Rose D. Friedman, *Two Lucky People*, Chicago: University of Chicago Press, 1998, 159. For a detailed discussion of Friedman's commitment to floating exchange rates, see Leeson, *Ideology and the International Economy*.

conceivable, if not likely.[55] From 1948 onwards, Friedman was the most vocal advocate of flexible exchange rates within the MPS and more broadly in the academic world. During the first crisis of the Bretton Woods system, Friedman played a not insignificant role in Canada's decision to allow the country's dollar to float freely; Friedman had met with Donald Gordon, the deputy general of the Bank of Canada, in April 1948, and advised him that 'the right policy was for Canada to float the dollar'.[56] Canada's decision to violate the Bretton Woods rules and in a 'piratical pursuit' (according to an IMF official)[57] to opt against capital and trade controls and for a flexible currency was to occupy an important place in the academic debates that followed: Canada's experience between 1950 and 1962 provided the empirical basis on which Friedman and some of his students at the University of Chicago built their arguments.[58]

Friedman's proposals dominated the discussion of monetary policy at the MPS conference held in Bloemendaal, the Netherlands, in

---

55 The first mention of flexible exchange rates in a publication by Friedman dates to 1948, a year after the first MPS conference and his contact with Graham. See Milton Friedman, 'A Monetary and Fiscal Framework for Economic Stability', *American Economic Review* 38, no. 3 (1948), 252. Friedman's arguments for floating exchange rates (e.g., 'Commodity-Reserve Currency' of 1951 and 'The Case for Flexible Exchange Rates' of 1953) are highly reminiscent of Graham, without ever mentioning him as a pioneer. Graham had already argued in the 1940s that a purely anti-inflationary gold standard was desirable, but that in an era of independent national monetary policy the most rational solution was flexible exchange rates. See Frank D. Graham, *Fundamentals of International Monetary Policy*, Princeton, NJ: Princeton University Press, 1943, 29; Frank D. Graham, 'Achilles Heels in Monetary Standards', *American Economic Review* 30, no. 1 (1940); and Frank D. Graham, *The Cause and Cure of 'Dollar Shortage'*, Princeton, NJ: Princeton University Press, 1949, 13.
56 Friedman and Friedman, *Two Lucky People*, 1998, 189. On this process, see Leeson, *Ideology and the International Economy*, 43–4. On Canada's decision to float the dollar, see Eric Helleiner, 'A Fixation with Floating: The Politics of Canada's Exchange Rate Regime', *Canadian Journal of Political Science* 38 (2005).
57 Quoted in Leeson, *Ideology and the International Economy*, 44.
58 See Egon Sohmen, *Flexible Exchange Rates: Theory and Controversy*, Chicago: University of Chicago Press, 1961, esp. 139. Sohmen: 'It is only fitting to remark, however, that one could hardly hope for a more persuasive empirical verification of the conclusions of this monograph than the one the Canadian experiment provides.' See also Harry C. Eastman and Stefan Stykolt, 'Exchange Stabilization in Canada, 1950–4', *Canadian Journal of Economics and Political Science / Revue canadienne d'Economique et de Science politique* 22, no. 2 (1956); Milton Friedman's entry in *International Payments Problems*; Friedman, 'Discussion', in Federal Reserve Bank of Boston, 1970, 116.

The Origins of Neoliberal Monetary Theory

September 1950. He was the only attendee to present two papers, each far longer than the other contributions, introduced in a highly appreciative spirit by Friedrich Lutz, one of the earliest proponents of flexibilisation.[59] The conference took place just as Friedman formulated his theory: at the time, he was working as the OEEC's special envoy to Europe and it was there that he made the provocative suggestion that the German current account deficit be resolved by floating the deutsche mark. Although this idea met with little sympathy on the part of West German authorities, the corresponding memorandum formed the basis of 'The Case for Flexible Exchange Rates', which Friedman composed at the end of 1950, after the year's MPS meeting.[60] In this pivotal article, generally regarded as the *locus classicus* of the theory of floating exchange rates, Friedman presented the full range of arguments that were to shape debates inside the MPS and beyond over the coming decades.[61] He defined free or floating exchange rates as 'exchange rates freely determined in an open market primarily by private dealings and, like other market prices, varying from day to day', a definition later adopted by the MPS.[62] After explaining that flexible exchange rates constitute the sole possible monetary system for free societies, Friedman then undertook to refute the most significant objections to them.[63] In so doing, he focused primarily on the central and widespread counter-argument that floating exchange rates would fluctuate widely, as they had in the 1920s, and that destabilising

---

59   The *NZZ* ('Freiheit, Gleichheit, und Gerechtigkeit') reported that questions of money and credit were the most important at the meeting, and that Lutz had made 'the rather extensive preparatory work for the monetary policy topics'.

60   Friedman, 'The Case for Flexible Exchange Rates'. The memo was entitled: 'Flexible Exchange Rates as a Solution to the German Exchange Crisis'. Cf. Friedman and Friedman, *Two Lucky People*, 156–82; Leeson, *Ideology and the International Economy*, 44 and 131f.

61   On this assessment, see Peter Isard, *Exchange Rate Economics*, Cambridge: Cambridge University Press, 1995, 187–91; Richard N. Cooper, 'Exchange Rate Choices', Conference Series, Federal Reserve Bank of Boston, June, 1999, 103.

62   Friedman, 'The Case for Flexible Exchange Rates', 157; see also the virtually identical definition in Gottfried Haberler, *Currency Convertibility*, Washington, DC: American Enterprise Institute, 1954, 14; Gottfried Haberler, 'Konvertibilität der Währungen', in *Die Konvertibilität der europäischen Währungen*, Zürich: Eugen Rentsch Verlag, 1954, 38.

63   Friedman, 'The Case for Flexible Exchange Rates', 157.

currency speculation would lead to 'chaos'.[64] On the contrary, Friedman argued that rates could be expected to fluctuate less than the fixed yet adjustable parities found in Bretton Woods, and he even claimed that speculation would in principle have a stabilising effect, since by generating profits it would lead to an equalisation of the balance of payments:

> People who argue that speculation is generally destabilizing seldom realize that this is largely equivalent to saying that speculators lose money, since speculation can be destabilizing in general only if speculators on the average sell when the currency is low in price and buy when it is high.[65]

To advance this point, Friedman revised the dominant historiography by claiming that the instability of the inter-war years resulted from 'underlying instability in the economic conditions', not currency speculation.[66] Friedman further held that since speculators on average do earn a profit, the practice is thereby on average stabilising. He thus implicitly defined destabilising speculation as that which does not correspond to long-term trends in rates: 'There is at least as much reason to call [speculative movements] "stabilizing" as to call them "destabilizing."'[67]

Such arguments were to reappear in countless MPS contributions.[68] Particularly influential was the line of reasoning that speculation in floating exchange rates 'undoubtedly has a beneficial effect', as Friedrich Lutz put it in 1954[69] – from there, it developed into the 'classic case for

---

64 Ragnar Nurkse, *International Currency Experience: Lessons of the Inter-war Period*, Princeton, NJ: League of Nations Publications Department, 1944, 118, 128. Hayek had also criticised destabilising speculations in *Monetary Nationalism and International Stability*.
65 Friedman, 'The Case for Flexible Exchange Rates', 175.
66 Ibid., 173. See also Eichengreen, *Globalizing Capital*, 57.
67 Friedman, 'The Case for Flexible Exchange Rates', 177, and also 173.
68 In his article, Friedman already presented all the arguments which, according to Ronald MacDonald, were the most important arguments of the advocates of floating exchange rates in the 1950s and 1960s. See Ronald MacDonald, *Floating Exchange Rates: Theories and Evidence*, New York: Routledge, 1988, 1–5.
69 Friedrich Lutz, 'The Case for Flexible Exchange Rates', *Banca Nazionale del Lavoro Quarterly Review* (December 1954), published in German in the collection *Geld und Währung. Gesammelte Abhandlungen*, Tübingen: Mohr, 1962, 181. The quotation is translated from the German version.

speculation'.[70] But that Friedman was able to publish the article only in his own anthology in 1953, despite multiple attempts to place it in an academic journal, shows how little these ideas corresponded to the economic consensus of the early 1950s.[71] From then on, however, he repeatedly pushed the floating exchange rate argument across magazines, journals and books.[72]

The two essays that Friedman presented at the 1950 conference set out the discursive framework of his theory. Having first criticised competing market-liberal currency systems that had dominated at the founding meeting of the MPS, he now championed their domestic effects, transforming them into market-liberal reforms in their own right. In his 'Commodity-Reserve Currency', Friedman pointed out the shortcomings of the commodity reserve standard and gold standard, comparing them unfavourably with his preferred paper money standard combined with flexible exchange rates.[73] Friedman displayed particular energy in attacking the commodity reserve standard proposed by Graham, which he argued had all of the disadvantages of the gold standard and none of the popular support.[74] Thereafter, the commodity reserve standard dropped off the agenda at MPS

70 See Robert L. Hetzel, 'The Contributions of Milton Friedman to Economics', *Economic Quarterly* 93, no. 1 (2007), 12. Egon Sohmen (*Flexible Exchange Rates: Theory and Controversy*, Chicago: University of Chicago Press, 1961, 45–64) formalised this argument of stabilising speculation theoretically and mathematically and wrote a corresponding book on futures markets in 1966, *The Theory of Forward Exchange*. See also Friedman's 1970 discussion at the Federal Reserve Boston Branch. Milton Friedman, 'Discussion', in Federal Reserve Bank of Boston, *The International Adjustment Mechanism: Proceedings of the Monetary Conference*, Boston, MA: Federal Reserve Bank of Boston, 1970, 109–20, here 116; Harry G. Johnson and John Nash, *UK and Floating Exchanges: A Debate on the Theoretical and Practical Implications* (Hobart Paper 46, Institute of Economic Affairs), London: Institute of Economic Affairs, 1969, 25–9; Milton Friedman and Robert Roosa, *The Balance of Payments: Free versus Fixed Exchange Rates*, Washington, DC: American Enterprise Institute, 1967, 101–29.

71 See Friedman, letter to Robbins of February 22, 1952, quoted in Leeson, *Ideology and the International Economy*, 107; Friedman, 'The Case for Flexible Exchange Rates', 157.

72 In 1953, in the liberal journal *Freeman*, he explained the dollar shortage as a consequence of excessively fixed exchange rates, citing Canada as an example. See Milton Friedman, 'Why the Dollar Shortage?', *Freeman* 4, no. 6 (1953), 212.

73 Milton Friedman, 'Commodity-Reserve Currency', LA 1950; the essay was published in 1951 in the *Journal of Political Economy* and in Friedman's 1953 collection of *Essays in Positive Economics*.

74 Friedman, 'Commodity-Reserve Currency', LA 1950, 34.

conferences, as dissent within the Society focused on the other two reform proposals.[75]

In his critique, Friedman concentrated on painting the gold standard as unrealistic.[76] He had acknowledged in 1950, by way of backhanded praise, that it would in principle guarantee 'essentially complete automaticity and freedom from political control'; however, under the social and political conditions of the day, it was highly questionable whether any government could play by the rules, making the gold standard 'an inherently unstable monetary system' subject to 'political intervention'.[77] In 1953 Friedman noted that faced with the demands of strong trade unions and the welfare state, prices and especially wages were not downwardly flexible and that therefore the traditional mechanism of equalisation yielded unemployment and was inflationary.[78] This argument was not so much economic as political and pragmatic, as the debates clearly show – the gold standard was not rejected in principle on economic-theoretical and market-liberal grounds, but on the basis of doubts harboured by advocates of floating exchange rates regarding its ability to function in a liberal manner given the conjunctural factors of the 1950s (by contrast with the previous century).

Interestingly, this reasoning turned the central argument invoked in support of the gold standard against its boosters. Both Mises and Hayek along with Heilperin and Sennholz defended the gold standard primarily with a view to the hoped-for depoliticisation and automatisation of

---

75   The most important proponent of the commodity reserve standard, Frank Graham, died in 1949. For the further impact of Graham's ideas, see Anthony M. Endres, *Great Architects of International Finance: The Bretton Woods Era*, London: Routledge, 2005, 101.

76   At the MPS conference, Friedman also criticised the gold standard for being wasteful – he calculated that up to half of the average annual growth rates would have to be raised as reserves. Elsewhere, Friedman estimated that a gold standard would waste 4 per cent of the annual gross national product. See Milton Friedman, *Program for Monetary Stability*, New York: Fordham University Press, 1960, 5–7. This argument of wasting resources appears repeatedly (e.g., in Milton Friedman, *Dollars and Deficits: Inflation, Monetary Policy and the Balance of Payments*, Englewood Cliffs, NJ: Prentice-Hall, 1968, 177; Friedman and Roosa, *The Balance of Payments*, 72; Friedman, *Capitalism and Freedom*, 67).

77   Friedman, 'Commodity-Reserve Currency', LA 1950, 34; see also Friedman, 'The Case for Flexible Exchange Rates', 157.

78   Friedman, 'The Case for Flexible Exchange Rates', 165–7; see also Lutz, 'The Case for Flexible Exchange Rates'.

The Origins of Neoliberal Monetary Theory

monetary policy.[79] Although exponents of flexibilisation considered these to be worthy goals, they argued – and their position was therefore considerably less radical – that it was unrealistic to assume the outcome. Such criticism of the gold standard, which amounted to an 'argument of unrealistic assumptions', pervaded all future discussions at the MPS conferences and would be raised time and again in various iterations in communication aimed at the broader public.[80]

Inside the MPS, then, theorists of flexibilisation felt compelled to demonstrate that depoliticisation and automation of monetary policy were also feasible by way of floating exchange rates. This is exactly what Friedman set out to do in the second essay he presented at the 1950 conference. There, he justified the so-called monetarist rule, according to which the money supply increases in a rule-governed manner by a fixed ratio to economic growth. This held that governments should determine in advance how to expand the money supply continuously by 3 to 5 per cent (the values assigned to X), with taxes kept constant. The argument was no doubt directed at Keynesian attempts to regulate economic fluctuations by means of counter-cyclical intervention.[81] The monetarist version was to eliminate human control and political influence, in accordance with the command 'rules over authorities', as

---

79 See Mises, *The Theory of Money and Credit*, 4, 438; Hayek, *Monetary Nationalism and International Stability*, 74.

80 See Friedman, *Dollars and Deficits*, 177, for the classical formulation: 'the mythology and beliefs required to make it [gold standard] effective do not exist'. Cf. the exemplary contributions by Lutz, 'Case for Flexible Exchange Rates'; Milton Friedman, 'Real and Pseudo Gold Standards', LA 1961; Fritz Machlup, ' International Liquidity and International Money Creation', LA 1961; Fritz Machlup, 'Nationalism, Provincialism, Fixed Exchange Rates and Monetary Union', in *Convertibility, Multilateralism and Freedom: World Economic Policy in the Seventies, Essays in Honour of Reinhard Kamitz*, Vienna: Springer, 1972, 269; Gottfried Haberler, 'The International Monetary Mechanism', LA 1964; Haberler, 'Konvertibilität der Währungen', 40f.; Friedrich Lutz, 'Die Konvertibilitätsdiskussion', in Gottfried Haberler et al., eds, *Die Konvertibilität der europäischen Währungen*, Zürich: Eugen Rentsch, 1954, 308f. Even Friedman, the most radical advocate of flexible exchange rates and the most important critic of the gold standard in the MPS, repeatedly expressed himself (on a principled level) extremely favourably about a pure gold standard in his publications. Friedman, *Program for Monetary Stability*, 81; Milton Friedman and Anna J. Schwartz, *A Monetary History of the United States, 1867–1960*, Princeton, NJ: Princeton University Press (Studies for the National Bureau of Economic Research), 1963, 10.

81 For pro and contra arguments, see Milton Friedman and Walter W. Heller, *Monetary versus Fiscal Policy*, New York: Norton, 1969.

Friedman's teacher Henry Simons had put it.[82] Later, Friedman held that the central bank might even be replaced by a computer, programmed to execute the rule.[83]

In his remarks at the MPS meeting of 1950, Lutz stressed that such policy was the 'logical' equivalent of flexible exchange rates monetarism – in other words, it could be the means by which to introduce flexible exchange rates (and vice versa).[84] Friedman himself noted the following:

> Though here presented as a by-product of the proposed domestic framework, flexible exchange rates can be defended directly. Indeed, it would be equally appropriate to present the proposed domestic framework as a means of implementing flexible exchange rates. The heart of the matter is that domestic and international monetary and trade arrangements are part of one whole.[85]

To understand Friedman's theory of flexible exchange rates, it is essential to grasp the connection between the two proposals he described as 'parts of one whole'. From the outset, Friedman distinguished his advocacy of flexible exchange rates as a *neoliberal* strategy in contradistinction to the *Keynesian*-motivated proposals to use flexible exchange rates as one measure allowing national governments the leeway for an independent monetary policy. The most important advocate of flexible exchange rates in the early 1950s, apart from Friedman, was the Keynesian James Meade, who nevertheless favoured them primarily because he believed they afforded governments the autonomy to implement their chosen policies.[86] Robert Mundell, who had studied under

---

82   Henry Simons, 'Rules versus Authorities in Monetary Policy', *Journal of Political Economy* 44 (1936); cf. Henry Simons, *Economic Policy for a Free Society*, Chicago: Chicago University Press, 160–83. The essay 'A Monetary and Fiscal Framework for Economic Stability' was also published in the *American Economic Review* 38, no. 3 (1948).

83   Friedman, *A Program for Monetary Stability*, 100.

84   Friedrich Lutz, 'Comments', LA 1950; cf. for an almost identical point, Friedman, 'A Monetary and Fiscal Framework for Economic Stability', 252, and Friedman, 'The Case for Flexible Exchange Rates', 158.

85   Friedman, 'Monetary and Fiscal Framework for Economic Stability', 252, fn. 11.

86   James Meade, *The Balance of Payments* (vol. 1 of *The Theory of International Economic Policy*), Oxford: Oxford University Press, 1951, 218–31; see also Friedman, 'The Case for Flexible Exchange Rates', 187.

both Meade at the London School of Economics and Friedman in Chicago, described the difference in the following terms:

> Friedman, as you know, like Meade, championed flexible exchange rates. Their reasons were very different. Meade, the liberal socialist, saw flexible exchange rates as a device for achieving external balance while freeing policy tools for the implementation of national planning objectives. Friedman, the libertarian conservative, saw flexible exchange rates as way of getting rid of exchange and trade controls.[87]

Neoliberals distinguished their theory from Keynesian approaches in two ways: first, by emphasising free international capital movements and rejecting state intervention in foreign exchange markets; and second, through a monetarism geared towards restricting the scope of the policy itself.[88] The discipline promised by the gold standard, considered unrealistic by proponents of flexibilisation, was replaced in Friedman's conception by the monetary standard. In limiting the freedom created by flexible exchange rates, it established an automatic system, so as to preclude a Keynesian, social-planning-type policy.[89] Friedman thus addressed the second basic neoliberal precept – namely, the obstruction of democratic management of the economy. He thereby delivered an alternative to the gold standard, albeit a somewhat weaker one.

Within three years, at the 1953 MPS conference in Seelisberg, Switzerland, an entire session was given over to the topic of 'Free Exchange Rates and Convertibility'. Lutz, a student of Walter Eucken and previously an advocate of the gold standard, was the sole speaker to argue in favour of flexiblisation.[90] Lutz had backed a commodity reserve

---

87 Robert Mundell, 'Updating the Agenda for Monetary Union', in Leonardo Leiderman, ed., *Optimum Currency Areas: New Analytical and Policy Developments*, Washington, DC: International Monetary Fund, 1997, 30.
88 Friedman, 'The Case for Flexible Exchange Rates', 167–70; 187–9.
89 See Charles Kindleberger, 'The Case for Fixed Exchange Rates, 1969', in Federal Reserve Bank of Boston, ed., *The International Adjustment Mechanism: Proceedings of the Monetary Conference*, Boston, MA: Federal Reserve Bank of Boston, 1970, 95; and Charles Kindleberger, review of *Monetary Problems of the International Economy* (Mundell and Swoboda), *Journal of International Economics* 1, no. 1 (1971), 130.
90 Unfortunately, no documents pertaining to this debate are available in the archives. In the Liberaal Archief, the inventory shows Lutz as the only speaker in this discussion.

standard in 1949, more in line with classical liberalism, based as it was on a 'principle' identical to that of the gold standard, and he had rejected floating exchange rates for fear of the fluctuations they might engender, as well as the risks of capital flight, speculation and currency wars.[91] But Lutz also happened to be among the first inside the MPS to defect to the flexibilisation camp.[92] As early as 1935, in an essay promoting fixed exchange rates and the gold standard, Lutz had noted that, in view of the strength of trade unions, inflexible wages and regnant economic policy, a return to the gold standard would make sense only 'if the world ... once again makes free competition the organising principle of the economic system'. Failing that, the task at hand was to 'devise a new monetary system appropriate to the circumstances'.[93] Lutz then seems to have gradually adopted the solution to this dilemma presented by Friedman in 1950. Beginning in the early 1950s, and emphatically by the time of the 1953 MPS conference, he had transformed himself into one of the most tenacious spokesmen for floating exchange rates. The slow change of opinion is reflected in a 1951 article in which Lutz criticised the European Payments Union and proposed instead that surplus countries join together and establish full convertibility. To this end, he maintained, they should 'at least for a while ... pursue a flexible exchange rate policy', and he explicitly called for them to stabilise exchange rates through gold and foreign exchange interventions. Put another way, at this stage flexibilisation appeared merely as a risk to be regulated by the state, not as an independent demand, as it would in his work three years later.[94] In 1954, Lutz published some of these arguments using the same title as Friedman's 1953 paper, 'The Case for Flexible Exchange Rates';[95] here Friedman's influence on the ordoliberal Lutz is evident not only in the borrowed title but also in certain striking parallels of content,

---

91 See Friedrich Lutz, 'Geldpolitik und Wirtschaftsordnung', *Ordo* 2 (1949), 213.
92 Peter Bernholz, *Geldwertstabilität und Währungsordnung*, Tübingen: Mohr, 1989, 11.
93 Lutz, 'Goldwährung und Wirtschaftsordnung', 27; see also his criticism of the Bretton Woods Monetary Agreement in Friedrich Lutz, *International Monetary Mechanisms: The Keynes and White Proposals*, Princeton, NJ: Princeton University Press, 1943.
94 Friedrich Lutz, 'Europäische Währungsprobleme, 1946–1950', *Ordo* 4 (1951), 340.
95 Lutz, 'The Case for Flexible Exchange Rates'.

position and argumentation.[96] Still, Lutz adumbrated a new argument that was to prove influential concerning the *threat posed by controls*: fixed exchange rates, he maintained, could be preserved only under existing social conditions by way of the 'introduction of foreign exchange control or, at least, of quantitative restrictions on imports in the form of quotas or licences'. Furthermore, there was 'undoubtedly a grave danger that just this method will be chosen in the future'.[97] This case for flexible exchange rates – that they comprised the only method for preventing far-reaching capital and ultimately trade controls, and thereby for saving the free market economy – was later refined in the 1960s over the course of the debates on currency regimes, and became the leading strategy deployed by neoliberal evangelists for flexibilisation.

The arguments set out by Friedman and Lutz at MPS meetings in the early 1950s had an effect. Harvard professor Gottfried Haberler, a student of Mises and prominent adherent of the Austrian School who had emigrated from Austria to the US, once a committed devotee of the gold standard, had by the 1950s changed his mind and rallied to flexibilisation.[98] As late as 1945 he still backed the Bretton Woods regime and rejected flexible exchange rates as unstable. In 1936, in *The Theory of International Trade*, he offered the following argument (one remarkably close to the Bretton Woods consensus and Nurkse's analyses):

---

96 Lutz's argument was nearly identical to Friedman's of 1953: the possibilities of equalising balance of payments imbalances are not really given under current conditions, as, for one thing, wages and prices are not downwardly flexible; the equalisation system of 'regulated' devaluations within the framework of the IMF does not really work. It is particularly striking that, in contrast to the great scepticism expressed in 1949 about fluctuating exchange rates and speculation in his essays of 1954 and 1958, these are not regarded as problematic, but rather as 'undoubtedly beneficial' in Friedman's sense. Ibid., 183, 184; Friedrich Lutz, 'Das Problem der internationalen Währungsordnung', *Ordo* 10 (1958), 221; cf. Bernholz, *Geldwertstabilität und Währungsordnung*, 22.

97 Lutz, 'The Case for Flexible Exchange Rates', 178; see also Friedman, 'The Case for Flexible Exchange Rates', 203. Friedman also discussed controls, which he considered the 'least desirable method' of balance-of-payments equalisation – the assessment that controls would become the most important mechanism for balance-of-payments equalisation in the future appears for the first time in Lutz, 'The Case for Flexible Exchange Rates', but was taken up again and again by Friedman.

98 On Haberler's preference for the gold standard and fixed exchange rates, see Gottfried Haberler, *The Theory of International Trade, with Its Application to Commercial Policy*, New York: Macmillan, 1936, 44; and Haberler, *Prosperity and Depression: A Theoretical Analysis of Cyclical Movements*, Geneva: League of Nations, 1937, 431.

The instability of the exchange-rate between gold and the sterling-currencies has led to serious disadvantages. The conclusion seems therefore justified that stable exchange-rates, or in other words an international standard of one kind or another is indispensable in the long run for any extensive exchange of goods and credit on an individualistic basis.[99]

Nine years later, he wrote that 'it is certain that a system of free exchange rates would lead to extremely undesirable results. It would fuel capital flight and violent fluctuations'.[100] From the early 1950s, however, Haberler was converted: after discussing flexibilisation at the annual meetings of the AEA in 1953 and 1954, he published a pamphlet titled *Currency Convertibility*, published by the neoliberal American Enterprise Institute (AEI), calling on European countries to do away with exchange and capital controls and establish full convertibility and flexible exchange rates, as Canada had done in 1950.[101] Haberler's arguments were strikingly similar to Friedman's, likely as a result of the extensive discussions taking place within the MPS in the early 1950s, which probably contributed to Haberler's metamorphosis.[102] Friedman himself was conscious of their convergence of views, and noted in a letter to Haberler in February 1953 that 'the only difference' between them was that he was 'more extreme and less tolerant' than his Austrian co-thinker.[103]

But Haberler was not the only proselyte. A similar change of opinion can be traced in his close colleague and friend Fritz Machlup, the other famous 'American Austrian'.[104] Machlup, director of the International

---

99 Haberler, *The Theory of International Trade*, 45f. On Haberler's support for the Bretton Woods agreement, see 'Economists Back Bretton Program'.
100 Gottfried Haberler, 'The Choice of Exchange Rates after the War', *American Economic Review* 35, no. 3 (1945), 309.
101 See Gottfried Haberler, 'Reflections of the Future of the Bretton Woods System', *American Economic Review* 43, no. 2 (1953), 82; Gottfried Haberler, 'The Relevance of the Classical Theory under Modern Conditions', *American Economic Review* 44, no. 2 (1954), esp. 40f; and Haberler, *Currency Convertibility*.
102 Harold James and Michael Bordo, 'Haberler versus Nurkse: The Case for Floating Exchange Rates as an Alternative to Bretton Woods?', discussion paper no. 2001-08 of the University of St. Gallen, 2001.
103 Friedman's letter to Haberler of 3 February 1953, quoted in James and Bordo, 'Haberler versus Nurkse', 24.
104 Hartwell, *A History of the Mont Pelerin Society*, 230. Here, Hartwell describes Machlup and Haberler as 'American Austrians'. These two economists had 'assimilated'

Finance Section of Princeton University, had, like Haberler, plumped for the classical gold standard as a student of Mises but during the 1950s became a firm proponent of floating exchange rates, which he supported publicly for the first time in a lecture on the topic delivered at the 1961 MPS meeting.[105]

After 1953, the matter of international monetary order was not raised again until the MPS's eighth meeting, held in 1957 in St Moritz, Switzerland.[106] The discussion there focused primarily on the question of whether the European Economic Community promoted liberalism in general and the free movement of capital in particular; the members issued a call 'in unison' for immediate full convertibility of European currencies.[107] At previous MPS conferences, the boosters of flexibilisation were

---

so much in the US, both in terms of lifestyle and their academical mode of thinking, that they no longer described themselves as part of the Vienna School. See Karen Vaughn, *Austrian Economics in America: The Migration of a Tradition*, Cambridge: Cambridge University Press, 1994, 8, 92.

105   Machlup, a favourite student of Mises, had written a dissertation on the gold exchange standard in 1925. However, he had already raised critical questions about the traditional understanding of the gold standard in 1940 (Machlup, 'Eight Questions on Gold', *American Economic Review* 30 [February 1940]) and – like Haberler – supported the adoption of the Bretton Woods agreements in 1945 (cf. Jörg Hülsmann, *Mises: The Last Knight of Liberalism*, Auburn: Mises Institute, 2007, 479; 'Economists Back Bretton Program'). Machlup had already made positive mention of changes in exchange rates at an international expert conference in 1952 (Robert Triffin, 'The Impact of the Bellagio Group on International Reform', in Jacob S. Dreyer, ed., *Breadth and Depth in Economics: Fritz Machlup – The Man and His Ideas*, Lexington: Lexington Books, 1978, 145).

106   In the discussion chaired by Karl Brandt on 'The Common Market, The Integration of Europe and Exchange Stability', contributions were presented by Rueff, Haberler, Röpke and Hahn, and Heilperin, Mises, Pfister, Villey and de Graaf took part in the debate. Liberaal Archief, *Mont Pèlerin Society (1947– . . .). Inventory of the General Meeting Files (1947–1998)*, Ghent: Liberaal Archief, 2004, 32. Unfortunately, only two contributions have survived, and only the essay by Albert Hahn deals with the topic of international monetary order. L. Albert Hahn, 'Autonomous Monetary Policy and Fixed Exchange Rates', LA 1957; Wilhelm Röpke, 'Political Enthusiasm and Economic Sense: Some Comments on a European Economic Sense', LA 1957.

107   Helmut Schoeck describes this as one of the axioms of the MPS (Schoeck, 'Der Stand des liberalen Denkens'). MPS members were central to the European debates on the reintroduction of convertibility in the 1950s (cf. Helleiner, *States and the Reemergence of Global Finance*, 66, 71f.). The demand had also been featured in a 1954 anthology in which MPS members primarily and representatives of the 'neoliberal school' generally (according to one reviewer) had discussed possible means for achieving immediate convertibility. See Gottfried Haberler et al., *Die Konvertibilität der europäischen Währungen*, Zürich: Eugen Rentsch Verlag, 1954.

most outspoken in their criticism of the gold standard on the grounds of its unrealistic assumptions and the threat of excessive controls, but by 1957 the first stirrings of an internal controversy that was to dominate the 1960s began to be felt. From the beginning, sharp exchanges set the tone: MPS member Helmut Schoeck reported in the *NZZ* that at the conference 'the advocates of flexible exchange rates, at their head L. A. Hahn . . . were in the minority' and were 'accused by Prof. Heilperin of unliberal monetary nationalism'.[108] Hahn, a prominent German banker, economist and stock exchange expert, rejected the accusation.

Hahn was much feared as a 'censor and critic in Frankfurt' because of his public comments, especially with regard to balance of payments.[109] His dual role as theorist and practitioner, economist and banker, was important because – as historian Jan-Otmar Hesse has shown – it conferred for his contemporaries in economics the status of someone who had special insight into economics, and a 'special authority' based in practical knowledge.[110] Hahn had popularised the arguments for flexibilisation developed within the MPS and loyally cited Society members as references, nearly to the exclusion of all others.[111] At the 1957 MPS meeting, he introduced the concept of 'imported inflation', which caused a furore in the Bonn Republic of the late 1950s and early '60s.[112] The problem that arose with fixed exchange rates and the classical gold standard alike, Hahn argued, was the

---

The cited review is Wolfgang Stolper, review of Haberler et al. in *Journal of Political Economy* 64, no. 1 (1956), 79.

108   Schoeck, 'Der Stand des liberalen Denkens', with the majority of the panellists generally favouring the gold standard (Röpke, Rueff, Mises, Pfister, Villey, de Graaf).

109   Marion Gräfin Dönhoff, 'Eine kritische Stimme ist verstummt. Zum Tode Albert Hahn', *Die Zeit*, 11. October 1968 (41), 43, 50. For his critical contributions, see, for example, L. Albert Hahn, 'Die Kaufkraft stabil halten' *Die Zeit*, 19 September 1957.

110   This was also an argument in favour of his inclusion in the MPS. See Jan-Otmar Hesse, 'Some Relationships between a Scholar's and an Entrepreneur's Life: The Biography of L. Albert Hahn', *History of Political Economy* 39 (2007), 221.

111   For example, he quoted Friedman, Sohmen, Machlup and Johnson in a pamphlet. Cf. L. Albert Hahn, *Ein Traktat über Währungsreform*, Basel: Kyklos-Verlag, 1964, esp. 48; but also L. Albert Hahn, 'Monetäre Integration oder Realität?', in Günther Schmölders et al., eds, *Währungspolitik in der europäischen Integration*, Baden-Baden: Nomos, 1964.

112   Hahn had in the first place coined the term and the argument of 'imported inflation'. See Marion Gräfin Dönhoff, 'Eine kritische Stimme ist verstummt', *Die Zeit*, 11 October 1968.

internationalisation of individual countries' monetary policy (he primarily directed his criticism against US laxness) imposed internal inflation and capital controls on hard-currency countries like Germany. Mediated by international trade, excessive demand in the US market overwhelmed attempts at restraining inflation in West Germany, the critique went. In addition to other generally illiberal consequences, the upshot harmed stock market speculators and bankers particularly severely.[113] Floating exchange rates, so the argument held, could insulate hard-currency countries with strong anti-inflationary policies from external pressures, especially the expansionary policy of the US Federal Reserve. Imported inflation played a central role in the following years at MPS conferences and in the broader European context; by 1964 it constituted the main theme of that year's Annual Report of the West German Council of Economic Experts, overseen by Meyer with the collaboration of MPS members Egon Sohmen and Friedrich Lutz.[114]

The topic was also discussed at the MPS's 1960 conference in Kassel, but, with two exceptions, the contributions there focused mainly on the problems of European integration.[115] Some MPS members, notably Haberler and Hahn, again endorsed 'fully flexible exchange rates', claiming that these were 'most compatible with liberal doctrine'.[116] Hahn's paper argued against the proposal by some gold standard stalwarts to raise the price of gold in the face of looming American balance-of-payments difficulties.[117] To the

---

113 Hahn, 'Autonomous Monetary Policy and Fixed Exchange Rates', LA 1957, 3, 5f. Hahn argued in a similar way to his latest publication, *Autonome Konjunktur-Politik und Wechselkurs-Stabilität: geldtheoretische Betrachtungen zur Währungspolitik der Bank deutscher Länder*, Frankfurt am Main: Fritz Knapp, 1957.

114 See Sachverständigenrat zur Begutachtung der gesamtwirtschaftlichen Entwicklung, *Jahresgutachten 1964/65*, Nachdruck 1994 by Schmidt Periodicals GmbH, Bad Feilnbach, 1964; Egon Sohmen und Friedrich Lutz, 'Wie kann sich ein Land der importierten Inflation entziehen?', in ibid., 157–67. This is discussed in more detail in chapter 3.

115 Many members took part in the debate entitled 'Economic and Financial Problems of the West', moderated by Bruno Leoni and Lawrence Fertig: Ludwig Hahn, Clarence Philbrook, Otto Veit, Gottfried Haberler, Lord Grantchester, Michael Heilperin, Gerhard Winterberger, Gerhard Schwarz, Daniel Villey, Wilhelm Röpke, Benjamin Rogge, Ernest Spat and Milton Friedman.

116 'Die Leitlinien einer liberalen Wirtschaftspolitik. Tagung der Mont Pelerin Society in Kassel', *NZZ*, 26 September 1960, 3.

117 L. Albert Hahn, 'Gold-Revaluation and Dollar-Devaluation?', LA 1960. The essay was also published in German in the journal *Kyklos* in 1960: L. Albert Hahn, 'Goldaufwertung und Dollarabwertung?', *Kyklos* 13, no. 4 (1960).

argument put forward by Heilperin among others that the price of gold must be raised in order to guarantee sufficient international liquidity, the logical response was the threat to drop the obligation of central banks to buy unproductive gold at fixed prices.[118] Here, Hahn formulated a highly preliminary form of the proposal for unilateral abandonment of the gold exchange guarantee that Haberler further developed through the late 1960s in the US. This in turn would become a central component of Haberler's and Nixon's strategy of 'benign neglect', anticipating Nixon's decision to close the gold window. The other relevant contribution to the 1960 MPS conference was made by the Frankfurt-based ordoliberal Otto Veit, a gold standard enthusiast and outspoken opponent of floating exchange rates. Veit discussed the possibility of depoliticising monetary policy within the Bretton Woods framework. This should be spoken of 'only in whispers', he warned, since 'politicians, intellectuals, economists and pressure groups are usually no friends of sound monetary conditions' and might resist it.[119]

During the 1950s, various members in the MPS fundamentally changed their vision of neoliberal monetary reform. Meyer, for instance, backed the gold standard or a similar fixed exchange rate system on ordoliberal lines until the 1950s. As late as 1951, in a comparative analysis in *Ordo* of the two market-liberal, or as he called them, 'transport-economic' currency systems – the gold standard and 'floating exchange rates' – he stated that fixed exchange rates were a condition of the international division of labour and free movement of capital, the reason why the gold standard represented 'a system of balance of payments adjustment decidedly superior to the exchange rate mechanism'.[120] In 1958, he problematised the consequences of 'cementing' the German

---

118   The gold price increase was also to be rejected, as the gold standard would generally function even worse than the current 'gold-substitute standard' in contrast to flexible exchange rates. Hahn, 'Gold-Revaluation and Dollar-Devaluation?' An increase in the gold price was propagated above all by Michael Heilperin, both in his contribution to the 1957 MPS conference ('Die Leitlinien einer liberalen Wirtschaftspolitik') and in various publications; see the articles in Michael Heilperin, *Aspects of the Pathology of Money*, Geneva: M. Joseph for the Graduate Institute of International Studies, 1968.

119   Veit, 'A New Stage in International Monetary Policy', LA 1960, 4. Veit had long promoted the gold standard (see Otto Veit, *Volkswirtschaftliche Theorie der Liquidität*, Frankfurt: Vittorio Klostermann, 1948) and had spoken out forcefully against flexible exchange rates (Otto Veit, 'Pecunia in ordine rerum', *Ordo* 6 [1954], 74).

120   Fritz W. Meyer, 'Das Problem der deutschen Zahlungsbilanz', *Ordo* 10 (1958); Fritz W. Meyer, 'Stabile oder bewegliche Wechselkurse?', *Ordo* 4 (1951), 363.

exchange rate, but argued only for a one-time revaluation of the deutsche mark.[121] His reversal must therefore have occurred in the late 1950s or early 1960s, because as a member of the German Council of Economic Experts (Sachsverständigenrat, or SVR) he supported a flexible deutsche mark and floating exchange rates from 1964 on.[122] Likewise, William Fellner, who taught at Yale and also changed his mind on the exchange rate question, was to play a key role in shaping both the transnational and American debates of the 1960s, and later became a member of Nixon's Council of Economic Advisers (CEA).[123]

New advocates of floating exchange rates emerged as well. Sohmen, a colleague of Fellner's at Yale who went on to teach at Saarbrücken and Heidelberg, was pivotal in disseminating the theory internationally and in his capacity as adviser to the SVR.[124] Sohmen's close contact with MPS members is evident in his friendships with Machlup, Haberler and Fellner in the US – his dissertation on floating exchange rates is dedicated to his 'mentor and friend' Haberler – and his collaboration with

121 Meyer, 'Das Problem der deutschen Zahlungsbilanz', 153.
122 See Sachsverständigenrat, *Jahresgutachten 1964/1965*, 131f.; Fritz W. Meyer, 'Die internationale Währungsordnung im Dienste der stabilitätspolitischen Grenzmoral und die Möglichkeiten einer Reform', in Dieter Cassel et al., eds, *25 Jahre Marktwirtschaft in der Bundesrepublik Deutschland*, Stuttgart: Fischer, 1972; Hans Willgerodt, 'Fritz Walter Meyer. 8. März 1907–4. März 1980', in *In Memoriam Fritz Walter Meyer* (Alma mater 50: Beiträge zur Geschichte der Universität Bonn), Bonn: Bouvier Verlag, 1981, 11–37, esp. 25f.; Peter Bernholz, *Geldwertstabilität und Währungsordnung*, Tübingen: Mohr, 1989, esp. 11.
123 Fellner became close friends with Haberler and Lutz in the 1950s, and from the early 1960s onwards he called for floating exchange rates, and was particularly focused on those proposals concerning the establishment of a bandwidth as a transitional solution to complete flexibility (see James N. Marshall, *William J. Fellner: A Bio-Bibliography*, Westport, CT: Greenwood Press, 1992, 19; William Fellner, 'Rules of the Game, Vintage 1966', in William Fellner et al., eds, *Maintaining and Restoring Balance in International Payments*, Princeton, NJ: Princeton University Press, 1966; William Fellner, 'Specific Proposal for Limited Exchange-Rate Flexibility', *Weltwirtschaftliches Archiv*, March, 1970). As early as 1962, he called for 'market flexibility of exchange rates within suitable bandwidths'. William Fellner, *Amerikanische Erfahrungen mit der Lohninflation in den Fünfziger Jahren* (Walter Eucken Institut: Vorträge und Aufsätze), Tübingen: J.C.B. Mohr, 1962, 32.
124 The economist Kindleberger puts it succinctly: 'Sohmen played a significant part in the 1960s in making the case for flexible exchange rates respectable.' Charles Kindleberger, 'Egon Sohmen', in John Eatwell et al., eds, *The New Palgrave Dictionary*, vol. 4, London: Macmillan, 1987, 421; for a similar view, see Bernholz, *Geldwertstabilität und Währungsordnung*, 25.

Friedman, dating to the late 1950s, on controversial topics in their field.[125]

The support of Leland B. Yeager, an American economist and co-founder of the neoliberal Virginia School, was decisive for the academic formalisation and dissemination of Friedman's arguments. Already by the early 1960s, Yeager had advocated flexibilisation and an end to the American gold exchange guarantee.[126] In 1966, he published a highly successful textbook (translated in Europe and Japan), described as 'a landmark book that soon became the standard reference in the field of international money and finance'.[127] In this text, Yeager recapitulated and formalised Friedman's arguments for floating exchange rates in a highly technical register. Two years later, he published a similar introductory-level textbook.[128]

Likewise Harry Johnson, who abandoned his Keynesian positions in the 1950s, by 1960 had become one of the most active exponents of floating exchange rates, shortly after moving to the University of Chicago. Discovery of a monetary approach to explaining balances of payments had the effect of 'the liberating force of an epiphany' for the erstwhile Keynesian.[129] He had previously accused Friedman and

---

125 See Egon Sohmen, *Flexible Exchange Rates: Theory and Controversy*, Chicago: University of Chicago Press, 1961; Herbert Giersch, introduction to Herbert Giersch, ed., *Money, Trade, and Competition: Essays in Memory of Egon Sohmen,* Berlin: Springer, 1992, vi. On the controversy, see Egon Sohmen, 'Demand Elasticities and the Foreign-Exchange Market', *Journal of Political Economy* 65, no. 5 (1957), 431–6; Egon Sohmen, 'Notes on Some Controversies in the Theory of International Trade: A Comment', *Economic Journal* 71, no. 282 (1961), 423–6; Harry G. Johnson and Jagdish N. Bhagwati, 'Notes on Some Controversies in the Theory of International Trade', *Economic Journal* 70 (March 1960), 93; D. E. Moggridge, 'Biography and Autobiography: Harry Johnson', *History of Political Economy* 39 (2007), 315–41, here 331–3; Egon Sohmen, *International Monetary Problems and the Foreign Exchanges*, Princeton, NJ: International Finance Section, 1964.
126 Leland B. Yeager, 'The Triffin Plan: Diagnosis, Remedy, and Alternatives', *Kyklos* 14, no. 3 (1961).
127 Alan Rabin, 'The Contributions of Leland B. Yeager to International Economics', *Journal of Private Enterprise* 16, no. 1 (2000), 124–36.
128 See Leland B. Yeager, *International Monetary Relations. Theory, History, and Policy*, New York: Harper & Row, 1966, 97, 189–208, 466. The introductory textbook is Leland B. Yeager, *The International Monetary Mechanism*, New York: Holt, Rinehart and Winston, 1968.
129 Jacques Polak, 'The Two Monetary Approaches to the Balance of Payments: Keynesian and Johnsonian', in W. Young and A. Arnon, eds, *The Open Economy Macromodel: Past, Present and Future*, Boston: Kluwer, 2002, 27. According to this monetarist approach – which was a central element of the debates at the MPS

The Origins of Neoliberal Monetary Theory 71

Sohmen of 'propaganda' for their unscientific analysis of floating exchange rates, but upon his move to Chicago – he was brought there by Friedman, in fact – he 'dropped the outsider pose' and largely assimilated into the Chicago School, however critically.[130] Johnson's about-face was among the most abrupt; in 1962, only two years after a much-resented attack on Friedman and Sohmen, he cited both of them in support of the assertion that 'the theoretical case in favour of floating exchange rates is, in my opinion, virtually incontestable'.[131]

Whether such changes of opinion were determined by the discussions taking place within the MPS network cannot be established definitively. Yet the connection is difficult to dismiss out of hand, since the MPS was the only forum in which those mentioned here met and exchanged views, and because nearly all economists who promoted floating exchange rates in the late 1950s and early 1960s were MPS members. At the time, however, the political and intellectual activities of the MPS were overshadowed by an internal power struggle unrelated to monetary debates. With the resolution of this so-called Hunold–Hayek crisis, some of the main backers of the gold standard resigned from the MPS, and the position of those advocating floating exchange rates within the organisation was strengthened. The crisis itself concerned a dispute between supporters of Albert Hunold, who favoured greater and more immediate politicisation of the MPS, and Hayek and his followers, who continued to prioritise long-term strategic calculations. Among others, Wilhem Röpke, Karl Brandt (later readmitted) and Alexander Rüstow left the MPS along with Hunold in 1961. With Jacques Rueff, Röpke had been the most important MPS advocate of the gold standard.[132]

---

conferences – balances of payments are interpreted exclusively as an 'essentially monetary phenomenon', a formulation that ran like an anti-Keynesian 'mantra' through Johnson's work.

130   Moggridge, 'Biography and Autobiography'; Harry G. Johnson, 'The Keynesian Revolution and the Monetarist Counterrevolution', *American Economic Review* 61 (May 1971). On the accusation of propaganda, see Johnson and Bhagwati, 'Notes on Some Controversies in the Theory of International Trade', 93.

131   Harry G. Johnson, 'International Liquidity – Problems and Plans', in Herbert G. Grubel, ed., *World Monetary Reform: Plans and Issues*, Stanford, CA: Stanford University Press, 1963, 376; Moggridge overlooked this in his analysis.

132   On the Hunold crisis, see Hartwell, *A History of the Mont Pelerin Society*, 100–33, and Walpen, *Die offenen Feinde und ihre Gesellschaft*, 131–51.

The 1960s

In the first half of the 1960s, an intensely acrimonious controversy over monetary issues erupted within the MPS. The terms of the debate are well illustrated by the 1961 Turin meeting, site of the longest and most divisive dispute in the Society's history up to that point, which also attracted its broadest participation. At its centre stood the question of the ideal neoliberal monetary system.[133]

In his opening remarks, Röpke, who had replaced Hayek as president of the MPS in 1961 (he would serve only a short term, lasting until 1962), insisted that the Society 'place common ground above what divides us' and suppress personal rivalries.[134] He emphasised repeatedly that no other issue provoked more disagreement than the currency question and suggested that discord had already reached a high pitch by the end of the 1950s.[135] Several participants of the debate emphasised that the inability to reach agreement after a long period of discussion was a 'disgrace' – Kemp even argued that the 'bitter controversy' within the liberal camp had 'given aid and encouragement to a common enemy'.[136] He recommended that such

---

133 At least thirteen men took part in the panel bearing the rather neutralised title 'The International Monetary System': Michael Heilperin, Philip Cortney, Jacques Rueff, Henry Hazlitt, Alexander Loveday, Hans Sennholz and Arthur Kemp spoke as advocates for a reintroduction of the classical gold standard. Friedman, Lutz, Machlup, Hahn and Hans Ilau spoke from the advocates of free exchange rates. It is the only MPS conference for which audio files exist, making it possible to supplement the reconstruction of the sometimes heated debates from the written essays in the Liberaal Archief by their oral arguments. See also the audio recordings of the MPS conference in Turin in 1961, available at http://web.archive.org/web/20091210075110/http://www.brunoleoni.it/riscoprirebl/interna.aspx?codice=0000000012, henceforth MPS, audio recording of Turin meeting 1961. See also Arthur Kemp, 'The International Monetary Order', LA 1961, 1. A report on the conference by Carlo Mötteli is also useful. Carlo Mötteli, 'Big Business, Developing Countries and the Monetary System', *Swiss Review of World Affairs*, November 1961.

134 On Röpke and his attitude to the gold standard, which he had adopted from his mentor Mises, see John Zmirak, *Wilhelm Röpke: Swiss Localist, Global Economist*, Wilmington: ISI Books, 2001, 197f.

135 Friedman, 'Real and Pseudo Gold Standards', LA 1961, 1; Kemp, 'The International Monetary Order', LA 1961, 1; Röpke, in MPS, audio recording of Turin meeting 1961.

136 Cortney, in MPS, audio recording of Turin meeting 1961; Friedman, 'Real and Pseudo Gold Standards', LA 1961, 1; Machlup, 'International Liquidity and International Money Creation', LA 1961, 1.

conflicts be dealt with internally, covered by a public-facing emphasis on unity.[137]

Philip Cortney, a leading American industrialist and chairman of the International Chamber of Commerce, ended his own intervention with an urgent appeal to 'the professors' to transcend their bickering and offer 'the free world some kind of assessment of the problem [of] how to restore international monetary order'.[138] His plea would be realised two years later by the MPS's own Machlup and Fellner, with the founding of the Bellagio Group. But in the 1961 discussion, attempts to dismiss and discredit rival neoliberal concepts of reform remained the order of the day. Any convergence between the various positions – save the rejection of capital controls and democratic economic policy, and the commitment to automatic currency adjustment – was largely overlooked. Only Kemp bucked the trend, emphasising the shared 'desire to somehow eliminate the amount of administrative discretion in monetary matters and replace it with a more or less automatic system or mechanism'.[139]

In these discussions, it is especially notable that – as Friedman put it – 'liberals (in the sense of our Society) reach such divergent conclusions from the same underlying principles'.[140] Many of these viewpoints were indeed mirror images of one another, and the resulting debates more reminiscent of theological disputes than rational disagreements over economics.[141] Selected examples suffice to illustrate the dynamic. The central argument of all proponents of flexible exchange rates in the MPS held that it was impossible to establish a genuine gold standard consistent with free markets and liberal principles, given actually existing social and political power relations and the Keynesian orientation of so many governments. Hans Ilau, managing director of the Chamber of Commerce and Industry (IHK) in Frankfurt, put it this way: 'I don't think we will get anywhere today with a return to the gold standard what with the combination of poor economic judgement and increased

---

137 Kemp, 'The International Monetary Order', LA 1961, 1.
138 Cortney, in MPS, audio recording of Turin meeting 1961.
139 Kemp, 'The International Monetary Order', LA 1961, 1.
140 Friedman, 'Real and Pseudo Gold Standards', LA 1961, 1.
141 Cortney (in MPS, audio recording of Turin meeting 1961) summarises the depth of dissent in the MPS in the following clear words: 'I must disagree with practically everything Friedman says on this subject.'

political power' of governments and central bankers.[142] Parallel to this, Sennholz and Heilperin also argued that advocates of floating exchange rates made the unrealistic assumption that monetary policy could be stable and anti-inflationary absent the constraint and discipline of the monetary system.[143]

Each camp accused the other of tabling a reform proposal that did not represent an authentic improvement of the status quo, and both claimed that their respective reforms were the only way to avoid capital controls and potentially serious crises. One recurrent argument charged that the opposing position did not conform to the liberal principles of the MPS. Flexible exchange rates, according to the American Arthur Kemp, an economist at Claremont College, were not compatible with an internationalist liberalism that placed international equilibrium above the goals of the national welfare state.[144] By contrast, Friedman criticised gold standard torch bearers for advocating illiberal measures, thereby (unintentionally) giving succour to collectivist and *dirigiste* policies, and in so doing inflicting enormous damage on liberalism by demanding that the price of gold be fixed.[145] Both camps agreed on the fundamental principle that the 'rule of men instead of law' was contrary to liberalism.[146] But while Sennholz argued that flexible exchange rates put too much power to decide economic policy in the hands of governments, Friedman maintained that fixed exchange rates and the gold standard both concentrated excessive power in the hands of bureaucrats via government control of foreign exchange and gold prices.[147] Finally, both sides interpreted the negative experience of Bretton Woods as clear evidence that their preferred monetary system represented the 'only solution'.[148]

---

142 Ilau speaks in German here. See Hans Ilau, in MPS, audio recording of Turin meeting 1961, and, above all, Machlup, 'International Liquidity and International Money Creation', LA 1961.

143 Heilperin, 'Monetary Reform in an Atlantic Setting', LA 1961, 7; Hans Sennholz, 'From Dollar Gap to Dollar Glut', LA 1961, 6.

144 Kemp, 'The International Monetary Order', LA 1961, 5; and Sennholz, 'From Dollar Gap to Dollar Glut', LA 1961, 6.

145 Friedman, in MPS, audio recording of Turin meeting 1961; Friedman, 'Real and Pseudo Gold Standards', LA 1961, 2, 11.

146 Friedman, 'Real and Pseudo Gold Standards', LA 1961, 11.

147 Sennholz, 'From Dollar Gap to Dollar Glut', LA 1961, 6. Friedman, 'Real and Pseudo Gold Standards', LA 1961, 11.

148 Sennholz, 'From Dollar Gap to Dollar Glut', LA 1961, 8; Machlup, 'International Liquidity and International Money Creation', LA 1961, 7.

Although the gold standard still enjoyed a slight advantage in 1961, it was already apparent that advocates of floating exchange rates were gaining the upper hand within liberal circles and beyond. Partisans of the floating exchange rate benefited from disagreement in the ranks of their adversaries, who could not agree as to whether increases in the price of gold were an essential prerequisite for the reintroduction of the classical gold standard. While Cortney, Heilperin and Rueff considered a substantial price increase to be essential – most often they spoke of doubling it – some around the American think tank Economists' National Committee on Monetary Policy (ENCMP), above all Kemp, saw such an eventuality as disastrous and inflationary.[149]

Those backing the gold standard could muster only superficial criticism of the flexible exchange rate position, and they mainly resorted to reasserting the well-known advantages of their panacea.[150] The argument sought to disqualify the opposing position as insufficiently radical and ill-suited for a liberal economic order worthy of the name. On this view, the case for flexible exchange rates took for granted the social reality brought about by Keynesian economic policy and strong trade unions, rather than challenging their pernicious consequences. In Hans Sennholz's formulation, the upshot was 'an unfortunate capitulation to the forces of statism'.[151]

By contrast, advocates of flexibilisation invested a great deal of time in mounting a detailed critique of their MPS colleagues' plans to rehabilitate the gold standard, and they produced a highly cogent argument against it. They did not limit themselves to condemning the gold standard as a matter of principle; rather, Friedman, Machlup and Ilau criticised its conceptual shortcomings and the likely effects of its

---

149 See Cortney, in MPS, audio recording of Turin meeting 1961; Heilperin, 'Monetary Reform in an Atlantic Setting', LA 1961, 7; Kemp, 'The International Monetary Order', LA 1961; Jacques Rueff, 'Gold Exchange Standard: A Danger to the West', LA 1961. MPS members of the ENCMP were Karl Brandt, Henry Hazlitt, William Harold Hutt, Donald Kemmerer (president from 1967 to 1970), Arthur Kemp, Ludwig von Mises, Hans Sennholz, John van Sickle. The ENCMP was founded in 1933 by economists and bankers to campaign for the reintroduction of the classical gold standard and was very active as an 'action organisation' in influencing Washington government circles. The successor organisation Committee for Monetary Research and Education (CMRE), founded in 1971 by MPS member Kemmerer, is still active.

150 Paradigmatic is Heilperin, 'Monetary Reform in an Atlantic Setting', LA 1961.

151 Sennholz, 'From Dollar Gap to Dollar Glut', LA 1961, 6.

implementation. They furthermore accused their rivals of being partly responsible for the introduction of far-reaching capital controls.

Friedman was especially thoroughgoing in his criticism.[152] It was, as he put it, 'schizophrenia' to demand different political measures for gold (state fixing of the gold price) than for other products, he argued, in keeping with the location of the conference in Italy, with wine. Not only did he accuse his colleagues in the MPS of 'schizophrenia', alleging that they stumped for what amounted to a 'pseudo gold standard' that should be rejected by all MPS members as alien to liberal convictions, he even asserted that their theory had already done great damage to liberalism.[153] 'War aside,' he remarked, 'nothing that has occurred in the past half-century has, in my view, done more to weaken and undermine the public's faith in liberal principles than the pseudo gold standard.' Friedman's misguided fellows, according to his 'far-reaching indictment', supported restrictions and regulations on the international movement of capital and goods. Nothing less than 'the preservation and promotion of a free society' hinged on understanding this fact and the distinction between the real and the fake gold standard, which would shape future internal debates.[154]

While Friedman struck a confrontational posture, Machlup, who had himself switched from the gold standard to floating exchange rate viewpoint in the 1950s, positioned himself as mediator. In explaining his own change of heart Machlup articulated one of the most insightful variants of the argument against unrealistic assumptions and the threat of controls; in so doing, he identified flexible exchange rates as the only recourse:[155]

---

152 Friedman's essay 'Real and Pseudo Gold Standard' was devoted exclusively to the conflict of ideas within the MPS. It was published in the *Journal of Law and Economics* in 1961 and in *Ordo* in 1962.

153 Friedman, 'Real and Pseudo Gold Standards', LA 1961.

154 Ibid., 67. Cf. Milton Friedman, 'How Stands the Theory and Practice of Monetary Policy', LA 1978, 1.

155 Machlup, 'International Liquidity and International Money Creation', LA 1961, 1; Fritz Machlup, *Plans for Reform of the International Monetary System*, Princeton, NJ: Princeton University Press, 1962, 364, fn. 105. The argument here is nearly identical. It is well worth noting how cautiously Machlup proceeded: 'My endorsement of flexible exchange rates is not an absolute one. My mind is not made up as to whether, if I had to choose, I would prefer flexible money incomes and money prices with fixed exchange rates, or flexible exchange rates. But I do not see that there is a choice.' See Machlup, 'International Liquidity and International Money Creation', LA 1961, 7. In his book

I do not see that there is a choice . . . If we, as liberals, have to embrace a floating exchange rate, then we have to embrace a floating exchange rate. If we, as liberals, reject capital and trade controls, and most people and their governments reject the restriction of effective demand [the equalisation mechanism of the gold standard], I see only one possibility: flexible exchange rates.[156]

In subsequent debates, this seemingly logical argument, along with the postulate that there was no alternative to the current system and that flexible exchange rates were therefore the only option, would be repeated time and again.[157]

As at the MPS conferences of the 1950s, in 1961 substantive arguments for flexibilisation and corresponding strategic considerations were also advanced. Machlup, for example, characterised flexible exchange rates as an automatic and particularly effective mechanism against trade unions' excessive wage demands. With flexibilisation, according to this argument, undue wage increases would immediately translate into a decline in exchange rates, and the resulting increase in the cost of imports would put upward pressure on the general price level; thus, an increase in wages in monetary terms would not yield an increase in real purchasing power, forcing unions to curb their demands. 'Once this is more widely understood,' Machlup warned, 'organised

---

resulting from the lecture, Machlup distinguished himself and the other MPS members from Keynesian advocates of free exchange rates: 'But we must distinguish those who recommend an autonomous monetary policy – a credit policy independent of the balance of payments – from those who do not recommend it but regard it as a given and unalterable fact with which realistic observers should reckon.' See Machlup, *Plans for Reform of the International Monetary System*, 358.

156   Machlup, 'International Liquidity and International Money Creation', LA 1961, 7.

157   The argument also appeared, for example, in the contributions by MPS members at MPS or public conferences and can be found in the following archival material: Haberler, 'The International Monetary Mechanism', LA 1964; Milton Friedman, 'The Political Economy of International Monetary Arrangements', LA 1965; Gottfried Haberler, 'International Monetary Problems', LA 1968; Enoch Powell, 'The Fixed Exchange and Dirigisme', LA 1968. For published material, see Haberler in *International Payments Problems*, 134; Machlup, 'International Monetary Systems and the Free Market Economy', 73, 173; Friedrich Lutz, 'Money Rates of Interest, Real Rates of Interest, and Capital Movements', in Fellner, *Maintaining and Restoring Balance in International Payments*, 28; the contributions of MPS members to the AEI conference 1966, American Enterprise Institute, *International Payments Problems*.

labor and social-democratic parties will become the most ardent advocates of fixed exchange rates and of maintenance of the "gold standard" in its modern form, with plenty of fiat money, full-employment policies, and import controls.'[158] Friedman, for his part, attempted to fasten divergent opinions within the MPS to one view and suggested as a possible common demand the complete privatisation of the gold market. He specifically backed a commitment by governments not to buy or sell gold at fixed prices and to divest their gold reserves. Two years later, he elaborated on this point before a US congressional committee,[159] and Machlup publicly upheld a similar concept (that is, lowering the price of gold), as did Haberler at the MPS's 1965 meeting.[160]

In his 1961 intervention, Machlup refined his argument against the threat of capital controls, transforming it into a discursive strategy to be deployed in conservative-liberal circles. Machlup argued that the advocate of free and flexible exchange rates 'can be quite respectable – even in banking circles – in calling for floating rates as an emergency measure, even if he actually prefers it for libertarian reasons, because he has found that fixed rates so often lead to direct controls'. Key opponents of flexible exchange rates (and potentially important coalition partners) such as bankers and conservative liberals were seen as most likely to be persuaded to endorse flexible exchange rates as contingency suited to periods of crisis.[161]

The schematic essay that Machlup presented at the MPS meeting in Turin was an early draft of his well-known *Plans for Reform of the International Monetary System*. With this book, he catapulted himself into the centre of international monetary debates; the material was

---

158   Machlup, 'International Liquidity and International Money Creation', LA 1961, 8; cf. Fritz Machlup, *International Payments, Debts, and Gold*, 77, fn. 11.

159   Friedman, 'Real and Pseudo Gold Standards', LA 1961, 11; see also Odell, *U.S. International Monetary Policy*, 89f. This represented an internationalisation and radicalisation of the strategy of unilateral abandonment of the gold exchange guarantee presented by L. Albert Hahn, in 'Keynesian Monetary and Fiscal Policy and Its Consequences', LA 1960, at the previous MPS conference.

160   Fritz Machlup, 'Comments on the "Balance of Payments" and a Proposal to Reduce the Price of Gold', *Journal of Finance* 16 (May 1961); Machlup, *International Payments, Debts, and Gold*, 344f.; Gottfried Haberler, 'Some Remarks on Recent Discussions about the International Payments System', LA 1965.

161   Machlup, 'International Liquidity and International Money Creation', LA 1961, 6.

even presented to the Subcommittee on International Exchange and Payments of the US Congress.[162] Machlup's taxonomy divided proposals for monetary reform into five groups, each tasked with resolving three problems:

1. The liquidity problem. How is sufficient international liquidity to be ensured?
2. The adjustment problem. Which adjustment mechanisms compensate for imbalances in the balance of payments?
3. The confidence problem. How is confidence in the value of a currency secured; for example, the US dollar in relation to gold?[163]

Since the beginning of the 1960s, Keynesian-orientated economists such as Triffin had been agitating to solve adjustment difficulties by expanding international liquidity, which ultimately led to the creation of an international artificial currency.[164] In government-adjacent circles, such a focus had served to occlude market-liberal concepts that relied exclusively on the *adjustment* of internal prices (that is, the gold standard) or exchange rates.

By contrast, Machlup's division of the discursive field shifted attention to the adjustment problem and gave advocates of flexible exchange rates more opportunities to place their proposals on the reform agenda. As with Friedman, Machlup – along with the Bellagio Group, discussed below – defined adjustment in a clearly neoliberal sense:[165] only price and wage inflation or deflation (i.e., the mechanisms of the gold standard) or currency appreciation and depreciation (i.e., the mechanisms of flexible exchange rates) were to be considered 'legitimate adjustment

---

162 See Machlup, *Plans for Reform of the International Monetary System*. His essay also appeared in 1962 in the edited collection *Factors Affecting the United States Balance of Payments*, published on behalf of the US Congress. In 1964 there was a second, revised edition, and translations were produced in German (1962, by the Kiel Institute for the World Economy), Italian (1962) and Japanese (1963).

163 See Machlup, 'International Liquidity and International Money Creation', LA 1961; Machlup *Plans for Reform of the International Monetary System*, 292–99. In his written contribution to the MPS conference, he discussed only the first two problems. For the popularisation of this subfield of economics, see chapter 3.

164 See Odell, *U.S. International Monetary Policy*, 79–160.

165 'The system of floating exchange rates' is 'the free market solution'. Friedman, *Capitalism and Freedom*, 67.

forces', whereas all others got 'another label', with their associated policy measures characterised as 'compensatory corrections'.[166]

This classification relegated Keynesian concepts of reform, which inclined towards financing payment imbalances by expanding international re-servicing and credit facilities, to the rank of the merely cosmetic and superficial, unable to solve either the adjustment or the confidence problems.[167] Flexible exchange rates, by contrast, were said to do both. Moreover, they could be presented as eliminating the need for reserves.[168] Defenders of flexibilisation emphasised its ability to resolve the adjustment problem, which they took to be one of the most fundamental; in the following years, such rhetoric appeared across publications and public talks by MPS members.[169] Machlup and

---

[166] Fritz Machlup, *Adjustment, Compensatory Correction, and Financing of Imbalances in International Payments*, Princeton, NJ: Princeton University Press, 1965, 206; cf. Friedman, *Capitalism and Freedom*, 67. On the effectiveness of such definitions and the 'politics of meaning', see generally Peter Sederberg, *The Politics of Meaning: Power and Explanation in the Construction of Social Reality*, Tucson: University of Arizona Press, 1984; and in relation to economic ideas, A. W. Coats and David Colander, eds, *The Spread of Economic Ideas*, Cambridge: Cambridge University Press, 1989.

[167] Charles Kindleberger, 'How Ideas Spread among Economists: Examples from International Economics', in Colander and Coats, *The Spread of Economic Ideas*.

[168] Machlup, *Plans for Reform of the International Monetary System*, 351.

[169] Gottfried Haberler and Thomas D. Willett, *U.S. Balance-of-Payments Policies and International Monetary Reform: A Critical Analysis*, Washington, DC: American Enterprise Institute, 1968, 59. Here, Haberler and Willett developed the paradigmatic formulation: 'The adjustment problem is much more important than the liquidity problems. Despite this, official and academic discussion has dwelt more on liquidity than on adjustment; and we have seen that adjustment policy has been woefully inadequate and misguided.' Cf. especially Machlup, *Adjustment, Compensatory Correction, and Financing of Imbalances in International Payments*, but also Fritz Machlup, 'The Cloakroom Rule of International Reserves: Reserve Creation and Resources Transfer', *Quarterly Journal of Economics* 79, no. 3 (1965); Fritz Machlup, *Remaking the International Monetary System: The Rio Agreement and Beyond*, Baltimore: Johns Hopkins University Press, 1968; Haberler, 'The International Monetary Mechanism', LA 1964; Gottfried Haberler, *Money in the International Economy: A Study in Balance of Payments Adjustment, International Liquidity and Exchange Rates* (Hobart Paper), London: Institute of Economic Affairs, 1965, 44; Gottfried Haberler, 'The International Payments System: Postwar Trends and Prospects', in *International Payments Problems*, 15; Haberler, 'International Monetary Problems', LA 1968, 4–7; Haberler and Willett, *U.S. Balance-of-Payments Policies and International Monetary Reform*, 59–63; Leland B. Yeager, 'Unilateral Action on International Monetary Policy', in Lawrence Officer and Thomas D. Willett, eds, *The International Monetary System: Problems and Proposals*, Englewood Cliffs, NJ: Prentice-Hall, 1969, 215; Friedman and Roosa, *The Balance of Payments*, 11.

Haberler were instrumental to the change of perspective in economics that resulted from these discussions, in which adjustment rose to the fore, and with it flexible exchange rates.[170]

After the 1961 meeting, some in the Society began to promote their views more forcefully and publicly. Rueff's campaign to return to the gold standard, launched that same year, was exemplary. In addition to a flurry of articles – some eighty-five, translated into multiple languages – and several books, his influence as a senior adviser to de Gaulle also figured in this effort.[171] His significant but in the end only partly successful attempt to shape French monetary policy did not match that of lobbyists for flexibilisation, however, who from 1963 onwards pitched their position to the public with great success, just as the popularity of the gold standard began to wane.

The topic was addressed again at the 1964 meeting in Semmering, Austria. Here, only Machlup and Haberler presented papers. The programme notes designated them as 'experts' who had proposed an objectively 'correct' resolution to the question of currency reform. Lutz, as of that year president of the MPS, advertised the debate under the somewhat bewildering title 'What Are the Critical Issues as between Experts as to Correct Domestic and International Monetary Arrangements? [sic]'.[172] Haberler labelled his lecture a small contribution to the meeting on 'conflicts of ideas within the Mont Pèlerin Society', and presented himself as an unbiased expert; his argument closely resembled Machlup's from the 1961 meeting.[173] Haberler's aims were to resolve and clarify in objective terms the conflict that had escalated over

170 Thomas D. Willett, 'Gottfried Haberler on Inflation, Unemployment, and International Monetary Economics: An Appreciation', *Quarterly Journal of Economics* 97, no. 1 (1982), 166; and Anthony Y. Koo, introduction to Anthony Y. Koo, ed., *The Liberal Economic Order*, vol. 1, *Essays on International Economics*, Brookfield: Edward Elgar, 1993, xv.
171 On Rueff's influence on the French government and de Gaulle, see Christopher Chivvis, 'Charles de Gaulle, Jacques Rueff and French International Monetary Policy under Bretton Woods', *Journal of Contemporary History* 41, no. 4 (2006), esp. 706, 712f.; Michael D. Bordo, Dominique Simard, and Eugene N. White, 'An Overplayed Hand: France and the Bretton Woods International Monetary System', Departmental Working Papers, Rutgers University, Department of Economics, 1994, esp. 11ff.
172 Liberaal Archief, *Mont Pèlerin Society (1947– . . .). Inventory*, 46. Unfortunately, Machlup's essay is not preserved in the archives.
173 Haberler, 'The International Monetary Mechanism', LA 1964, 1; see also Machlup, 'International Liquidity and International Money Creation', LA 1961.

the previous three years, and to cement the status of flexible exchange rates as the superior reform proposal on pragmatic grounds. He implored that the dispute 'not be raised to the level of economic "*Weltanschauung*"', for both the gold standard and flexible exchange rates were 'perfectly compatible . . . with the free market system'. Rather than wade into an ideological contretemps, Haberler focused on the objective question of which alternative was better suited to contemporary realities. He introduced new arguments against the gold standard, above all stressing the difficulties of its concrete implementation. He returned to the theme that the equalisation mechanism could no longer function as it once had, and claimed that free exchange rates were therefore the only appropriate path forward.[174] Haberler adopted many of the same formulations in a widely read 1965 pamphlet, published by the MPS-affiliated think tank IEA, in which he also assailed the assumption that fixed exchange rates would discipline national monetary policy.[175]

Haberler's attempt at the 1964 conference to establish flexibilisation as *the* neoliberal reform project, understood from an ostensibly neutral, expert perspective, did not succeed. At another conference the following year, an entire day was devoted to the contentious issue, once more inflaming the neuralgic point. In 1965, at the General Meeting of the MPS in Stresa, Italy, the currency controversy again provoked serious dissensus; however, it was the last meeting at which any member of the Society seriously promoted the gold standard.[176] The question posed in

---

174   Haberler, 'The International Monetary Mechanism', LA 1964, 7.
175   The book was published as a Hobart Paper under the title *Money in the International Economy: A Study in Balance of Payments Adjustment, International Liquidity and Exchange Rates*, London: Institute of Economic Affairs, 1965; see also Clyde H. Farnsworth, 'Flexible System for Money Urged', *NYT*, 22 February 1965, 29. Haberler's argument (e.g., against Kemp, 'The International Monetary Order', LA 1961, 3; Sennholz, 'From Dollar Gap to Dollar Glut', LA 1961, 7) that 'a falling exchange rate is just as strong a deterrent to more inflation as a falling gold reserve' (Haberler, *Money in the International Economy*, 34) was repeatedly put forward in subsequent debates and played a central role, especially in discussions with representatives of international bankers. See also Machlup, 'International Monetary Systems and the Free Market Economy', 161; Haberler, 'International Monetary Problems', LA 1968, 12; Johnson and Nash, *UK and Floating Exchanges*, 29f.; and Harry G. Johnson et al., 'Three Experts on the Reform Plans', in Grubel, *World Monetary Reform*, 396f.
176   Apart from William Hutt's defence of the gold standard at the 1968 conference in a brief commentary (William H. Hutt, 'The Fixed Exchange and Dirigisme: Comment on Mr. Enoch Powell's Paper', LA 1968), the topic is no longer discussed according to the

the title of the panel, 'International Monetary Problems: Return to the Gold Standard?', was answered with an unequivocal 'No' in reasoned essays by its chairman Machlup along with Haberler, Hahn, Friedman and Sohmen. A decisive vote in favour of floating exchange rates followed, with only Heilperin and Rueff dissenting.[177]

The progressive displacement of the gold standard as the dominant liberal monetary theory in the MPS, and its eventual replacement by flexibilisation, was evident not only in terms of the composition of the Society's membership but also substantively. The fronts between the two antagonistic positions had hardened with respect to previous conferences. Advocates of floating exchange rates rehearsed the argument of unrealistic assumptions in increasingly vehement language: Haberler considered the gold standard 'wholly unworkable and utopian'. 'No, the automatic gold standard is a thing of the past', he stressed, 'it cannot and should not be resurrected.'[178] Sohmen, presenting a paper for the first time at an MPS conference, made a conciliatory gesture, noting that the two positions, generally regarded as 'diametrically opposed (yet allegedly similarly insane) ends of the spectrum of opinion' on the international monetary order, were in principle rather similar – but in the end he voted in favour of floating exchange rates. It 'is safe to predict', he went so far as to venture, that an attempt to return to the strict discipline of the gold standard, given the 'present inflexibility

---

inventory of the Liberaal Archief. There were contributions on monetary systems at the following MPS conferences, which, however, mainly dealt with the effects of floating exchange rates, domestic monetary stability and, increasingly, the creation of a European monetary union: 1970, 1972, 1974, 1978, 1988, 1990, 1996.

177 According to the inventory of the Liberaal Archief, these (and Allais) are the people who presented papers, although the papers by Hahn and Rueff are missing from the archive.

178 Haberler, 'Some Remarks on Recent Discussions about the International Payments System', LA 1965, 1. Haberler's contribution was published in German in *Ordo* (Gottfried Haberler, 'Einige Bemerkungen zur gegenwärtigen Diskussion über das internationale Währungssystem', *Ordo* 17 [1966]). Haberler reworked his contribution to the 1965 MPS conference into the opening speech of an AEI monetary conference to be held in September 1965 (Haberler, 'The International Payments System', 4–8, 10–11). Milton Friedman repeated his argument from the 1961 MPS conference and declared that it was 'currently impossible' to establish a genuine gold standard in line with liberal principles. See Friedman, 'The Political Economy of International Monetary Arrangements', LA 1965, 1, 8. Friedman's contribution was published in a 1968 anthology, *Dollars and Deficits: Inflation, Monetary Policy and the Balance of Payments*.

of prices', would lead not only to a deepening stagnation of the world economy but to a 'gradual abandonment of liberal trade and payments policies everywhere'.[179]

Heilperin's arguments were also decidedly sharp in tone. He blamed flexible exchange rates for the world currency crisis of the 1930s and wondered why, despite this 'totally negative experience' that had settled his personal view of the matter, one could find 'in the 1960s, ardent and indeed highly persuasive advocates of that type of monetary system'.[180] Even when compared to the strident rhetoric used by advocates of floating exchange rates, however, Heilperin's apocalyptical plea for the gold standard stands out. Only a systemic collapse, he foretold, would make possible its reintroduction: 'And then, finally, when the storm has subsided, the sun will rise'; in this delirious prophecy, the gold standard would rise 'out of the chaos' created by the collapse of the present international monetary order, as the only functioning monetary system.[181]

Haberler advanced an early version of the motion to abandon the gold exchange guarantee at the 1965 MPS conference, in a foretaste of the 'benign neglect' strategy he was to employ in his capacity as the chairman of Nixon's Task Force on US Balance of Payments Policies in subsequent years.[182] One of the central dangers anticipated by critics of the Bretton Woods system was that other countries might follow France's example and cash in their dollar reserves for gold, thereby undermining the Federal Reserve's ability to make good on its obligations. Following Hahn's suggestion at the 1960 MPS conference, Haberler pushed for unilateral abandonment of the gold exchange guarantee, now to be combined with a threat to float the dollar. 'The answer should be to

---

179 Egon Sohmen, 'International Monetary Problems: Return to the Gold Standard?', LA 1965, 3. Sohmen advanced a similar argument to that of Haberler at the 1964 MPS conference. See Haberler, 'The International Monetary Mechanism', LA 1964, 1–2.

180 Heilperin, 'International Monetary Problems: Return to the Gold Standard?', LA 1965, 3; cf. also Michael Heilperin, 'Appendix: Memorandum on the Reason for Raising Substantially the World Price of Gold', 1965 LA.

181 Heilperin, 'International Monetary Problems: Return to the Gold Standard?', LA 1965, 5.

182 See Haberler and Willett, *U.S. Balance-of-Payments Policies and International Monetary Reform*; Gottfried Haberler and Thomas D. Willett, *A Strategy for US Balance of Payments Policy*, Washington, DC: American Enterprise Institute, 1971.

continue to sell gold at $35', he proposed, 'but at the same time to make clear that the US will not be ready in the future to buy gold at $35 per ounce or at all, and is determined to let the dollar float when all the gold is gone, whatever that may mean for the value of gold.'[183]

In addition to these contributions, reviving old arguments combined with newer strategies, the meeting in Stresa illustrated above all the personal costs of the intellectual divisions that roiled the Society. During the proceedings, Machlup broke with his teacher Mises, who remained a strict advocate of the gold standard even in the mid-1960s. Mises had not participated much in the MPS debates on monetary questions, but he had a definite view, on which he had published in the 1950s. When Cortney had asked him in 1965 why he was not writing anything on the subject, Mises replied that he had already said everything he had to say and added that the gravity of the current crisis only confirmed his long-standing convictions: 'If our civilisation will not in the next years or decades completely collapse, the gold standard will be restored.'[184]

Machlup, as chairman of the 1965 meeting, had compared calls for the price of gold to be hiked with trade union demands for wage increases.[185] Such an analogy between the traditional market-liberal monetary system and the interests of the MPS's main antagonists showcases just how far enmity between the two camps had progressed. Machlup's comment offended his mentor so profoundly as to cause Mises to sever their friendship.[186] The significance of this break is underscored by the closeness of their relationship up until that point: as favourite pupil and

---

183   This was to reduce drastically interest in hoarding gold, and harm those attacking the dollar and thereby 'blackmailing' the US government (Haberler, 'Some Remarks on Recent Discussions', LA 1965, 7). For further elaboration, see Haberler and Willett, *U.S. Balance-of-Payments Policies and International Monetary Reform*, 81f.

184   See, above all, Mises, *The Theory of Money and Credit*; Hartwell incorrectly dates the break between Mises and Machlup to 1961. See Hartwell, *A History of the Mont Pelerin Society*, 119.

185   See Machlup, 'Ludwig von Mises', 13, for a detailed description of this process in a homage to Mises.

186   According to his wife, Mises said afterwards: 'He was in my seminar in Vienna . . . he understands everything. He knows more than most of them and he knows exactly what he is doing.' (Margit von Mises, *My Years with Ludwig von Mises*, Cedar Falls: Center for Futures Education, 1978, 192f.) Machlup had already spoken out against the gold standard earlier that year before a committee of the American Congress, of which Mises, who was not very pleased, had been informed by a letter from Rueff (Hülsmann, *Mises*, 1032).

intimate of Mises and his wife, Margit, Machlup was no mere colleague.[187] Only after some years could Mises be persuaded by his wife to resume contact with the 'intellectual apostate'.[188] Machlup, for his part, never discussed the matter again in Mises's presence, which was evidently painful for both of them.[189] Nor was their estrangement the only casualty of the ongoing controversy, which also dissolved Mises's friendship with Haberler, another one of his students and best man at his wedding.[190]

The ascendancy of the floating exchange rate faction within the MPS, already coming into view in 1965, was undeniable by the 1968 General Meeting at the Scottish town of Aviemore. There, the subject of 'International Money' was entrusted to two champions of flexibilisation, Haberler and the long-time ultra-conservative British MP Enoch Powell.

Powell had already backed floating exchange rates in 1957 as chancellor of the exchequer. A decade later, he debated the issue with Friedman and Senator Paul Douglas in Washington and published a combative paper on 'Exchange Rates and Liquidity' at the MPS-affiliated London think tank IEA; he would go on to pursue his campaign in a lecture tour of the US.[191] Powell's arguments resembled those of others at the MPS, but in his contribution to the 1968 conference he pushed the matter, presenting fixed exchange rates as the 'key instrument of *dirigisme*' and 'supreme "commanding height" of a controlled economy'.[192] Fixed exchange rates and the corresponding justification

---

187   Machlup was the only participant in the famous Mises Private Seminar, whose dissertation Mises personally supervised. Friedrich von Hayek, in the introduction to *Ludwig von Mises (1978). Erinnerungen* (Stuttgart: G. Fischer, 1978, xi–xvi, xii), writes: 'Strictly speaking, only Fritz Machlup was originally a disciple of Mises.' And Mises praised Machlup's 1931 work 'Börsenkredit, Industriekredit und Kapitalbildung' as a 'masterpiece', which is unique. Cf. Hülsmann, *Mises*, 477–8; but also Israel Kirzner, *Ludwig von Mises: The Man and His Economics*, Wilmington: ISI Books, 2001, 7, and Ludwig von Mises, *Erinnerungen*, Stuttgart: G. Fischer, 1978, 66.

188   Margit von Mises, *My Years with Ludwig von Mises*, 146.

189   Machlup, 'Ludwig von Mises', 13.

190   Bruce Caldwell, *Hayek's Challenge: An Intellectual Biography of F. A. Hayek*, Chicago: University of Chicago Press, 2004, 147 fn. 18. Hayek's biographer does not, however, comment on the timing of this break. On the closeness between Mises and his students Haberler and Machlup, see Hayek, introduction to *Ludwig von Mises*, xii, and Mises's own contribution in Mises, *Erinnerungen*, 66.

191   Enoch Powell, *Exchange Rates and Liquidity*, London: Institute of Economic Affairs, 1967; Leeson, *Ideology and the International Economy*, 109.

192   Powell, 'The Fixed Exchange and Dirigisme', LA 1968, 5.

to 'defend the value of money' through capital controls, he asseverated, had been used by *dirigiste* forces like 'Circe's wand' to 'turn free men into slaves and rational men into obedient cattle'. The rhetoric clearly reveals what Powell and other MPS members believed to be at stake in their struggle. Powell decried a menace to the most fundamental freedoms: 'to buy or invest overseas, or to own, let alone purchase, gold'.[193] In his memo to Nixon barely six weeks after the MPS conference, Friedman praised Powell as 'the most intelligent and courageous of the Tory leaders', who would 'jump at the chance' to introduce floating exchange rates.[194]

Haberler took a more diplomatic approach in his contribution to the 1968 meeting but reached a similarly unambiguous conclusion. Starting from a decidedly fierce critique of the regulations and controls on international capital movements and foreign direct investment that had been increasingly relied upon in recent years, he dismissed any restoration of the gold standard, which had been rejected 'by the overwhelming majority of economists' as 'totally inadequate' and 'utterly impossible and undesirable'.[195] Haberler argued that MPS members' extensive activities to popularise free exchange rates in the 1960s could be justified strategically, given the ignorance and suspicion that beset prominent decision-makers:

> The main reason why practical men, central bankers, ministers of finance, directors of the IMF, etc. are so reluctant to experiment with floating exchange rates is probably a mixture of inertia, tradition, suspicion of the unknown and fear of transitional difficulties.[196]

Haberler therefore presented his recommendations for 'how to influence the transition' and underscored that limited flexibility, though less effective than unlimited, was practical as a transitional solution.

---

193 Ibid., 1.
194 Milton Friedman, 'A Proposal for Resolving U.S. Balance of Payments Problems', in Leo Melamed, ed., *The Merits of Flexible Exchange Rates: An Anthology*, Fairfax, VA: George Mason University Press, 1988, 438.
195 Haberler, 'International Monetary Problems', LA 1968, 5, 8.
196 Ibid., 12.

This strategy was advanced with particular enthusiasm at the Bürgenstock conferences from 1969 onwards.[197] Haberler, along with a younger colleague at Harvard, Thomas Willett, developed these points in a 1968 pamphlet published by the think tank AEI, now regarded as a blueprint for the doctrine of 'benign neglect'.[198] At the Aviemore meeting, the sole defence of the gold standard appeared in an exceedingly brief commentary by the economist William Harold Hutt, then teaching in South Africa and a close associate of the Austrian School. Hutt argued that no one would 'use the term *dirigisme*' for the nineteenth-century gold standard system and that 'whatever the advantages of floating over fixed exchange rates', he did not believe the latter was responsible for the 'expansion of government control over the individual'.[199] Only in passing did Hutt dispute the assimilation of the gold standard to *dirigisme*, in an intervention focused primarily on the mathematical aspects of Powell's critique of inflation. Hutt's marginal contribution only highlighted the newfound dominance of flexibilisation within the Society. Haberler had perhaps anticipated some other conclusion to the most intense debate in the history of the MPS; in any case, he ended his speech at the 1968 meeting with the following appeal to the membership: 'The upshot of this discussion is that all those who wish to preserve a free competitive enterprise economy without direct controls and regimentation should, under modern conditions, favour flexible exchange rates.'[200]

---

197   Ibid., 10f., 13. Haberler also explained to what extent the American controls on international payments could be used as a 'temporary cover' for a transition to floating exchange rates (ibid., 13). The 'temporary but comprehensive embargo on capital transfers' recommended by Haberler for the US was replaced by Nixon in August 1971 with a 10 per cent surcharge on imports when the gold window was closed.

198   The 1968 paper by Haberler and Willett was entitled 'U.S. Balance-of-Payments Policies and International Monetary Reform: A Critical Analysis'; in 1971 the AEI published a follow-up study, 'A Strategy for U.S. Balance of Payments Policy', in which the 'policy of benign neglect' was further elaborated. Haberler was himself (together with Friedman and others) a member of the AEI's advisory board.

199   Hutt, 'The Fixed Exchange and Dirigisme. Comment on Mr. Enoch Powell's Paper', LA 1968, 2.

200   Haberler, 'International Monetary Problems', LA 1968, 13. Friedman's attempt at characterising the internal MPS conflict and to solidify the emerging consensus by listing points of agreement between the opposing positions will be discussed in the following chapter, as it condenses and summarises important matters.

A transnational epistemic expert community of floating exchange rate advocates

During the 1950s and 1960s, debate on the currency question at MPS conferences was characterised not only by fundamental conflict and jostling for position between two opposing camps – advocates of floating exchange rates and proponents of the gold standard – but also by repeated attempts to establish unity and consensus. Milton Friedman devoted much effort to this end at the 1968 MPS conference: he presented a 'list of propositions agreed to by both proponents and opponents of free exchange rates', but in it he formulated not only the agreement but also the dissent.[201] Under the title 'Free vs Fixed Exchange Rates', Friedman listed eight points as key words, though fundamental agreement existed regarding only six of them, which succinctly reflected the basis of any consensus that might have emerged in the MPS:

1. Repeal all current prohibitions on 'private ownership, purchase, sale, and coinage of gold'.
2. Enact legislation to ensure that courts can enforce such contracts which provide for repayment in gold or foreign currencies.
3. Abolition of all capital controls and government regulation of private capital movements.
4. Abolition of all trade controls.
5. Demand 'non-inflationary national monetary policy'.
6. A monetary system with strong and volatile fluctuations of exchange rates is worse than one with less irregular exchange rate movements.[202]

Two further points revealed the essence of the controversy roiling the Society: alongside the classical liberal monetary system of the gold standard, the floating exchange rate idea had established itself internally

---

201 Milton Friedman, 'Free vs Fixed Exchange Rates: List of Propositions Agreed to by Both Proponents and Opponents of Free Exchange Rates', LA 1968. The page-long numbered list is attached to the essays by Powell and Hutt.

202 Ibid. The last point implicitly refers to the claim of the advocates of floating exchange rates that flexible exchange rates would fluctuate less than the fixed but adjustable exchange rates of the Bretton Woods monetary system (see also Friedman, 'The Case for Flexible Exchange Rates', 175–7).

as an alternative neoliberal concept for reforming Bretton Woods.[203] The question of which of the two utopias was preferable from a neoliberal perspective was never settled conclusively at the MPS – and two points remained contentious until the end. First, advocates of floating exchange rates doubted whether a gold standard consistent with liberal principles could be realised under the prevailing socio-political conditions of the 1960s; and second, the dwindling number of advocates of the gold standard claimed that floating exchange rates would not be an improvement to the Bretton Woods arrangement at all, which, they noted, was at least formally linked to gold.

With reference to the policy trilemma outlined in the introduction, one might argue that gold standard boosters placed greater emphasis on the prevention of autonomous monetary policy, while the advocates of floating exchange rates prioritised avoiding capital account controls.[204] The first camp issued their criticism principally on the grounds that advocates of floating exchange rates took the autonomy of national monetary policy anchored in Bretton Woods as given and intransigent, while their adversaries held that attempts to maintain the gold standard in the post-war socio-economic context indirectly supported capital controls. The heated controversies that emerged from this disagreement, which have already been discussed at length, belie Hartwell's euphemistic assertion in his history of the MPS that 'the mix of Austrian and Chicago [Schools]' had always existed 'in tolerant partnership and mutual respect'.[205]

That the floating exchange rate theory achieved a certain hegemony within the MPS, albeit never uncontested, and that various members were 'converted' from the gold standard to the flexible exchange rate position, can be attributed to a number of factors. Foremost among them were the crisis-like distortions of the Bretton Woods system

---

203 Friedman attempted to expand the zone of consensus further. First, he repeated, as all advocates of floating exchange rates had emphasised in the MPS debates, that a 'fully effective gold standard' would be better than the Bretton Woods monetary system. Second, he argued that 'fully free market exchange rates between national fiat currencies' would be better than a system of fixed rates implemented by widespread direct controls'. Friedman, 'Free vs Fixed Exchange Rates', LA 1968.

204 Interestingly, Machlup also referred indirectly to the trilemma in his contribution to the 1961 MPS conference, see Machlup, 'International Liquidity and International Money Creation', LA 1961, 7.

205 Hartwell, *A History of the Mont Pelerin Society*, 230.

already alluded to: fixed parities came under increasing pressure, liberalised capital flows threatened the balance of payments of core countries, and some states responded by strengthening capital controls or introducing new ones. All these developments could plausibly be integrated into the case for floating exchange rates. Several more specific reasons also help to explain why this position gained so much support.

First, the rhetorical and metaphorical persuasiveness of the theory itself was important.[206] Paul Volcker, himself a conservative economist and member of the Nixon administration, considered Friedman's theory an 'attractive doctrine' that offered politicians an 'appealing escape'. Friedman, in Volcker's opinion, painted 'an idyllic picture of a benign world in which the natural operation of foreign exchange markets . . . automatically correct international disequilibrium. There would be no need for controls.' What is more – this was certainly particularly central – Friedman 'and others left the impression that this would all actually happen rather smoothly and painlessly . . . that floating exchange rates could work their magic without wide fluctuations'.[207] The extensive use of the term 'free' exchange rates, as opposed to 'fixed', or as Friedman put it, the 'strait jacket of fixed exchange rates', no doubt further recommended them to the MPS neoliberals.[208] The harmonious picture of free and automatically equilibrating exchange markets sketched by Friedman was, as Charles Kindleberger has pointed out, supported by powerful metaphors. Kindleberger described the theory of floating exchange rates propagated by 'Milton Friedman, Gottfried Haberler, Fritz Machlup, Harry Johnson, and, especially vociferously, Egon Sohmen', as the best example of 'the powerful idea, widely accepted, and buttressed by metaphor, that proves wrong'.[209] The strongest analogy to appear in nearly all writings and conference papers of the free exchange faction compared currencies to ordinary commodities – meaning that under competitive conditions, a changing, flexible price should allow the market for any

---

206   See Deirdre N. McCloskey, *The Rhetoric of Economics*, Madison: University of Wisconsin Press, 1998, esp. 15–51. McCloskey refers to metaphors as easily the most important of the master tropes conferring legitimacy to economic theories.

207   Paul A. Volcker and Toyoo Gyohten, *Changing Fortunes: The World's Money and the Threat to American Leadership*, New York: Times Books, 1992, 46f.

208   Friedman, *Capitalism and Freedom*, 71. See McCloskey, *The Rhetoric of Economics*, 16, where such mechanisms are identified as powerful elements of economic argumentation.

209   Kindleberger, 'How Ideas Spread among Economists', 53f.

good to be tapped efficiently without adverse feedback.[210] For Kindleberger, however, the metaphor, like others found in Friedman, Sohmen and Machlup, obscured more than it explained.[211]

Second, the concept of floating exchange rates was novel and radical. It challenged fundamental assumptions and opened up promising questions and avenues for research, especially for younger economists, eager for a chance make their mark in a burgeoning field.[212] By contrast, the antiquated image of the gold standard could not be shaken off in terms of either its substance or the cohort of its adherents. It found hardly any supporters outside of a dwindling coterie of aging economists.

Third, the increasing dominance of floating exchange rate theory in the MPS had much to do with the different academic styles that defined the two positions, and the corresponding schools of economics representing them. Mark Skousen's general characterisation of the difference between Austrians and Chicagoans aptly applies to this study: advocates of the gold standard were uncompromising idealists who, with their unwavering, unrestrained (or even blind) belief in the balancing effect of market forces and the discipline of the gold standard, alarmed not only the majority of Keynesian economists but increasingly their neoliberal colleagues as well.[213] Those who took up the banner of flexible exchange rates, by contrast, proposed a pragmatic approach, justified internally as a second-best solution but nevertheless one to be promoted

---

210 See, for example, Friedman, *Essays in Positive Economics*, and Friedman and Roosa, *The Balance of Payments*, 5.

211 See also Kindleberger, review of *Monetary Problems of the International Economy*, 127–40, here 131. For a general discussion of the rhetorical and discursive strategies of neoliberal think tanks, see Diane Stone, *Capturing the Political Imagination: Think Tanks and the Policy Process*, London: Frank Cass, 1996, which focuses in particular on the metaphors of war, faith and the market.

212 The attractiveness of a new research paradigm for young economists was first addressed by Harry Johnson in relation to Keynesianism. See Harry G. Johnson, 'The Keynesian Revolution and the Monetarist Counterrevolution', *American Economic Review* 61, 1971.

213 In a study of the two neoliberal schools, Mark Skousen describes the typical representative of the Austrian School as an 'uncompromising idealist and recluse' with a 'steadfast, unwavering, complete and perfect faith (critics would call it blind faith) in the free market', and characterises the average Chicagoan as a 'pragmatic and extroverted activist' who has 'great faith in capitalism', but under certain circumstances accepts state intervention and demands 'often second-best solutions'. See Skousen, *Vienna and Chicago, Friends or Foes?*, 266–8.

in a decidedly activist and extroverted manner. They were less ideological, were more open to counter-arguments, did not shy away from academic debates and, above all, enjoyed greater success in providing answers to the real political problems of the time.[214] It was certainly not unimportant that Friedman, in particular, was a gifted rhetorician and powerful debater.[215] Their success likewise converged with a general ideological shift inside the MPS from an Austrian to a Chicago School orientation over the course of the 1960s.[216]

Fourth, flexibilisation as a concept profited from the inability of economic theory to respond adequately to the difficult social and political realities confronting it.[217] Floating exchange rate theory, unlike the gold standard, was not in direct and irreconcilable opposition to the prevailing economic theories and policies of the voting population and elites. While it was not possible to combine Keynesian economic and welfare state policies with the disciplining mechanisms of the gold standard and hardly any theoretical points of contact between Keynesian economics and the classical liberalism of the gold standard existed, the theory of floating exchange rates could at least be partially accommodated by this paradigm because it did not directly contradict it. The fading of the gold standard owed something to 'the climate of world opinion' in the 1960s, as the economist Francis Cassel put it, in which 'plans for reforming the international monetary system encounter

---

214 Hartwell describes the reasons for the general success of the Chicago School quite similarly. Hartwell, *A History of the Mont Pelerin Society*, 230. See also Friedrich A. von Hayek, *Hayek on Hayek: An Autobiographical Dialogue*, ed. Stephen Kresge and Leif Wenar, Chicago: University of Chicago Press, 1994, 145, and Ebenstein, *Friedrich Hayek*, 273.

215 This is emphasised again and again. See, for example, George Stigler, *Memoirs of an Unregulated Economist*, Chicago: University of Chicago Press, 1988, 154.

216 The increasing influence of the Chicago School in economics is demonstrated by the fact that two of its most important protagonists became presidents of the AEA, Stigler (1964) and Friedman (1967). On the declining importance of the Austrian School in the US, to which less than 1 per cent of economists belonged in the 1960s, see Richard Vedder and Lowell Gallaway, 'The Austrian Market Share in the Marketplace of Ideas, 1871–2025', *Quarterly Journal of Austrian Economics* 3, no. 1 (2000), 33.

217 For, as Peter Hall rightly noted, 'persuasiveness is an inherently relational concept, determined as much by the shape of contemporary economic and political circumstances as by the shape of the ideas themselves'. See Hall's conclusion in Peter Hall, ed., *The Political Power of Economic Ideas: Keynesianism across Borders*, Princeton, NJ: Princeton University Press, 1989, 369–70.

resistance roughly in proportion to the surrender of national sovereignty they entail'.[218] The gold standard was, after all, a viewpoint defined by the complete abandonment of monetary sovereignty.

Internal debates on the matter not only helped to convince MPS members themselves but, through the Society's conferences, served above all to fine-tune the theoretical justification for floating exchange rates, to focus discussions and to disseminate it across a broad transnational network. MPS conferences therefore contributed to the development of a *transnational elite network* and an *epistemic expert community* of campaigners for flexibility, and so dramatically enlarged a group which had in the early 1950s consisted of a few lonely stalwarts at a time when 'Friedman was nearly alone with his views'.[219] With regard to *shared normative assumptions and principles*, it is striking that despite their differences, proponents of both flexibilisation and the gold standard in the MPS advocated the same monetary norms and principles, in direct conflict with the basic presuppositions of Bretton Woods and the majority of Keynesian economists. In his systematic evaluation of the most consequential monetary theories of the 1950s and 1960s, the economic historian Anthony Endres notes the conspicuous ideological convergence within the MPS on normative monetary assumptions, although these were left tacit rather than openly mooted.[220] Schematically

---

218 Francis Cassell, *Gold or Credit? The Economics and Politics of International Money*, London: Pall Mall Press, 1965, 109.

219 Richard N. Cooper, 'Exchange Rate Choices', Conference Series, Federal Reserve Bank of Boston, June 1999, 103. The development has been summarised well by Peter Haas, 'Introduction: Epistemic Communities and International Policy Coordination', in *International Organization* 46, no. 1 (Winter 1992), 3. Haas defines 'epistemic communities' by enumerating four points, discussed below in relation to the relevant expert community: 'Although an epistemic community may consist of professionals from a variety of disciplines and backgrounds, they have (1) a shared set of normative and principled beliefs, which provide a value-based rationale for the social action of community members; (2) shared causal beliefs, which are derived from their analysis of practices leading or contributing to a central set of problems in their domain and which then serve as the basis for elucidating the multiple linkages between possible policy actions and desired outcomes; (3) shared notions of validity – that is, intersubjective, internally defined criteria for weighing and validating knowledge in the domain of their expertise; and (4) a common policy enterprise.'

220 Endres (*Great Architects of International Finance*, 214) describes almost all MPS members together as 'architects who condoned or advocated free market processes as a way of delivering an appropriate outcome in international finance', without any further elaboration.

the Society's members all agreed that the market stabilises the international economy, took for granted the existence of well-functioning international capital markets, preferred minimal international cooperation, supported an automatic and self-differentiating monetary system; and believed in the tendency of international financial institutions to malfunction spectacularly.[221]

During the 1950s and 1960s, as Endres indicates, there were two 'epistemic communities' in economics: the majority of Keynesians, who dominated the field, and the neoliberals, almost all of whom were MPS members. The MPS in turn comprised two competing epistemic communities: those backing the gold standard and those backing flexible exchange rates. The latter shared a common analysis of contemporary problems and began from certain assumptions – that, for example, wages and prices are not downwardly flexible and that autonomous monetary policy is a central goal of national governments. They argued that fixed exchange rates and attempts to maintain them could not fly in the face of socio-political facts and were therefore *causally* related to the introduction of capital controls. Such arguments (of unrealistic assumptions and imminent controls) employed powerful narratives to explain the linkages among economic problems, political actions and desired goals.[222] Only flexible exchange rates, according to the political strategy resulting from this interpretation of the causal relationship, could bring about a liberalisation of the international financial markets in view of unchangeable social realities. The same might be accomplished with regard to other shared assumptions.[223]

---

221   By contrast, the more Keynesian-oriented economists Alvin Hansen, Williams, Triffin, Roy Harrod and Mundell believed that market processes did not have a stabilising effect; that capital markets fail; that global cooperation through strong management and political coordination is desirable; and that international financial institutions are essential (with the exception of Williams). See Endres, *Great Architects of International Finance*, 209, Table 10.1.

222   See Haas, 'Epistemic Communities and International Policy Coordination', 3. This argumentation also fulfils the exact criteria of 'story lines' as articulated in McCloskey, *The Rhetoric of Economics*, 17f.

223   Other key shared assumptions were: fluctuating exchange rates are caused solely by irresponsible monetary policy, while flexible exchange rates are inherently stable and not susceptible to destabilising speculation; international reserves are not necessary with flexible exchange rates, as balance of payments imbalances are automatically offset and do not need to be financed; fixed exchange rates internationalise the monetary policy of individual countries, while flexible exchange rates insulate countries from external changes.

Finally, in addition to their agreement as to the standards for judging the validity of arguments – here agreement with liberal principles was held in particularly high esteem – the pro-flexibilisation epistemic expert community within the MPS was united by practical pursuits arising from these principles and ideas, what Peter Haas has called 'a common policy enterprise'.[224] It is to these pursuits, specifically attempts to hegemonise floating exchange rates, that the next chapter turns.

---

224   Haas defines this as 'a set of common practices associated with a set of problems to which their professional competence is directed, presumably conviction that human welfare will be enhanced as a consequence'. Haas, 'Epistemic Communities and International Policy Coordination', 3.

3

Freedom Fighters in Action

The Hegemonisation of Flexible Exchange Rate Theory in the 1960s

Hegemonic possibilities: Target groups, conferences, persons, institutions

Over the course of the 1960s, champions of flexible exchange rates within the MPS established the theoretical basis of their position in a community of academic experts, thereby transforming what had been a marginal view into the dominant consensus. They also worked to familiarise and convert key policymakers to their position, among them central and private bankers along with prominent employers. MPS members inside the Nixon administration came to play a significant role in ensuring that flexible exchange rates prevailed.[1] Hartwell has rightly pointed out that since the MPS remained 'almost invisible' to the public until the 1980s, it exerted influence 'primarily through its members' – that is, through influential think tanks and the placement of some members in governmental circles, 'directly influencing political

---

1   The chapter aims at making these arguments plausible, rather than directly proving them. This results from general methodological difficulties of analyses of the influence of epistemic expert communities or think tanks, which cannot directly be 'measured'. See Donald E. Abelson, *A Capital Idea: Think Tanks and US Foreign Policy*, Montreal: McGill-Queen's University Press, 2006, xi; Josef Braml, *Think Tanks versus 'Denkfabriken'? US and German Policy Research Institutes' Coping with and Influencing Their Environments*, Baden-Baden: Nomos, 2004, 548.

platforms and thus public policy'.[2] The present chapter traces these activities in the transnational context of the MPS, though the Society as such was entirely 'invisible' to the public at the time and is hardly mentioned in contemporary published sources.[3] All three of Hartwell's strategies, the impact of the MPS 'through its members', via think tanks and (especially academic) institutions, and by way of direct influence on policy, are discussed in this chapter.

To grasp properly the dissemination of economic ideas, it must be conceptualised in relation to diverse target groups. Among the most significant of those to be treated here are the discipline of economics, the lay public, politicians and representatives of the banking and business sectors.[4] MPS members attempted to win acceptance for flexible exchange rates across all four fields or groups, but convincing the public was not a priority, given the subject's complexity (a notable exception being Friedman's extensive popular-scientific and journalistic activities).[5]

---

2   Ronald Max Hartwell, *A History of the Mont Pelerin Society*, Indianapolis: Liberty Fund, 1995, 202.

3   A keyword search with ProQuest for 'Mont Pèlerin Society' in major American newspapers (*Los Angeles Times, NYT, WSJ, WP, Boston Globe*) between 1947 and 1973, for example, yields only six relevant hits (four reports of conferences and two references to von Mises's membership in the MPS). The only published mentions of the MPS I have found are in Friedman's published contributions to the MPS conferences and in a contribution by Ferrero to the AEI conference in 1966 and in a book by Haberler's students Lawrence Officer and Thomas Willett, in which they quote Haberler's contribution to the 1968 MPS conference. See American Enterprise Institute, ed., *International Payments Problems: A Symposium Sponsored by the American Enterprise Institute for Public Policy Research*, Washington, DC: American Enterprise Institute, 1966, 96, and Lawrence Officer and Thomas Willett, eds, *The International Monetary System: Problems and Proposals*, Englewood Cliffs, NJ: Prentice-Hall, 1969, 219.

4   In their 1989 book *The Spread of Economic Ideas*, Colander and Coats addressed only the target groups of economists (part I), the lay public (part II) and politicians (part III). In the preface, however, 'groups of businesspeople and bankers' are also mentioned as an audience (A. W. Coats and David C. Colander, *The Spread of Economic Ideas*, Cambridge: Cambridge University Press,1989, 12).

5   The issue was generally a matter for academic experts and policymakers and was little discussed in public. John S. Odell (*U.S. International Monetary Policy: Markets, Power, and Ideas as Sources of Change*, Princeton, NJ: Princeton University Press, 1982, 126) points out that in the 1960s and early 1970s virtually no organised groups were interested in currency issues or organised corresponding campaigns. An exception that contradicts this observation is the treatment of the issue initiated by Giersch and Sohmen in the 1969 West German election campaign (Herbert Giersch, introduction to

The Society's public relations initiatives encompassed lectures; articles and appeals in newspapers, magazines and academic journals; and the organisation of public discussions and media appearances. Networks of economists and a variety of venues featured prominently in this endeavour, and indeed from 1963 onwards there emerged a 'new industry', as Kindleberger termed it, 'of conferences on the international monetary system by academic economists with an occasional admixture of central and commercial bankers'.[6] These fora offer a clear and manageable source base for analysing how this constellation of experts functioned.

In the 1950s and 1960s, three series of conferences hosted the most consequential discussions of the international monetary order, according to the overwhelming opinion of historians, and each was addressed to one of the three target groups mentioned above: the Bellagio conferences of the Group of 32 Economists in 1963 and 1964, attended chiefly by economists; the Bellagio conferences from 1964 onwards, which served primarily to promote discussion between economists and central bankers and politicians; and the 1969 Bürgenstock Conferences, aimed specifically at international private bankers and business representatives.[7] Analysis of these conferences reveals the extent to which

---

Herbert Giersch, ed., *Money, Trade, and Competition: Essays in Memory of Egon Sohmen*, Berlin: Springer, 1992, vi). Friedman repeatedly filled his columns in the American *Newsweek* at the end of the 1960s with arguments in favour of closing the gold window and floating exchange rates (some of the articles are reprinted in Milton Friedman, *Dollars and Deficits: Inflation, Monetary Policy and the Balance of Payments*, Englewood Cliffs, NJ: Prentice-Hall, 1968, 236–46). In May 1969, for example, Friedman discussed flexible exchange rates with Samuelson in a television debate. Charles Kindleberger, 'The Case for Fixed Exchange Rates, 1969', in Federal Reserve Bank of Boston, *The International Adjustment Mechanism: Proceedings of the Monetary Conference*, Boston, MA: Federal Reserve Bank of Boston, 1970, 95.

6   Charles Kindleberger, review of *Monetary Problems of the International Economy* (Mundell and Swoboda), *Journal of International Economics* 1, no. 1 (1971), 127; cf. Charles Kindleberger, 'How Ideas Spread among Economists: Examples from International Economics', in Colander and Coats, *The Spread of Economic Ideas*, 46–9.

7   Anthony M. Endres, *Great Architects of International Finance: The Bretton Woods Era*, London: Routledge, 2005, 7, 10; J. Keith Horsefield and Margaret G. de Vries, *The International Monetary Fund 1945–1965: Twenty Years of International Monetary Cooperation*, vol. 2, *Analysis*, Washington, DC: International Monetary Fund, 1969, 50; Harold James, *International Monetary Cooperation since Bretton Woods*, Washington, DC: International Monetary Fund, 1996, 213; Kindleberger, 'How Ideas Spread among Economists', 47; Robert Leeson, *Ideology and the International Economy: The Decline*

advocates of flexible exchange rates, who were by then transnationally networked through the MPS, contributed to introducing and popularising the theory.

Not only were MPS members instrumental in organising the most significant monetary policy conferences of the 1960s, they dominated them in terms of personnel and orientation: 9 out of 32 participants in the Bellagio conference (or 28 per cent), 5 out of 14 of the leading economists at the follow-up conferences with politicians (36 per cent), and 9 out of 17 economists at the Bürgenstock Conferences (53 per cent) were MPS members.[8] They were not generally the majority, but they were nevertheless able to shape the content of the conferences thanks to their positions as sponsors and keynote speakers, and because they formed a coherent group and coordinated their activities through the epistemic community of the MPS (operating with shared normative principles and causal assumptions). By contrast, Keynesian-orientated conference participants were not organised as a bloc via any well-defined network.[9] This is particularly evident in the fact that the only economists to participate in all three conference series were MPS members: Machlup, Haberler, Fellner, Johnson and Lutz.[10]

Why did MPS members become so involved in the conception and implementation of these conferences? It is reasonable to assume that the subject was raised at MPS meetings.[11] Some insight can be gleaned

---

and Fall of Bretton Woods, New York: Palgrave Macmillan, 2003, 48; Odell, U.S. International Monetary Policy, 92, 182; Robert Solomon, International Monetary System, 1945–76: An Outsider's View, New York: Joanna Cotler Books, 1977, 70f, 169.

8 Two MPS members of the Bellagio conference in 1963 were representatives of the classical gold standard position and therefore do not belong to the group of advocates of flexible exchange rates in the MPS discussed here.

9 The only other organised group were the economists from the Brookings Institution – only one economist from this organisation took part in the first two Bellagio conferences and only two in the Bürgenstock conferences.

10 Those taking part in the most significant monetary policy conferences of the 1960s are listed in table 3 (see p. 163). The US is the focus of what follows (along with a particularly notable West German case), given the centrality of the US for every fundamental change in the international monetary order, which required that state's support or even initiation (a dynamic persisting into the early 1970s). Because of this fact, MPS efforts at popularisation of their views were increasingly concentrated on the US itself.

11 For example, the regular MPS Newsletter, which was founded in 1973, reports not only on the latest publications by MPS members but also on the participation of MPS members in conferences.

from the monetary policy symposium of the neoliberal think tank AEI in 1965, at which MPS members emphasised the need for political as well as academic lobbying: if politicians were not prepared to 'discuss, let alone adopt', flexible exchange rates, Machlup held, their backers 'should not resign themselves to a ten-year period of inaction, but, should instead get busy teaching the politicians', for they were '[lagging] in their intellectual development' – or, according to a critical remark by the banker Charles Walkers on Machlup's speech at the AEI conference, to be 'uneducated dunderheads'.[12]

Friedman argued that there were two means by which the introduction of floating exchange rates may be achieved: in a crisis situation or directly following a change of government. They could be effective in a serious currency crisis, in other words, but only when – and here the importance of the MPS becomes clear – decision-makers were already familiar with the theory and the relevant arguments had gained some academic recognition. The deliberate implementation of neoliberal policy measures in crisis situations has been studied in detail by Naomi Klein, both theoretically and historically, with particular emphasis on Friedman's role as the ideological godfather of this 'disaster capitalism'.[13] Yet, according to Friedman, floating exchange rates could also be established 'the first month after a new government of the formerly opposition party takes office'; within three years he had written a memorandum to presidential candidate Nixon.[14]

In his lecture 'The Role of Networks of Economists in International Monetary Reform' (now unfortunately lost), Harry Johnson stressed that many of the conferences – the Bellagio series among them – concerned themselves less with the development and discussion of *new* theories and more with the distribution of concepts and strategies that had already been produced. Johnson also stated that he preferred meetings that 'not only produced new ideas, but enforced them'.[15] MPS

12   Fritz Machlup, 'International Monetary Systems and the Free Market Economy', in American Enterprise Institute, *International Payments Problems*, 159f., 188.
13   See Naomi Klein, *The Shock Doctrine: The Rise of Disaster Capitalism*, New York: Metropolitan, 2007, esp. 49–97.
14   See Friedman's contribution to American Enterprise Institute, *International Payments Problems*, 90.
15   This lost paper, which Johnson presented at a conference at the University of Pennsylvania in November 1976 was summarised by its commentator. See Kindleberger, 'How Ideas Spread among Economists', 47. For further discussion, see also Johnson's

members did not trust that the theory of floating exchange rates would automatically prevail in a free competition of ideas on the basis of its inherent superiority; great effort and discipline went into planning its triumph. Such efforts far exceeded typical academic activity: close cooperation with think tanks and well-financed foundations along with lobbying associations, the extremely time-consuming preparation of dozens of conferences, and mobilisation of government members or advisers – especially in the Nixon administration – all attest to MPS members' commitment to bringing about the changes on which so much depended.

The individual figures of greatest significance in the eventual hegemony of floating exchange rates were the MPS economists who actively took part in the three primary conference series on monetary policy. Together with Machlup, the main organiser of the meetings and a tireless populariser skilled at mediating between contested positions, Haberler, Fellner, Johnson and Lutz must be counted as key actors, and Friedman was of course also central.[16] In addition to participating in the conferences themselves, the latter shaped debate through the combined impact of publications and public appearances, and in his capacity as adviser to Nixon. Friedman took on the role of the radical, intransigent 'extremist'.[17] Notably, four of the six most

---

taxonomy of conference types. Some, like consumer goods, provide answers to politically relevant questions and those, analogous to plant and equipment, concentrate on the production of fundamental knowledge. Harry G. Johnson, 'The "Problems" Approach to International Monetary Reform', in Robert Mundell and Alexander Swoboda, eds, *Monetary Problems of the International Economy*, Chicago: University of Chicago Press, 1969, 393.

16 Even if the other conferences discussed in this paper are included (some of which had a more neoliberal orientation due to the selection and were not as generally significant as the Bellagio and Bürgenstock conferences), the same figures dominate: of a total of fifteen conferences or conference series listed in table 3 (p. 163), Haberler participated in eleven, Machlup in ten, Johnson in eight, and Lutz and Fellner in seven conferences each. Of all other economists, only Roy Harrod took part in eight and Robert Triffin, Walter Salant and Robert Mundell in seven of the fifteen conferences, all other economists in fewer. In addition to the organisational and journalistic efforts described below, Machlup gave dozens of lectures on currency issues in a wide variety of countries (as found in the Hoover Institution Archives, 'Register of the Fritz Machlup Papers', 2008).

17 Friedman had turned down a CEA post under Eisenhower with the following justification: 'I prefer being independent and more useful. I think society needs a few kooks, a few extremists. If you're in the Administration, it's right and natural to

active MPS key actors were erstwhile advocates of the gold standard who had converted to the floating exchange rate viewpoint during the 1950s. By the mid-1960s, these men – then aged sixty to sixty-five – were at the peak of their scholarly reputations. Through their academic and political work, they had established themselves as authorities on monetary questions, both inside academia and for a broader public. Machlup, Haberler, Friedman and Fellner served as presidents of the American Economic Association (AEA) in this period, and save Fellner and Johnson they were energetic participants in the relevant MPS conferences.[18]

Aside from this '"vital few" in the great battle of ideas', as MPS historian Hartwell put it, a host of MPS members propagated flexibilisation via other outlets or as political advisers: Rómulo Ferrero, Eugênio Gudin, Arnold Harberger, Bertrand de Jouvenel, Wolfgang Kasper, Paul McCracken, Alan Meltzer, Frank W. Paish, Herbert Stein, George Stigler, Thomas F. Johnson. Because they often pursued a similar line of argumentation to that of their MPS colleagues, they may be counted – in Hartwell's words – among 'the many followers' who 'accept the new ideas and circulate them in the academies, the media and the public'. Hartwell stressed that while only a few may 'initiate intellectual change', the 'impetus to significant changes in the tide of human ideas' is the work of this avant-garde.[19]

In the process of popularising and disseminating economic ideas, institutions also played a role. The following were paramount in the establishment of the idea of flexibilisation over the course of the 1960s:

---

compromise.' (Marylin Bender, 'Chicago School Goes to the Head of the Class', *NYT*, 23 May 1971, F3). Other important MPS members at the public conferences besides Egon Sohmen were John Exter, Michael Heilperin and Philip Cortney, who were also very active representatives of the classical gold standard in the MPS. Friedman took part in five of the fifteen conferences discussed, while Sohmen, Cortney, Exter and Heilperin each took part in four.

18   With the exception of Albert Hahn, the people who had participated particularly frequently in the MPS conferences were also the most active in the broader scientific environment. At the age of seventy-five, Hahn still took part in the first Bellagio conference in 1963, but then withdrew completely. See Jan-Otmar Hesse, 'Some Relationships between a Scholar's and an Entrepreneur's Life: The Biography of L. Albert Hahn', *History of Political Economy* 39 (2007), 218.

19   Ronald Max Hartwell, *A History of the Mont Pelerin Society*, Indianapolis: Liberty Fund, 1995, 228.

University institutes. Of central importance was the International Finance Section at Princeton University, led by Machlup, host of one of the pivotal series of conferences on monetary policy. Machlup was most active from 1960 to 1971 as holder of a chair previously occupied by Frank Graham, who had developed a theory of flexibilisation at the start of the 1930s. The Princeton programme was established by Edwin Kemmerer, father of MPS member Donald Kemmerer, who headed it until 1945.[20] Of equal importance was the University of Chicago's Economics Department, home to Friedman, Thomas F. Johnson, George Stigler, Allan Meltzer and Herbert Stein.[21]

Think tanks and journals. MPS members founded a number of think tanks for the purpose of popularising their ideas.[22] These fulfiled three central functions, in Diane Stone's schema: as 'research brokers', publishing important writings and pamphlets; as 'discourse managers', arranging conferences and symposia; and as 'policy entrepreneurs', through their close ties to business interests and the Nixon administration.[23] Most important in these respects were the AEI and the British Institute of Economic Affairs (IEA). The AEI published a range of influential books and pamphlets and organised conferences and other

---

20 Those Walker professors before Machlup were MPS member Frank Graham (1945–1950) and the founder of the Chicago School Jacob Viner (1950–1960). See Anthony M. Endres, 'Frank Graham's Case for Flexible Exchange Rates: A Doctrinal Perspective', *History of Political Economy* 40, no. 1 (2008). On the prolific publication activity of this chair, see Robert Triffin, 'The Impact of the Bellagio Group on International Reform', in Jacob S. Dreyer, ed., *Breadth and Depth in Economics: Fritz Machlup – The Man and His Ideas*, Lexington: Lexington Books, 1978, 146.

21 On the Chicago School, see Robert Van Horn and Philip Mirowski, 'The Rise of the Chicago School of Economics and the Birth of Neoliberalism', in Philip Mirowski and Dieter Plehwe, eds, *The Road from Mont Pèlerin: The Making of the Neoliberal Thought Collective*, Cambridge: Harvard University Press, 2009; Melvin W. Reder, 'Chicago Economics: Permanence and Change', *Journal of Economic Literature* 20, no. 1 (1982).

22 Bernhard Walpen, *Die offenen Feinde und ihre Gesellschaft. Eine hegemonietheoretische Studie zur Mont Pèlerin Society*, Hamburg: VSA Verlag, 2004; see also Mirowski and Plehwe, *The Road from Mont Pèlerin*, 2009.

23 See Diane Stone, *Capturing the Political Imagination: Think Tanks and the Policy Process*, London: Frank Cass, 1996, 122; pp. 26–37 provide a good overview of research on think tanks, which distinguishes analytically between different research directions. See also Donald E. Abelson, *Capitol Idea: Think Tanks and US Foreign Policy*, Montreal: McGill-Queen's University Press, 2006.

events.[24] Founded on Hayek's instructions in 1955 by MPS member Antony Fisher as the 'hegemonic apparatus' of the MPS, the IEA can be regarded as the first think tank of a new 'partisan' type.[25] Fisher had already argued for free exchange rates in a 1949 publication, and the IEA was quite active in the field of currency and capital market reforms.[26] It repeatedly backed the adoption of floating exchange rates, beginning with its inaugural publication, and would go on to bring out a series of works by MPS members on the subject: Haberler's 'Money in the International Economy'; 'A Study in Balance of Payments Adjustment'; 'International Liquidity and Exchange Rates'; a pamphlet by politician Enoch Powell; and a debate between Harry Johnson and John Nash, in which Johnson urged the UK to adopt floating exchange rates.[27]

Also key was the Walter Eucken Institute (WEI) in Freiburg, which maintained close relations with the MPS and in the 1960s provided a forum for numerous MPS members to lecture on currency issues, on which it itself published widely. The German journal *Ordo* brought out a plethora of articles on monetary policy, with growing attention to the floating exchange rate concept. *Ordo* was first edited by Walter Eucken and Franz Böhm, and from 1951 to 1972 by Lutz, Meyer and Böhm with the participation of Brandt, Hayek, Röpke and Rüstow (all members of the MPS), among others, and published treatments of the currency problem by Society members in almost every issue, often by editors Lutz and Meyer.

24   See Gottfried Haberler, *Currency Convertibility*, Washington, DC: American Enterprise Institute, 1954; Gottfried Haberler and Thomas D. Willett, *U.S. Balance-of-Payments Policies and International Monetary Reform: A Critical Analysis*, Washington, DC: American Enterprise Institute, 1968; Gottfried Haberler and Thomas D. Willett, *Presidential Measures on Balance of Payments Control*, Washington, DC: American Enterprise Institute, 1968; Gottfried Haberler and Thomas D. Willett, *A Strategy for U.S. Balance of Payments Policy*, Washington, DC: American Enterprise Institute, 1971; Milton Friedman and Robert Roosa, *The Balance of Payments: Free versus Fixed Exchange Rates*, Washington, DC: American Enterprise Institute, 1967.
25   On the founding of the IEA, see Walpen, *Die offenen Feinde und ihre Gesellschaft*, 124–31.
26   Antony Fisher, *The Case for Freedom*, London: Runnymede, 1949.
27   George Winder's *The Free Convertibility of Sterling* (London: Institute of Economic Affairs, 1955) calls for, among other things, the abolition of capital controls and flexible exchange rates for the UK. See also John Blundell, *Waging the War of Ideas*, London: Institute of Economic Affairs, 2016, available at iea.org.uk.

Expert advisory bodies on policy. MPS members likewise seized on bodies such as the West German Sachsverständigenrat (German Council of Economic Experts, or SVR) and the American Council of Economic Advisers (CEA) to promote flexible exchange rates and liberalised capital markets.

Academic economists

The collective effort to popularise MPS thinking on currency questions dates to 1963. It was aimed first at an academic readership, and then broadened to reach a more general public.[28] In the wake of Robert Triffin's provocative prediction that Bretton Woods would soon collapse due to the precipitous loss of confidence in the US dollar as the reserve currency, an international debate over potential reforms flared up at the beginning of the decade, yielding an unmanageable multiplicity of proposals along with much strife in the field of economics.[29] At the IMF's annual meeting in October 1963, heads of state of the major industrialised countries responded by commissioning a thorough study of the international monetary system, to be carried out by economists close to the governments involved, since independent economists were considered 'so much in disagreement with one another that their advice was practically useless to those in charge of decision-making'.[30] This study, as a second stipulation, was to reflect the consensus that the 'underlying structure of the present monetary system – *based on fixed exchange rates and the established*

---

28   Before the Bellagio conferences of April 1963 (discussed below), Albert Hunold, a founding member of near equal stature to Hayek in the early-phase MPS, had organised a panel discussion at the University of Zurich, whose participants, with the notable exception of Robert Triffin, were all Society members. See Albert Hunold, ed., *Inflation und Weltwährungsordnung* (Sozialwissenschaftliche Studien für das Schweizerische Institut für Auslandsforschung), Zürich: Eugen Rentsch Verlag, 1963.
29   On the Triffin dilemma, see above all Robert Triffin, *Gold and the Dollar Crisis: The Future of Convertibility*, New Haven, CT: Yale University Press, 1960; see also Endres, *Great Architects of International Finance*, 102–26, and on the influence of this theorem Odell, *U.S. International Monetary Policy*, 89–164.
30   Quoted in Fritz Machlup and Burton Malkiel, eds, *International Monetary Arrangements: The Problem of Choice. Report on the Deliberations of an International Study Group of Thirty-Two Economists*, Princeton, NJ: Princeton University Press, 1964, 6.

price of gold – has proven its value as the foundation for present and future arrangements'.³¹

Not only did this explicitly challenge the competence of academics and their expertise as policy advisers, but when the IMF confirmed the underlying soundness of the Bretton Woods consensus, it categorically ruled out more fundamental reforms, not least those discussed within the MPS. Three economists present at the IMF meeting who felt excluded by its verdict immediately reacted by forming a group of 'non-government economists'.³² Machlup, Fellner and Triffin organised the Group of 32 Economists, also called the Bellagio Group or the Machlup Group, which met four times in 1963 and 1964 in Princeton and Bellagio, Italy, and published a widely acclaimed report timed to rival the government economists' study.³³ Financed by the Ford and the Rockefeller Foundations, the group enjoyed the use of luxury premises in Bellagio.³⁴

The Bellagio Group is generally regarded as the most important international association of economists dealing with the monetary questions arising in the 1960s.³⁵ Yet the pronounced MPS role in it has, to date, been overlooked in histories of the period. The group's main organiser and vital source of ideas was Machlup, its 'undisputed intellectual leader and mentor'.³⁶ In addition to Machlup and his co-convener Fellner, nine of the thirty-two economists were Society members: Haberler, Hahn, Sohmen, Johnson and Lutz – all advocates of flexible exchange rates – as well as gold standard die-hards Rueff and Heilperin.³⁷

---

31   Quoted in ibid., 5, emphasis in original.
32   This is one of the strategies of epistemic expert networks described by Haas. See Peter Haas, 'Introduction: Epistemic Communities and International Policy Coordination', in *International Organization* 46, no. 1 (Winter 1992), 4.
33   On the formation of the Bellagio Group, see the comments in the report of the International Study Group, Machlup and Malkiel, *International Monetary Arrangements*, and Triffin, 'The Impact of the Bellagio Group on International Reform', 147f.
34   Triffin, 'The Impact of the Bellagio Group on International Reform', 147.
35   Horsefield and de Vries, *The International Monetary Fund 1945–1965*, vol. 2, 50; Leeson, *Ideology and the International Economy*, 48; Solomon, *International Monetary System, 1945–76*, 70f.
36   This is emphasised by various people, most importantly by co-organiser Triffin, 'The Impact of the Bellagio Group on International Reform', 156; cf. Robert Triffin, *The World Money Maze: National Currencies in International Payments*, New Haven, CT: Yale University Press, 1966, 317; Solomon, *International Monetary System, 1945–76*, 70.
37   A journalist from the *Economist* also took part in the Group of 32. Two other MPS members, Milton Friedman and Eric Lundberg, were invited but were unable to

From the outset, the Bellagio Group had two main functions. First, it concerned itself with rehabilitating the interpretative autonomy of independent specialists on questions of international monetary order. With the 'formation of a non-governmental group of experts' from different countries, obvious differences of opinion were to be worked through in a way that was potentially useful for politicians and decision-makers.[38] Through exacting analysis of the different 'factual and normative assumptions' underlying various reforms, these non-governmental 'experts' (the term was emphasised repeatedly) undertook to give politicians a basis for making 'rational decisions'.[39] The group thus endeavoured to restore the 'collective intellectual authority' of economists while demonstrating that a fractious professions could nonetheless agree on certain principles (according to Haberler's characterisation of Machlup's motives).[40]

Second, the group delivered a substantive challenge to the IMF's view that the basic structure of Bretton Woods, 'based on fixed exchange rates and the established price of gold', had been vindicated.[41] As distinct from IMF- and government-sponsored analyses, which exempted both the gold standard and flexible exchange rates from serious scrutiny, the Bellagio Group placed these at the centre of the reform debate. Its second policy statement noted that 'the price of gold or flexible exchange rates, which the Group of Ten has excluded from its agenda, deserve and will receive our full attention in our next meeting'.[42]

Machlup's circle exercised a lasting influence on the monetary policy

---

attend due to time constraints. Friedman originally accepted membership of the group and later regretted very much that he was unable to attend (Milton Friedman, Edward M. Bernstein and Milton Gilbert, 'Discussion', *American Economic Review* 55, nos 1/2 [1965], 178). Economists close to the MPS included Machlup's student at Princeton Burton Malkiel. For further discussion, see the corresponding chapter in Dreyer's *Breadth and Depth in Economics*.

38   Machlup and Malkiel, *International Monetary Arrangements*, 6.
39   Ibid., 7–8. The invitation text stated: 'The purpose of the conference is an experiment: to find out whether we can identify the differences in factual and normative assumptions that can explain the differences in prescriptions for solving the problems of the international monetary system ... [This would] be a major step toward a better understanding of the present conflict of ideas.'
40   Coats and Colander, *The Spread of Economic Ideas*, 4; Gottfried Haberler, 'Fritz Machlup: In Memoriam', *Cato Journal* 3, no. 1 (1983), 1.
41   Machlup and Malkiel, *International Monetary Arrangements*, 5, 7.
42   Triffin, *The World Money Maze*, 323.

discussions of the 1960s, anticipating many developments in political economy. It is exemplary of the force transnational expert communities exert in agenda-setting.[43] Peter Haas has formulated the process succinctly: such groups 'framed the issues for collective debate, thereby influencing subsequent negotiations and bringing about their preferred outcomes to the exclusion of others'.[44] To begin with, the Bellagio Group accomplished this by establishing and defining a common terminology.[45] The exchanges it fostered were then mobilised to shift economics away from liquidity and towards adjustment. It promoted Machlup's taxonomic differentiation between the liquidity, adjustment and confidence problems (first introduced at the 1961 MPS meeting), which became nearly universally accepted in subsequent years.[46] The 'Machlup-Fellner-Triffin schema', as Kindleberger termed it, enabled advocates of flexible exchange rates to push their solutions onto the reform agenda with increasing frequency.[47]

Third, the Bellagio Group divided the multitude of reform proposals into four categories, a heuristic division that contributed significantly to moving flexible exchange rates from the fringes of the debates to the centre and establishing them as a serious alternative among other proposals for reform:

1. The centralisation of international reserves
2. A multiple currency standard

---

43   Triffin, 'The Impact of the Bellagio Group on International Reform', 149f.
44   Haas, 'Epistemic Communities and International Policy Coordination', 5.
45   Definitions were one of Machlup's specialities. See Fritz Machlup, *Plans for Reform of the International Monetary System*, Princeton, NJ: Princeton University Press, 1962, and Fritz Machlup, 'Liquidité, internationale et nationale', *Bulletin d'Information et de Documentation, Banque Nationale de Belgique* 37 (February 1962). Differences of a semantic nature were resolved by a glossary appended to the 1964 report. There is also a chapter on 'Notes on Terminology' in the Bellagio Group anthology published in 1966 (William Fellner et al., eds, *Maintaining and Restoring Balance in International Payments*, Princeton, NJ: Princeton University Press, 1966, 243–54). Many definitions in this volume followed Machlup's own definitions. See Fritz Machlup, *Adjustment, Compensatory Correction, and Financing of Imbalances in International Payments*, Princeton, NJ: Princeton University Press, 1965, 206, and also chapter 2, above.
46   Fritz Machlup, 'International Liquidity and International Money', LA 1961; Machlup, *Plans for Reform of the International Monetary System*.
47   Kindleberger, review of *Monetary Problems of the International Economy*, 127–8.

3. The gold standard
4. Flexible exchange rates (with or without state intervention).[48]

The latter two had long been tabled nearly exclusively by MPS members.[49] These neoliberal positions, given equal space in the report, at the time had few true adherents within academia and politics, and so were in fact overrepresented, in the taxonomy. As was emphasised time and again, the organisers had selected participants in such a way as to prize contradictory viewpoints.[50]

It should be understood that such a presentation, by juxtaposing flexibilisation with the gold standard, would have made the former appear as the less extreme alternative, since the latter was by then widely seen to be a fringe viewpoint. Some contemporaries noticed that the schema contradicted the Bellagio Group's self-description as a 'representative group of non-governmental economists', giving disproportionate space to market-liberal reforms unrepresentative of academic discourse on the topic.[51] BIS chief economist Milton Gilbert, for example, complained that he could 'count on his fingers' economists in the AEA who favoured either the gold standard or flexibilisation without state intervention. The prominence of these views within the Bellagio Group therefore constituted a 'gross overrepresentation'.[52]

---

48 Just how arbitrary this categorisation was is shown by the twenty-four proposals and commentaries written independently in the anthology *World Monetary Reform Plans and Issues* published by Grubel in 1963. The arbitrariness was also criticised by Milton Gilbert (in Friedman, Bernstein and Gilbert, 'Discussion', 187).

49 The two economists who favoured a classical gold standard (Rueff and Heilperin) and those who advocated flexible exchange rates without government intervention were almost exclusively MPS members. Although no names are mentioned in the 1964 report for flexible exchange rates, the economists in the group who were not MPS members were in favour of non-floating exchange rates – with the exception of Machlup's student Malkiel (see Friedman, Bernstein and Gilbert, 'Discussion', 187; Triffin, *The World Money Maze*, 3f.).

50 See Machlup and Malkiel, *International Monetary Arrangements*, 8f. and the chapter 'Stress on Disagreement', 17–20, and 106.

51 Machlup and Malkiel, *International Monetary Arrangements*, 7f.

52 Gilbert on a discussion of the AEA with Friedman and Bernstein (in Friedman, Bernstein and Gilbert, 'Discussion', 186) described these two groups as 'laissez-faire economists'. This division also influenced the Bellagio conferences with central bankers, to be discussed in the following section. See Haas, 'Epistemic Communities', 16.

Bringing flexible exchange rates into the academic mainstream was no doubt an intent of Bellagio's organisers. Machlup and Fellner made this plain in their contributions, and the first meeting was devoted to the advantages and disadvantages of flexible or fixed exchange rates, with the merits of other reforms to be dealt with at a later date.[53] Bellagio Group discussions were, as Triffin once recalled, very much influenced by Machlup's 'Plans for Reform of the International Monetary System', itself a reiteration of his lecture at the 1961 MPS conference, where the topic had been central.[54]

Along with self-stylisation as 'representative', 'independent' and 'international', much emphasis fell on the diversity of the invited economists' points of view.[55] This highlighted the contrast between the Bellagio Group and the government economists of the IMF, seen by implication as representing entrenched national interests, outdated modes of thought and the baser side of workaday politics.[56] Bellagio furthermore provided an ideologically neutral setting for the introduction of concepts hatched inside the MPS.

Despite the much-touted heterogeneity of the Bellagio Group, a consensus coalesced in favour of both the centralisation of international reserves and greater flexibilisation of exchange rates. The organisers did not hesitate to boast publicly of this 'miraculous' meeting of the minds.[57] After each of the three conferences, press releases underscored the enthusiasm for flexibilisation. Although no similar convergence could be reached on the complete flexibility of market-determined exchange rates favoured by most MPS members, individuals inside the group vigorously upheld it.[58] The group's 1964 report circulated widely among

53 Machlup and Malkiel, *International Monetary Arrangements*, 12–23. Interestingly, all MPS members were also authors of the respective reports on the four proposals (nine out of twenty-four authors were thus MPS members), which indicates that they took the conferences quite seriously and had not left earlier as had eight other economists.

54 See Triffin, 'The Impact of the Bellagio Group on International Reform', 149f.; Fritz Machlup, 'International Liquidity and International Money Creation', LA 1961; Machlup, *Plans for Reform of the International Monetary System*.

55 Machlup and Malkiel, *International Monetary Arrangements*, 7f.

56 On this, see Fritz Machlup, 'Why Economists Disagree', *Proceedings of the American Philosophical Society* 109, no. 1 (1965).

57 Machlup and Malkiel, *International Monetary Arrangements*, 20. Haberler, 'Fritz Machlup: In Memoriam', 12.

58 Reports were published after the following three conferences: from 17 to 23 January 1964, 21 and 22 March 1964 and from 24 May to 6 June 1964 (the meeting lasted

economists, to a generally positive reception, and it attracted considerable attention from officials and central bankers.[59] By 1965, Machlup was presenting the Bellagio findings to the AEA.[60]

The Bellagio conferences enthroned the flexibilisation of exchange rates as a credible reform and successfully represented it – though perhaps to a lesser degree – as the settled opinion of the most highly regarded, independent experts. No equivalent acceptance attached to the traditional market-liberal or classical gold standard position, defended by Heilperin and Rueff, against which the group's report could marshal arguments first presented within the MPS itself.[61] No proponent of the gold standard would take part in the Bellagio Group's follow-up conferences with central bankers and politicians or any of the related Bürgenstock conferences.

Apart from its report, the Bellagio Group also published a statement by twenty-seven American and European economists in support of greater flexibility in exchange rates. Released internationally in February

---

fourteen days!). For the first two declarations, see Triffin, *The World Money Maze*, 320–6; for the last, see Machlup and Malkiel, *International Monetary Arrangements*, 101–7.

59 Triffin, 'The Impact of the Bellagio Group on International Reform', 147. Triffin writes that the report 'attracted considerable attention and praise from the officials attending the 1964 annual meeting of the IMF'. One of the most favourable reviews is Richard S. Thorn, 'Review, *International Monetary Arrangements: The Problem of Choice*', *Journal of Finance* 20, no. 1 (1965), 161–3. Friedman's assessment of the Bellagio conferences is exemplary: 'The resulting report is a model of its kind. No student of international monetary arrangements, however profoundly he has studied the subject, can fail to be instructed by its careful unravelling of the strands that combine to form a judgment in favour of one or another policy'. Friedman, Bernstein and Gilbert, 'Discussion', 178. Cf. also Richard E. Mooney, 'Economist Group Plans Fund Move', *NYT*, 27 January 1964, 35.

60 Machlup, 'Why Economists Disagree'. The speech to the AEA was published in the *American Economic Review* under the title 'The Report of the Nongovernment Economists' Study Group' (see Fritz Machlup, 'The Report of the Nongovernment Economists' Study Group', *American Economic Review* 55, nos 1/2 [1965]). In it, Machlup compared the non-government economists' study with the official studies and emphasised its advantages.

61 The internal conflict within the MPS also divided the Bellagio Group. Fellner, for example, published a statement at the end of the report in which he firmly rejected the gold standard as well as a multiple currency standard or a centralisation of reserves (Machlup and Malkiel, *International Monetary Arrangements*, 111–13). Heilperin declared similarly: 'I am opposed to "flexible" exchange rates and even to a widening of admissible fluctuations around a fixed parity'. For these arguments, see the characterisations of the two positions found in Machlup and Malkiel, *International Monetary Arrangements*, 74–80, 94–100, 116.

1966, this was reproduced and debated in the *New York Times*, among other international dailies, and in sympathetic journals such as *Ordo*. Notably, the appeal appeared only three weeks after the first US plan for a new reserve currency became known, an eventuality addressed in its first sentence: 'The discussion of possible reforms of the present system of international payments has been largely focused on the problem of "international liquidity"', neglecting the 'no less important issue of exchange rates'.[62]

Thus, as at the Bellagio conferences, the priority was to shift the focus of reform: from the idea of (state-controlled, discretionary) financing through international reserves, which dominated public debates, to (market-controlled, automatic) adjustment through flexible exchange rates.[63] The 1966 statement, conceived by Machlup, Haberler, Fellner and Tibor Scitovsky, the only non-MPS member of the group, called for a considerable widening of the range of permissible exchange rate fluctuations (to 4–5 per cent in both directions) as well as floating parity, or the option for central banks to alter exchange rate parities on their own authority if they did not deviate by more than 2 per cent from the previous year.[64] A compromise proposal, as Machlup put it at an annual meeting of the AEA, was 'all that could reasonably be demanded at present'.[65] Almost half of the signatories were MPS members.[66]

---

62 Edwin Dale, 'Economists Offer a Currency Plan', *NYT*, 21 February 1966, 63; in German in the neoliberal journal *Ordo* in 1966, cf. Fritz Machlup et al., 'Vorschlag für eine Reform der internationalen Währungsordnung', *Ordo* 17 (1966), esp. 9. Robert Mundell recalls: 'A follow-up of those discussions [of the Bellagio Group] was the circulation of a petition in 1966 urging the generalised adoption of flexible exchange rates.' See Robert Mundell, *Optimum Currency Areas: New Analytical and Policy Developments*, ed. Leonardo Leiderman, Washington, DC: International Monetary Fund, 1997.

63 This is also emphasised by John S. Odell, who notes, however, that the economists' proposal (relayed erroneously that it was signed by twenty-one economists) remained a 'fringe activity' until the end of the 1960s. See Odell, *U.S. International Monetary Policy*, 92–3.

64 Machlup had already made similar considerations in 1962. See Machlup, *Plans for Reform of the International Monetary System*, 364.

65 Machlup, 'The Report of the Nongovernment Economists' Study Group', 176; see also Machlup, *Plans for Reform of the International Monetary System*, 364; Gottfried Haberler, *Money in the International Economy: A Study in Balance of Payments Adjustment, International Liquidity and Exchange Rates* (Hobart Paper), London: Institute of Economic Affairs, 1965, 34.

66 Twelve of twenty-seven were members: Friedman, Haberler, Arnold Harberger, Hahn, Johnson, Lutz, Machlup, Meyer, Fellner, Sohmen, Bertrand de Jouvenel and Allan

Bringing together many of the advocates of flexibilisation who would take centre stage in subsequent debates, the declaration set the framework for what by the end of the decade was the majority opinion among economists.[67]

If these developments marked the beginning of organised advocacy for flexible exchange rates, the years to come witnessed a slew of MPS-organised or -affiliated conferences in which the Society's members played central roles and arguments for flexible exchange rates and liberalised capital markets enjoyed ever greater prominence. The conferences discussed below may also be read as part of the process of academic persuasion, since economists were present, even if bankers, politicians and businessmen constituted the main audience.

The activities of MPS members in the American Economic Association (AEA) also contributed to the growing acceptance of flexible exchange rates within academic economics. During the 1960s, half of the presidents of the AEA were MPS members who favoured flexibilisation: Haberler (1963), Stigler (1964), Machlup (1966), Friedman (1967) and Fellner (1969).[68] The considerable prestige associated with the post of president, elected by members of the discipline's oldest and

---

Meltzer. For Meltzer, it could not be verified whether he was already an MPS member in 1964 or joined the MPS only later. A number of other economists who signed up to the MPS network can also be counted among its close circle, above all Herbert Giersch, later president of the MPS, but also Lloyd Metzler, George N. Halm and Hendrik Houthakker. However, it was also important for the credibility of the declaration that, in addition to liberals, some prominent Keynesian economists of the time, like James Meade and Alvin Hansen, also signed on – this meant that the arguments in the text could be presented as non-ideological.

67   In addition to the ideologically and organisationally most important people (Machlup, Haberler, Johnson, Fellner, Lutz and Friedman), three of the five economists on the German Council of Economic Experts, or SVR (Meyer, Giersch, Bauer), two future members of Nixon's CEA (Houthakker, Fellner) and two of Nixon's closest advisers (Friedman, Haberler) also signed. The German Economic Advisory body adopted the demand in its annual report of 1966 (Sachverständigenrat, *Jahresgutachten 1966/67*, Stuttgart/Mainz: Kohlhammer, 1966, 275; see also Ansgar Strätling, *Sachverständiger Rat im Wandel. Der theoretische Argumentationshintergrund des Sachverständigenrats zur Begutachtunng der gesamtwirtschaftlichen Entwicklung zur Beschäftigungspolitik von 1964 bis 1999*, Marburg: Metropolis-Verlag, 2001, 87).

68   Apart from Stigler, these were four of the most important experts who played key roles at the conferences discussed in this chapter. Previous presidents of the AEA who were also MPS members are Howard Ellis (1949), Frank Knight (1950) and Arthur Burns (1959).

most important professional association, did nothing to hurt their cause, which MPS members zealously defended at the AEA's annual meetings.[69]

This was particularly evident at the 1969 AEA annual conference, where MPS backers of flexibilisation dominated the cluster of sessions on the 'future of gold'. Machlup used the forum to declare that currency speculation is 'usually a "good thing", especially when the speculators are making money'; he encouraged currency and gold speculators to seek 'better financial advisers' and ignore political attempts to curb their activities. This was justified because, 'as a rule, their profits can be taken as proof that . . . their actions were in the national interest'.[70] In a discussion among well-regarded experts at the same 1969 meeting, the 'Roundtable on Exchange Rate Policy', Machlup, Haberler and Friedman all took the same line. 'Frankly', Haberler confessed, 'I find it exceedingly difficult to think of valid objections to flexible exchange rates', while Friedman called on the US to close the gold window. Machlup, for his part, brought the discussion to a conclusion in his capacity as a 'neutral' moderator by pressing for limited flexibility.[71]

---

69   In the 1960s half of the presidents of the AEA were members of the MPS. See Hartwell, *History of the Mont Pelerin Society*, 202. See also the following contributions at the annual conferences of the AEA: Gottfried Haberler, 'Reflections of the Future of the Bretton Woods System', *American Economic Review* 43, no. 2 (1953); Gottfried Haberler, 'The Relevance of the Classical Theory under Modern Conditions', *American Economic Review* 44, no. 2 (1954); Harry G. Johnson, 'Equilibrium under Fixed Exchanges', *American Economic Review* 53, no. 2 (1963); Harry G. Johnson, 'The Gold Rush of 1968 in Retrospect and Prospect', *American Economic Review* 59, no. 2 (1969). In his much-discussed presidential address to the AEA in 1968, Milton Friedman ('The Role of Monetary Policy', *American Economic Review* 58, no. 1 [1968], 4) put forward the argument that was very prominent in MPS debates: full employment policy under a fixed exchange rate system would lead to direct trade and capital controls.

70   Fritz Machlup, 'Speculations on Gold Speculation', *American Economic Review* 59, no. 2 (1969), 332; see also Johnson, 'The Gold Rush of 1968', esp. 348. The third essay was by Friedman's colleague in Chicago Mundell.

71   On Haberler, see Fritz Machlup et al., 'Round Table on Exchange Rate Policy', in *American Economic Review* 59, no. 2 (1969); Papers and Proceedings of the Eighty-First Annual Meeting of the American Economic Association (May 1969), 359; on Friedman, see ibid., 365. The other two were Henry C. Wallich, who was closely networked with MPS members and joined the MPS in the 1970s – he defended fixed exchange rates – and Peter Kenen, who problematised the debate and discussed the advantages and disadvantages of both options.

How important were MPS members in securing the hegemony of flexible exchange rates by the end of the 1960s? Over the course of the period ever more economists grew to accept that this view might be a sensible alternative to Bretton Woods. Cascading currency crises and the increasingly obvious discrepancy between growing sums of foreign US dollars and shrinking American gold reserves undermined confidence in the post-war monetary system, and surely contributed to this ideological transformation. That these crises were conceptualised in a certain manner – mainly as a sign of insufficient monetary flexibility – and that flexibilisation at this point was no longer regarded by so many as 'a kind of lawbreaking behaviour' as it had been previously, was also in part a result of the persuasiveness of its many well-known advocates in the MPS.[72] Recurrent currency crises led more and more economists to question the theoretical underpinning of Bretton Woods and seek alternatives. These crises also appeared to confirm hitherto marginal views, such as the notion that fixed rates could be maintained only through capital controls.[73] Acceptance of the taxonomy advanced by the Bellagio Group, Machlup in particular, was integral to this sea change. At an AEA debate in 1969 three of the 'five economist giants', as the *New York Times* had labelled them the previous December, called for flexible exchange rates (these were Haberler, Friedman, Machlup); only one, Henry C. Wallich, defended fixed exchange rates. Such shifts illustrate the inroads made by flexible exchange rates over the prior decade, thanks in no small measure to the efforts of the MPS.[74]

---

72   Endres, *Great Architects of International Finance*, 9.

73   Crises generally confirm the arguments of previously minority positions. See Paul A. Sabatier and Christopher Weible, 'The Advocacy Coalition Approach: Innovations and Clarifications', in Paul A. Sabatier, ed., *Theories of the Policy Process*, Boulder, CO: Westview Press, 2007, 207. The authors describe shock-like changes within a political subsystem as internal shocks – in this case the international monetary order – and argue that 'internal shocks confirm policy core beliefs in the minority advocacy coalition(s) and increase doubt within the dominant coalition'.

74   See 'Exchange Rates Lack Consensus; University Experts Suggest Various Policy Changes', *NYT*, 30 December 1968, 47. The five 'giants': Gottfried Haberler of Harvard; Milton Friedman of the University of Chicago; Henry C. Wallich of Yale; Peter B. Kenen of Columbia; Fritz Machlup of Princeton.

Central banks and policy

Along with bolstering the academic credibility of flexible exchange rates, reformers also needed to convince policymakers in international organisations, central banks and the finance ministries of the capitalist core.[75] Outright rejection or ignorance of the issue was particularly pronounced among members of government and affiliated experts. Throughout the 1960s, official declarations proscribed flexible exchange rates along with alterations in the price of gold from the repertoire of future reforms. This state of affairs was exemplified in the 1964 report of the ten largest industrial nations (the Group of Ten), in the 1964 and 1965 annual reports of the IMF and in the 1964 declaration of the CEA.[76] Friedrich Lutz made the point quite clear: 'There is no question of flexible exchange rates being introduced, since the monetary authorities in all countries are opposed.'[77]

Despite the growing number of economists speaking out in favour of flexible exchange rates, the idea was not seriously discussed in government circles until late 1968.[78] Governments feared above all that the instability posed by flexibilisation and accompanying speculative capital flows could hinder trade and unleash global economic chaos. Until the end of the 1960s, government representatives in Europe also assumed that 'it was only the "discipline" of the balance of payments that made it possible for them to make restrictive fiscal and monetary policies palatable to their own citizens'.[79] Moreover, most governments had a political

---

75 For a general introduction to the influence of economists and economic ideas on governments, see A. W. Coats, 'Economic Ideas in Government', in Colander and Coats, *The Spread of Economic Ideas*.

76 Group of Ten, *Ministerial Statement of the Group of Ten and Annex Prepared by Deputies*, Paris, 1964, 1. See also Solomon, *International Monetary System, 1945–76*, 60; Horsefield and de Vries, *The International Monetary Fund 1945–1965*, vol. 2, 50.

77 Lutz in Hunold, *Inflation und Weltwährungsordnung*, 175; see also Triffin, 'The Impact of the Bellagio Group on International Reform', 146.

78 Solomon (*International Monetary System, 1945–76*, 167) investigated the question of when flexible exchange rates began to be seriously discussed within government circles and dates it to the end of 1968. It was not until 1969 that the arguments of the opponents of the Bretton Woods system began to be discussed in the wider public and taken up by newspapers and public figures. See also Horsefield and de Vries, *The International Monetary Fund 1945–1965*, vol. 2, 173.

79 Solomon, *International Monetary System, 1945–76*, 170; see, for a similar view, Milton Friedman, 'Why the Dollar Shortage?', *Freeman* 4, no. 6 (December 14, 1953), 217.

interest in maintaining the monetary status quo. The US, for instance, sought to avoid losing its position as issuer of the leading currency, and the Europeans resisted a devaluation of the dollar as they pursued their own financial and competition policies.[80]

Just as they had contributed to academics' gradual acceptance of floating exchange rates, the Bellagio Group, and through it some MPS members, also helped to persuade policymakers and central bankers to lend their support. In 1964, at the request of central bankers familiar with that year's Bellagio Group report, Machlup, Fellner and Triffin organised nearly twenty joint conferences with international economists and high-level representatives of central banks in the industrialised countries – along with international organisations – over a period of several years. The participating economists prepared for the conferences in advance and then spent days debating with 'high officials from national Central Banks and Treasuries, the IMF, the European Community, the OECD, the BIS, and, on one occasion, from UNCTAD'.[81]

The Bellagio conferences offered politicians and technocrats a forum in which they could discuss matters that, if mentioned in public, might have triggered dramatic and destabilising speculation, and which were taboo in political circles for this reason alone. According to Triffin, the most consequential and delicate topics were those vexing foundational principles of Bretton Woods: 'fixed exchange rates and the price of gold at $35 an ounce!'[82]

The exact nature of what was discussed at these meetings remains secret to this day.[83] The sole publicly accessible source is a widely circulated collective volume, containing papers presented by fourteen economists at three separate meetings. Among the authors, five – Machlup, Fellner, Haberler, Johnson and Lutz – were MPS members who had

---

80   Francis J. Gavin, 'Ideas, Power, and the Politics of America's International Monetary Policy during the 1960s', in Jonathan Kirshner, ed., *Monetary Orders: Ambiguous Economics, Ubiquitous Politics*, Ithaca, NY: Cornell University Press, 2002; Seymour Harris, ed., *The Dollar in Crisis*, New York: Harcourt, Brace and World, 1961, 33.
81   Triffin, 'The Impact of the Bellagio Group on International Reform', 147; Fritz Machlup, 'Preface: The Story Behind the Symposium', in Fellner et al., *Maintaining and Restoring Balance in International Payments*.
82   Triffin, 'The Impact of the Bellagio Group on International Reform', 148.
83   'In order to ensure fullest and frankest discussion, no record of these joint meetings was ever kept or will ever be published.' Ibid., 147.

already attended the Group of 32 Economists meetings in 1963 and 1964.[84]

Transnational expert communities can influence states by direct advocacy of certain policies, or indirectly by placing certain options on the agenda and framing decisions about them.[85] The Bellagio Group did both: some participants – including all the MPS members – argued for greater flexibility of exchange rates and the free movement of capital. But they also engaged in more purely academic pursuits: the reconceptualisation of monetary issues, the enumeration of potential reforms, and the condensation of expert opinion so as to be 'potentially useful to decision-makers'.[86]

Organisers introduced their anthology with summaries that – in a feature that was stressed as 'striking' and 'most encouraging' – overlapped substantially despite the respective authors' 'different backgrounds, political leanings, and past contributions to economics'.[87] As in the 1964 Bellagio Group report, diversity was touted to illustrate the weight and objectivity of the emerging consensus, by now familiar: all three organisers favoured exchange rate adjustments in the event of imbalances, and Machlup and Fellner generally advocated greater flexibility, 'as indeed', the introduction stated, did 'most of the academic specialists today'.[88] Fellner advised that policymakers solve international coordination difficulties by floating exchange rates: 'By letting free-market processes perform more of the equilibrating function, alternatives of this kind would take part of the burden off the direct collaborative effort'.[89] Machlup illustrated the simplicity of flexible exchange rates in a long paper, 'In Search of Guides for Policy'. In it, he explained

---

84   As no more than eighteen economists took part in the more than twenty conferences of the Bellagio Group, it seems reasonable to assume that the authors of this collection of essays were the lead economists in the Bellagio conferences.
85   Haas, 'Epistemic Communities', 4.
86   Here, analysis was based on the aforementioned 1964 report of the Group of 32 Economists. See Machlup and Malkiel, *International Monetary Arrangements*, 6; cf. above all, the chapter 'Notes on Terminology'.
87   Machlup and Malkiel, *International Monetary Arrangements*, 4.
88   Ibid., 5–6.
89   William Fellner, 'Rules of the Game, Vintage 1966', in Fellner et al., *Maintaining and Restoring Balance in International Payments*, 12. William Fellner, 'On Limited Exchange-Rate Flexibility', in ibid., esp. 117. Fellner here argued in favour of 'limited flexibility'.

in detail why, due to insufficient information, politicians will often err in monetary decision-making, even when they follow established guidelines. Machlup contrasted the complexity of political decisions under a fixed exchange rate paradigm – he argued it comprised eleven parameters politicians were obliged to follow – with the slimmed-down flexible exchange rate regime, guided by only two basic principles.[90] With the statement issued by the twenty-seven economists in favour of flexibilisation, a claim for an emerging consensus could be made, though it in fact had not yet cohered among economists.[91]

In their contributions, MPS members held that either national monetary policies must be harmonised internationally (an unrealistic prospect in view of inflexible wages and prices as well as dramatically divergent inflation rates) or flexible exchange rates had to be introduced in order to prevent capital controls.[92] The MPS bloc thus appealed to politicians' need to circumvent unpleasant restrictive measures – meaning unemployment if wages were inflexible – by way of flexibilisation, and argued that only this approach could allow for continued national variation.[93] These contributors placed special emphasis on the rejection of capital controls as instruments of monetary policy because, according to Machlup, these had 'serious side effects on economic and political freedom'.[94] Machlup stressed that the use of controls instead of flexible exchange rates was 'either a thoughtless perversion of thought or a disingenuous use of a pretext for a concealed real purpose of the restrictions'.[95] And both Machlup and Haberler made plain that flexible exchange rates were realistically the

---

90   See Fritz Machlup, 'In Search of Guides for Policy', in Fellner et al., *Maintaining and Restoring Balance in International Payments*.

91   Fellner, 'Rules of the Game, Vintage 1966'.

92   Fellner, in his discussion, focused on the concerns of central bankers. See ibid., 12, and Machlup, 'In Search of Guides for Policy', 84; Haberler in American Enterprise Institute, *International Payments Problems*, 134, Lutz in ibid., 166.

93   Machlup, 'In Search of Guides for Policy', 77 and 74–7. Gottfried Haberler, 'Adjustment, Employment, and Growth', in American Enterprise Institute, *International Payments Problems*, 133. There, Haberler argued almost identically, but at the same time defended the 'tough school' of conservative European central bankers and his MPS colleague Lord Robbins, who considered internal adjustments of wages and prices to be sensible (ibid., 128–33).

94   Machlup, 'In Search of Guides for Policy', 72; Haberler, 'Adjustment, Employment, and Growth', 133. Haberler also criticised the 'drift towards direct controls'.

95   Machlup, 'In Search of Guides for Policy', 73.

'only genuine alternative' and means 'to halt the drift towards more and more controls'.[96]

By establishing the long-running Bellagio Group conference series, MPS members had created a transnational institution for academic-political debate that far exceeded reach and influence of typical venues for economic theory. Johnson later recalled that their principal aim was to 'influence central bankers and finance ministry officials'.[97] Indeed, the Bellagio series had a significant impact on the participating policymakers and central bankers, in that it initiated a gradual shift in opinion in favour of flexibilisation. James Marshall held that it 'is widely believed that these joint meetings were instrumental in convincing the governments of the West that there was no alternative to a shift from the system of fixed exchange-rates to one of flexible rates'.[98] Triffin's assessment, which also emphasised Machlup's close contacts to international economists and central bankers, was as follows:

> These discussions undoubtedly initiated a slow but radical evolution in the thinking of our official colleagues, preparing them at least for the decisions that were finally forced upon them by the events rather than as a deliberate choice many years later in 1971 and 1973.[99]

But Bellagio was only the best-known forum for this transnational debate that helped win newfound acceptance for neoliberal ideas. International currency meetings furnished another venue for MPS members to confront public officials with their arguments for floating exchange rates. In September 1966, for example, a University of Chicago

---

96   Ibid., 73; see also Haberler's introduction to American Enterprise Institute, *International Payments Problems*, 15; 128, 134.

97   Unpublished contribution by Johnson to a conference in Pennsylvania, quoted from Kindleberger's notes in Kindleberger, 'How Ideas Spread among Economists', 47.

98   James N. Marshall, *William J. Fellner: A Bio-Bibliography*, Westport, CT: Greenwood Press, 1992, 19.

99   Triffin, 'The Impact of the Bellagio Group on International Reform', 148, is here referring to the flexibilisation of exchange rates. Also see Herbert G. Grubel, 'Gold and the Dollar Crisis: Twenty Years Later', in Richard N. Cooper et al., eds, *The International Monetary System under Flexible Exchange Rates: Global, Regional, and National. Essays in Honor of Robert Triffin*, Cambridge: Ballinger, 1982, 193. On the impact of the Bellagio and Bürgenstock conferences, see also George N. Halm, 'Floating and Flexibility', in Dreyer, *Breadth and Depth in Economics*.

conference dealing specifically with the theoretical problems of the international monetary system, in order to 'solve' them politically, featured MPS members – including Valéry Giscard d'Estaing – and foregrounded their calls for greater flexibility in exchange rates.[100] Held biennially from 1967 onwards, the Bologna-Claremont conferences were another particularly noteworthy series, at which economists discussed problems of the international monetary order with senior bankers and journalists. As Machlup stated after the 1969 meeting, 'a consensus [emerged] that closely approaches unanimity' and which he, as chairman, showed were statistically in favour of the gold standard. Only two participants favoured gold backing, while 79 per cent called for increased flexibility in the form of floating parities.[101]

A particularly interesting case concerns the influence of MPS members on the German Council of Economic Experts (SVR). Founded

---

100   Robert A. Mundell and Alexander K. Swoboda, eds, *Monetary Problems of the International Economy*, Chicago: University of Chicago Press, 1969, 22. The conference was initiated by Johnson and the Chicago economist Robert A. Mundell and published in 1969. Three of the five sessions were chaired by MPS members (Haberler, Johnson, Machlup) and nine of the thirty-four participants were members of the MPS (Philip Cortney, Gerard Curzon, Giscard d'Estaing, Gottfried Haberler, Harry Johnson, Fritz Machlup, Pascal Salin, Egon Sohmen, Leland B. Yeager). Another participant, Herbert Grubel, a student of Triffin and an advocate of centralisation of reserves, converted in 1966 to a convinced advocate of floating exchange rates. See Herbert G. Grubel, *The International Monetary System*, Harmondsworth: Penguin Books, 1969, esp. 14–15, 109. This was mainly due to his close collaboration with Harry Johnson in Chicago. Grubel later joined the MPS. See also Kindleberger, review of *Monetary Problems of the International Economy*.

101   Fritz Machlup, 'Concluding Observations', in Randall Hinshaw, ed., *The Economics of International Adjustment*, Baltimore: Johns Hopkins University Press, 1971, 143f. The conference papers and discussions were edited by Randall Hinshaw in 1969, 1971 and 1972. Various MPS economists took part in all three conferences, mostly in central positions (Maurice Allais, Philip Cortney, John Exter, Lord Robbins, Jacques Rueff, Michael Heilperin, Fritz Machlup, Gottfried Haberler). It is interesting to note that due to the dominant role of some advocates of a classical gold standard, MPS members at these conferences represented the two radical extreme positions that were perceived as opposing each other: a pure gold standard and completely flexible exchange rates. The former position was represented by Rueff, who dominated the first conference (see Jacques Rueff, 'The Rueff Approach', in Hinshaw, *The Economics of International Adjustment*), Cortney, Exter and Heilperin (in ibid., 118ff.); the latter position by Machlup, Haberler and the Chicago economist Lloyd Metzler. Machlup – in his function as a moderator endeavouring to mediate – argued in favour of limited flexibility. See Hinshaw, *The Economics of International Adjustment*, 12, 31, 41, 81, 118, and also Machlup, 'Concluding Observations'.

in 1963 by MPS member and West German Chancellor Ludwig Erhard, with the participation of Sohmen and Giersch, the SVR sought to make economic policy 'objective'.[102] The SVR pressed for floating exchange rates from its inception, at a time when virtually no one in academia and politics was interested in the matter. How this came about can partly be explained by its conspicuous personal and ideological closeness to the MPS itself, a proximity completely overlooked in scholarly treatments of the organisation.[103]

In 1964, the five-member SVR included industry-affiliated economist Wilhelm Bauer, an early promoter of flexible exchange rates, as well as MPS member Fritz W. Meyer and soon-to-be member Herbert Giersch.[104] Both Meyer and Bauer had co-signed the 1966 declaration of twenty-seven economists, while Erhard had spoken positively about flexible exchange rates as early as 1952.[105] In its very first annual report, the SVR adopted without qualification the position of Sohmen and Lutz, the two most prominent German advocates of free exchange rates. The two MPS economists were engaged as advisers, their expert opinion included as an annex to the SVR's annual report.[106]

---

102 See Gabriele Metzler, 'Versachlichung statt Interessenpolitik. Der Sachverständigenrat zur Begutachtung der gesamtwirtschaftlichen Entwicklung', in Stefan Fisch, ed., *Experten und Politik: wissenschaftliche Politikberatung in geschichtlicher Perspektive*, Berlin: Duncker & Humbolt, 2004, 129–37; on the SVR, see also Alexander Nützenadel, *Stunde der Ökonomen: Wissenschaft, Politik und Expertenkultur in der Bundesrepublik 1949–1974*, Göttingen: Vandenhoeck & Ruprecht, 2005, 152–64; Giersch, introduction to *Money, Trade, and Competition*, vi; and the contributions in *Vierzig Jahre Sachverständigenrat: 1963–2003*, Wiesbaden: Statistisches Bundesamt, 2003.

103 Leeson, *Ideology and the International Economy*, 131f. Leeson argues that Friedman's memorandum written for German authorities in 1950 (published as Friedman, 'The Case for Flexible Exchange Rates') explains the early and decisive advocacy of German politicians and the SVR in favour of flexible exchange rates. However, any concrete tracking of personal or ideological continuities over this period is missing.

104 Sachverständigenrat, *Jahresgutachten 1964/65*, Stuttgart/Mainz: Kohlhammer, 1964.

105 Leeson, *Ideology and the International Economy*, 131; James 1996, 101f.

106 The SVR met with both of them as early as July 1964. Lutz had already propagated floating exchange rates as an adviser to the BIS in the late 1950s. See Verena Veit-Bachmann, 'Friedrich A. Lutz: Leben und Werk', in Viktor Vanberg, ed., *Währungsordnung und Inflation: Zum Gedenken an Friedrich A. Lutz (1901–1975)*, Tübingen: Mohr-Siebeck, 2003, 36. Sohmen had written a relevant dissertation on floating exchange rates in 1958 and since the late 1950s had tirelessly and passionately 'propagated . . . the introduction of flexible exchange rates in West Germany' (Peter Bernholz, *Geldwertstabilität und Währungsordnung*, Tübingen: Mohr, 1989, 25).

Following Sohmen and Lutz, the advisory council demanded that the deutsche mark be allowed to float completely, since a country could avoid the greatest danger of the present, 'imported inflation', only through exchange rate flexibalisation. Their argument was based on the German private banker Hahn's intervention at the 1957 MPS Conference.[107] But the SVR's recommendation, repeated in its subsequent annual reports, was rejected vehemently. The ensuing debates, as they played out dramatically across the German media and in the Bundestag, illustrated how fragile support for flexible exchange rates was in the mid-1960s.[108] In the lively discussions occasioned by the SVR's first report, the federal government had accused the council of having an 'unrealistic preference' for 'fluctuating exchange rates [that] ran like a red thread' through the report and thus violated its mandate, which forbade the recommendation of specific measures.[109] But once a

---

107 The report by Lutz and Hahn is entitled 'How Can a Country Escape Imported Inflation?'; Egon Sohmen and Friedrich Lutz, 'Wie kann sich ein Land der importierten Inflation entziehen?', in Sachverständigenrat, *Jahresgutachten 1964/65*, repr., Bad Feilnbach: Schmidt Periodicals, 1994 [1964], Anhang IV, 157–67. See also Heinz-Peter Spahn, *Zur Stabilitätspolitik des Sachverständigenrates: Zur Abhängigkeit ökonomischer Paradigmenwechsel von wirtschaftspolitischen Handlungsimperativen*, Frankfurt: Campus-Verlag, 1979, 55. The demand for full flexibility in particular, which was not to gain majority support among economists until the end of the 1960s, points to the influence of the expert contributors drawn from the MPS network.

108 See Sachverständigenrat, *Jahresgutachten 1966/67*, 275; Sachverständigenrat, *Jahresgutachten 1969/70*, Stuttgart/Mainz: Kohlhammer, 1969, 88–95. A great deal of material – discussions with members of the SVR, the debate in the Bundestag, press reports on the SVR's reports, etc. – has been compiled in a volume of sources published by the German Economic Society (1966). See Nützenadel, *Stunde der Ökonomen*, 164–74. Strätling argues that the SVR and its reports were based on Keynesian positions in the first phase from 1964 to 1974 but overlooks the truly non-Keynesian but rather neoliberal roots of the SVR's economic policy ideas. See Strätling, *Sachverständiger Rat im Wandel*, 72.

109 This is particularly striking given that 'neutrality' of economic expertise was central to the concept of the SVR (see Metzler, 'Versachlichung statt Interessenpolitik', 143). In addition to the SVR, Meyer and Lutz also propagated floating exchange rates in the Scientific Advisory Council of the Federal Ministry of Economics and within the framework of the Social Market Economy Action Group. Meyer was a member of the Advisory Council from 1950, Lutz from 1965. In his 1967 report, for example, Lutz problematised fixed exchange rates and thus supported the SVR's demand (see Nützenadel, *Stunde der Ökonomen*, 170, cf. also 340f.). On the propagation of floating exchange rates in the Aktionsgemeinschaft Soziale Marktwirtschaft, see Friedrich Lutz, 'Das Internationale Währungssystem', in Aktionsgemeinschaft Soziale Marktwirtschaft, ed., *Freiheitliche Politik für eine freie Welt* (Tagungsprotokoll Nr. 32), Ludwigsburg: Martin Hoch, 1969.

respected panel of expert advisers to a major economic power had pushed for fully flexible and market-determined exchange rates, the concept had to be taken seriously. This probably did more for the fortunes of flexible exchange rates than many of the conferences devoted to the topic itself.[110]

In the second half of the 1960s, advocates of flexibilisation were also particularly active in the US, as it was apparent that fundamental changes in the international monetary order would have to originate there. Central to this effort was the insistence that Washington should unilaterally abandon the gold exchange guarantee and 'cut the link between the dollar and gold', as first formulated by Haberler at the MPS conference in 1965; it was then popularised by American MPS members such as Haberler, Machlup, Friedman, Yeager and Johnson in a range of influential publications.[111] At a 1967 discussion organised by the AEI, Friedman concretised this strategy by sketching four demands, summarised as follows: (1) abolition of all exchange controls; (2) declaration that the US would not support exchange rates relative to other currencies; (3) declaration that the US would sell all gold at thirty-five dollars per ounce or stop gold trading immediately; and (4) a stable internal monetary and fiscal policy.[112] Machlup called for a similar strategy in a study for the American industrial lobby association Committee for Economic Development, as did Johnson at a conference at the University of Chicago.[113]

---

110   Furthermore, it is also thanks to the influence of the *Wirtschaftsweisen* that in 1974 the German Bundesbank was the first central bank in the world to follow Milton Friedman's guidelines and introduce monetarist money supply management, which became established worldwide in the 1980s.

111   Haberler and Willett, *U.S. Balance-of-Payments Policies and International Monetary Reform*, 81; cf. similarly Gottfried Haberler, 'Some Remarks on Recent Discussions about the International Payments System', LA 1965, 7; Haberler and Willett, *Presidential Measures on Balance of Payments Control*; Haberler and Willett, *U.S. Balance-of-Payments Policies and International Monetary Reform*, 5; Fritz Machlup, *Remaking the International Monetary System: The Rio Agreement and Beyond*, Baltimore: Johns Hopkins University Press, 1968, 120. For a contemporary critique of this strategy, see Robert Triffin, 'Neither Gold nor the Dollar', *New Republic* 158, no. 4 (1968).

112   Friedman and Roosa, *The Balance of Payments*, 19, 77–8.

113   Machlup, *Remaking the International Monetary System*, esp. 118–21; Harry G. Johnson, 'Balance-of-Payments Controls and Guidelines for Trade and Investment', in George P. Shultz and Robert Z. Aliber, eds, *Guidelines, Informal Controls, and the Market Place: Policy Choices in a Full Employment Economy*, Chicago: University of Chicago Press, 1966, 181.

Pro-flexibalisation MPS members garnered publicity for their positions in the press, before the US Congress and relevant committees, and as advisers to the Federal Reserve. As early as December 1962, for example, Machlup and Johnson testified at a hearing of the Congressional Monetary Policy Committee, together with finance expert Edward Bernstein and US congressman Henry S. Reuss.[114] In 1963, Friedman pushed the US Congress to float the dollar unilaterally,[115] a demand repeated three years later by Yeager.[116] Johnson, and more frequently Machlup, pushed the same line as political advisers.[117] In 1965, Friedman was invited to address the Board of Governors of the US Federal Reserve on the subject of his statistical-historical studies of American economic history; there, invoking his academic research, he argued for the necessity of floating exchange rates. The appearance brought him considerable recognition, setting him on the path to receiving a Nobel Prize.[118]

---

114   It is interesting that the two (as two of three 'experts') were able to dominate this hearing with their arguments at such an early stage, when floating exchange rates were still receiving little attention. They jointly rejected Bernstein's fashionable plan to expand liquidity as a 'technical gimmick' that would not solve the fundamental problems. Harry G. Johnson et al., 'Three Experts on the Reform Plans', in Herbert G. Grubel, ed., *World Monetary Reform: Plans and Issues*, Stanford, CA: Stanford University Press, 1963, 404.

115   Odell, *U.S. International Monetary Policy*, 89f. In the early 1960s, Friedman complained to Thomas Curtis (House of Representatives) and Jacob Javits (Senate) about the fact that free exchange rates were not mentioned in the report of the Congressional Monetary Policy Committee and succeeded in having the committee repeatedly point out the lack of serious discussion of free exchange rates from 1964 onwards (Leeson, *Ideology and the International Economy*, 118).

116   Leland B. Yeager, 'Unilateral Action on International Monetary Policy', in Lawrence Officer and Thomas D. Willett, eds, *The International Monetary System: Problems and Proposals*, Englewood Cliffs, NJ: Prentice-Hall, 1966, esp. 215. Note the indicative title of the lecture.

117   Harry G. Johnson, 'The Case for Flexible Exchange Rates, 1969', *Review* (Federal Reserve Bank of St. Louis), June 1969. Machlup spoke before the subcommittee of the Joint Economic Committee of the US Congress dealing with monetary issues in 1962, 1963, 1966 and 1968 and made a statement to the Board of Governors of the Federal Reserve in 1968. Cf. Hoover Institution Archives, 'Register of the Fritz Machlup Papers, 1911–1983', 2008, available at oac.cdlib.org.

118   Friedman wrote in 1965: '[American monetary history's] key lesson on this point [balance of payments] is that, *so long as exchange rates are fixed*, the money stock must adjust itself sooner or later so as to keep prices in the U.S. in line with prices abroad.' (emphasis in original). See Milton Friedman, 'Lessons of U.S. Monetary History and Their Bearing on Current Policy: Memorandum Prepared for Consultant's Meeting, Board of Governors, Federal Reserve System, October 7, 1965', in *Dollars and Deficits*, 151.

In November 1967, Friedman, Fellner, Machlup and Johnson wrote a joint letter to the editor in the New York Times calling on the US to introduce 'exchange rate flexibility in free markets' and to abolish any 'controls' that 'suppress the forces of the market.'[119] This document, signed by four of the six most important and active advocates of floating exchange rates in the MPS, is exemplary of the Society's organisational power: the four were based at three different universities (Chicago, Princeton and Yale) and adhered to various schools of economics, but the MPS provided the key linkage for them on this point.

There was also official institutional support in the US for flexibalisation. MPS member Homer Jones, director of the Research Department and later vice president of US Federal Reserve Bank in St. Louis, developed this branch of the Fed into the 'unofficial statistical arm of the Chicago School.'[120] The St. Louis Fed was the only US central bank to advocate monetarism, and various staff members called for flexible exchange rates in a series of articles and speeches in the late 1960s.[121]

---

119 William Fellner, Milton Friedman, Harry G. Johnson and Fritz Machlup, 'Strong Dollar Seen in Free Markets', Letter to the Editor, *NYT*, 26 November 1967, E13. The editors of the *NYT* moved to support floating exchange rates by the end of 1968, earlier than other daily newspapers, and the *WSJ* followed shortly afterwards. See Odell, *U.S. International Monetary Policy*, 182, and Leeson, *Ideology and the International Economy*, 109, on this letter specifically.

120 Walter Heller in Milton Friedman and Walter Heller, *Monetary versus Fiscal Policy*, New York: Norton, 1969, 20. Johnson described the central bank of St. Louis as an 'oasis in the desert of Keynesian economics'. See Beryl W. Sprinkel, 'Confronting Monetary Policy Dilemmas: The Legacy of Homer Jones', *Review* (Federal Reserve Bank of St. Louis), November 2013, 5. The branch was regarded as the 'Medina' of the Chicago School (Bender, 'Chicago School Goes to the Head of the Class'). In addition to Jones, MPS member Jerry L. Jordan also worked at the Federal Reserve of St. Louis. See also A. F. Brimmer, 'The Political Economy of Money: Evolution and Impact of Monetarism in the Federal Reserve System', *American Economic Review* 62 (1972); Milton Friedman, 'Homer Jones: A Personal Reminiscence', *Journal of Monetary Economics* 2 (1976).

121 Johnson, 'The Case for Flexible Exchange Rates'; George W. McKenzie, 'International Monetary Reform and the "Crawling Peg"', *Review* (Federal Reserve Bank of St. Louis), February 1969; David C. Rowan, 'Towards a Rational Exchange Policy: Some Reflections on the British Experience', *Review* (Federal Reserve Bank of St. Louis), April 1969; Wolfgang Schmitz, 'More Flexibility in Exchange Rates – and in Methods,' *Review* (Federal Reserve Bank of St. Louis), March 1970; Milton Friedman, 'The Euro-Dollar Market: Some First Principles', *Review* (Federal Reserve Bank of St. Louis), July 1971. In 1971, the president of the Federal Reserve of St. Louis, Darryl Francis, spoke out in favour of completely flexible exchange rates at the World Trade Conference,

Reinhard Kamitz, MPS member and president of the Austrian central bank from 1960 to 1968, also repeatedly insisted on flexible exchange rates as an 'advocate of the adjustment process' – in October 1968 he was the first prominent central banker to suggest that the IMF examine the advantages and disadvantages of extending the range of exchange rate fluctuations, as the Fund did two years later.[122]

There was only mixed success when it came to persuading representatives of governments and central banks, who were typically highly critical of flexible exchange rates. Although central bankers and businesspeople were gradually familiarised with flexibilisation through international conferences, the governments of the major industrialised countries – with the exception of Canada – remained uniformly hostile to the idea until the end of the 1960s. Even the German government-appointed expert panel's demand for flexibilisation of the deutsche mark failed due to political resistance. Not until the Nixon presidency did the intellectual situation change. But the sudden transformations at the turn of the 1970s, which resulted in the establishment of a new international system of flexible exchange rates by decade's end, are difficult to imagine without the transnational debates of the preceding decade. It was through these protracted discussions that central bankers and politicians grew familiar with the views of the expanding layer of economists who pushed for flexibilisation.

Private banks and the economy

The advocates of flexible exchange rates confronted a particularly difficult challenge when it came to lobbying representatives of banks and large corporations, over and above what they faced when dealing with

---

basing himself primarily on Friedman's arguments. Darryl Francis, 'The Flexible Exchange Rate: Gain or Loss to the United States?', *Review* (Federal Reserve Bank of St. Louis), November 1971.

122 Fritz Diwok, 'The Achievements of Reinhard Kamitz', in Wolfgang Schmitz, ed., *Convertibility, Multilateralism and Freedom: World Economic Policy in the Seventies, Essays in Honour of Reinhard Kamitz*, Vienna: Springer, 1972, 30, 11. The IMF study was published in 1970 and reflected above all the IMF's general scepticism about floating exchange rates. Cf. International Monetary Fund, *The Role of Exchange Rates in the Adjustment of International Payments: A Report by the Executive Directors*, Washington, DC: International Monetary Fund , 1970.

academics, politicians and central bankers. For the most influential banks, the 'conventional conservative thinking on these matters, the thinking of the Wall Street banking community, was all for fixed exchange rates'.[123]

This split in 'conservative thinking' between economists and bankers can be explained, in one respect, by the fear of jeopardising profits by inducing strong fluctuations in exchange rates;[124] many bankers were also convinced that 'the obligation to maintain fixed exchange rates served as a discipline on governments, dissuading them from inflationary policy in general and from big expenditures in particular'.[125] American bankers and their lobby organisation, the American Bankers Association (ABA), were just as concerned that under flexible exchange rates the US dollar would lose its role as an international investment and payments currency, and with it the privileges that accrued to American banks.[126]

The task at hand was therefore to refute the bankers' most substantial criticisms and dispel their remaining doubts. First, they needed to be

[123] Herbert Stein, *Presidential Economics: The Making of Economic Policy from Roosevelt to Reagan and Beyond*, New York: Simon and Schuster, 1984, 165.

[124] Ibid., 164–5. Stein points to the interesting split in conservative thinking between the practitioners and the theorists; from early on, 'the standard doctrine of free market economists, led by Friedman, had favored floating, or free, exchange rates'. Bankers had resigned themselves to the relatively restrictive Bretton Woods system in the post-war period, as they assumed that 'a liberal financial order would not be compatible, at least in the short term, with a stable system of exchange rates and a more liberal trading order'. See Eric Helleiner, *States and the Reemergence of Global Finance: From Bretton Woods to the 1990s*, Ithaca, NY: Cornell University Press, 1994, 50.

[125] Stein, *Presidential Economics*, 165.

[126] This is emphasised by John Conybeare in his comprehensive study of American export capital controls. See John Conybeare, *United States Foreign Economic Policy and the International Capital Markets: The Case of Capital Export Controls, 1963–1974*, New York: Garland, 1988, 114f. After Chase Manhattan Bank and the Bank of America had advocated greater flexibility in April 1966, they were publicly criticised by the ABA and other bank colleagues. See also Odell, *U.S. International Monetary Policy*, 181. As early as 1961, David Rockefeller had presented the interests of the bankers to the US Congress and emphasised in particular that centralisation of reserves would mean that New York would lose influence and importance as a financial centre. In contrast to other reform proposals, he did not even mention flexible exchange rates. For this, see David Rockefeller, 'International Monetary Reform and the New York Banking Community', Hearings of the Joint Economic Committee's Subcommittee on International Exchange and Payments, originally published in 1961 and now found in Grubel's edited volume *World Monetary Reform*.

convinced that flexible exchange rates would not cause unmanageable fluctuation, and so posed no threat to profit-making. Second, it was necessary to show that flexible exchange rates would not arrest the anti-inflationary and government-expenditure-reducing discipline of the monetary system. Third, American bankers in particular had to be reassured that flexibilisation would not cause the US to recede as a global financial centre. Advocates of floating exchange rates were aided in this effort by intensive debates with internal conservative critics at the MPS conferences. Like the bankers, gold-standard boosters at the MPS had also criticised floating exchange rates for undermining international financial markets' ability to impose monetary discipline on governments.

Popularisation of floating exchange rate theory in the private sector had been promoted since the mid-1960s at a succession of conferences. The AEI was particularly active and exploited its extensive contacts to the business world to this end.[127] Five of the nine men on the AEI Advisory Board in 1965 were MPS members – in addition to Friedman and Haberler, Paul McCracken (chairman), Karl Brandt and Felix Morley – as were its president, William Baroody, and research department director, Thomas Johnson.[128]

As early as 1965, the AEI organised a symposium in Washington on international payment imbalances, at which eighteen experts – half of them MPS members – tried to convince about 300 top-class guests from academia, business and the banking lobby.[129] The arguments road-tested at the MPS conference in Stresa only a few weeks earlier played a central role.[130] The event was dominated by arguments in favour of flexible

---

127   Founded in 1943 by industrialists, the AEI was the most important American conservative think tank up to the early 1970s and was closely linked to the MPS.

128   American Enterprise Institute, *International Payments Problems*; on the AEI see Patrick Ford, 'American Enterprise Institute for Public Policy', in Carol Weiss, ed., *Organizations for Policy Analysis: Helping Government Think*, Newbury Park: Sage, 1992; Stone, *Capturing the Political Imagination*, 251f.

129   In addition to Friedman, Haberler, Machlup, Fellner and Lutz, the Peruvian Rómulo A. Ferrero, the Brazilian Eugênio Gudin and the Briton Frank Walter Paish spoke. The chairmen of the three panels were Karl Brandt, Paul McCracken and Thomas Johnson (all MPS). The contributions to the symposium were published by the AEI.

130   Haberler's opening lecture ('The International Payments System: Postwar Trends and Prospects', in American Enterprise Institute, *International Payments Problems*, 4–8, 10–11) is, word for word, identical to his contribution to the MPS conference ('Some Remarks on Recent Discussions about the International Payments System', LA 1965), though it is not indicated.

exchange rates, without excessive regard for the sensibilities of those who dissented.[131] Friedman exploited his authority as an academic expert to counter bankers' concerns that floating exchange rates might mean greater, and unwelcome, fluctuation. Studies clearly demonstrated that there had not been 'a single confirmed case of destabilizing speculation', he assured the audience.[132] Here, not surprisingly, Friedman referred only to the empirical research produced by his students, with his close cooperation, which tended to refer primarily to the rather ambiguous case of the Canadian floating dollar of the 1950s.[133] The predictions derived from these studies, to the effect that floating exchange rates were not susceptible to destabilising speculation, were to be entirely disproven over the course of the 1970s, but by then they had played their role in shaping debates on the question.[134]

In September 1971, the AEI organised a similar follow-up conference with representatives of international private and central banks.[135] In

---

131 For example, Alex N. McLeod, 'Discussion', in American Enterprise Institute, *International Payments Problems*, 104. Machlup devoted his entire contribution to the argument that only flexible exchange rates could save the free market system. See 'International Monetary Systems and the Free Market Economy', in ibid.

132 Friedman's discussion in American Enterprise Institute, *International Payments Problems*, 89.

133 The empirical studies Friedman referred to came from William Poole, Harry Eastman and Stefan Stykolt. William Poole studied under Friedman at the University of Chicago and wrote his doctoral thesis on 'The Canadian Experiment with Flexible Exchange Rates 1950–62' at his suggestion in 1966 (for a summary, see William Poole, 'The Stability of the Canadian Flexible Exchange Rate, 1950–1962', *Canadian Journal of Economics and Political Science / Revue canadienne d'Economique et de Science politique* 33, no. 2 [May 1967]; William Poole, 'Data, Data and Yet More Data', speech before the Association for University Business and Economic Research [AUBER] Annual Meeting, University of Memphis, 16 October 2006).

134 On the role of empirical studies on floating exchange rates in the 1960s, see Poole, 'Data, Data and Yet More Data'; on the historical experience with strongly fluctuating exchange rates in the 1970s, which was far removed from scientific forecasts, see Barry Eichengreen, *Globalizing Capital: A History of the International Monetary System*, Princeton, NJ: Princeton University Press, 1996, esp. 141.

135 Seventeen of the fifty-two participants were MPS members (see Fritz Machlup, Armin Gutowski and Friedrich Lutz, eds, *International Monetary Problems*, Washington, DC: American Enterprise Institute, 1972, 135–6). Machlup, Armin Gutowski and Lutz presented papers on the Eurodollar system and possible controls, the relationship between flexible exchange rates and capital controls, and possibilities for a European monetary union as keynote speakers of the three panels, published in their jointly edited volume.

May 1967, the think tank convened a large-scale roundtable discussion, heavily covered in the media, that provided Milton Friedman with a convenient platform and familiar setting to discuss flexible exchange rates with a top banking authority, Robert V. Roosa, former assistant secretary for monetary policy at the US Treasury. Roosa, then president of the American Finance Association (AFA), was also a partner at Brown Brothers Harriman and Co. in New York, among the largest private investment banks in the US. The two lectures, two responses and three discussion sessions with a select group of government representatives, academics and journalists were published by the AEI in 1967 as the fourth 'Rational Debate Seminar' under the title *Free Versus Fixed Exchange Rates*.[136]

In addition to the AEI, the University of Chicago was particularly active in organising dialogues with representatives of upper management and capital. In April 1966, for example, George Shultz (later Nixon's secretary of the treasury) and Robert Aliber set up a conference in Chicago on the initiative of MPS member George Stigler, at which Friedman, Harberger, Johnson, Meltzer, Stein and Stigler urged the adoption of floating exchange rates and liberalised capital markets before senior figures from the corporate world, banking sector and the trade unions.[137] In his summary of the event, Stigler remarked that what struck him most was 'how weak the criticism of floating exchange rates' was, criticism he also dismissed as 'inarticulate and unfounded':

> The opposition to floating exchange rates is not based upon analytically defensible criticisms of how the economy would behave. Rather the opposition rests upon an instinctive and possibly atavistic belief, on the basis of the century-old history of the gold standard, that a

---

136   The seminar was organised by Warren Nutter (1923–1979), together with James Buchanan, founder of the Virginia School of Political Economy, MPS member, former doctoral student of Friedman and Knight at Chicago. Other MPS members who took part in the discussion were Haberler, Stein and McCracken. See also *WP*, 19 May 1967, D9.

137   See above all Johnson 'Balance-of-Payments Controls and Guidelines for Trade and Investment', and Allan Meltzer, 'The Regulation of Bank Credits Abroad: Another Failure for Government's Balance-of-Payments Programs?', in Shultz and Aliber, *Guidelines, Informal Controls, and the Market Place*.

fixed price of gold serves to discipline dangerous fiscal and monetary tendencies.[138]

With the American campaign underway, flexibilisation advocates also launched a transnational effort to convert international capital to their side. In this effort, the National Industrial Conference Board (NICB) proved decisive. Founded in 1916 by New York industrialists, the NICB was among the largest international associations of large banks and corporations, helping forge connections between them through conferences and sympathetic research programmes.[139] In October 1965 and in September 1969, the NICB organised two conferences in Tarrytown, New York, and in San Francisco, at which MPS members worked to sway private bankers both to floating exchange rates and to the gold standard. The set-up was prompted by a coalition of gold standard advocates in the MPS around Philip Cortney and the international gold lobby.[140] Developments within the Committee for Economic Development (CED), another powerful US industrial and banking lobby, are noteworthy. Until the mid-1960s, the CED had supported capital controls in the interest of international stability, but starting in 1966, under the advisement of MPS members Machlup, Haberler and Harberger, it began to promote a neoliberal form of financial market liberalisation (as found in the CED's 1966

---

138 George Stigler, 'Report on Workshop Discussions', in Shultz and Aliber, *Guidelines, Informal Controls, and the Market Place*, 278.

139 See conference-board.org.

140 The majority of the economists were MPS members (Philip Cortney, John Exter, Gottfried Haberler, Michael Heilperin, Allan Meltzer, Henry Wallich; Jacob Viner was at the 1964 MPS conference). Other participants included nine presidents, vice-presidents or directors of major American banks, high-ranking representatives of the gold industry and other economists (NICB 1966, vii–xi). For the second conference, see Robert Wright, 'Money Experts Debate Status of Gold at Industrial Meeting', *NYT*, 17 September 1969, 57. The alliance of advocates of the gold standard in the MPS and representatives of the international finance and gold lobby also organised a conference on the international monetary order at the Graduate Institute for International Studies in Geneva in April 1968, at which a resolution was passed recommending a doubling of the gold price – representatives of flexible exchange rates were not invited (Graduate Institute for International Studies, *On International Monetary Order: Agenda for Action, by a Group of Monetary Experts*, reports and papers presented at the Conference on International Monetary Order, Geneva, 18–20 April 1968, Geneva: Graduate Institute for International Studies, 1968, 10). Mises had also been invited by Cortney, but refused to attend as the resolution had already been agreed in advance (Jörg Hülsmann, *Mises: The Last Knight of Liberalism*, Auburn: Mises Institute, 2007, 1034).

report *The Dollar and the World Monetary System*).[141] In 1968 the CED commissioned Machlup to study possibilities for reforming the international monetary system. In his analysis, Machlup argued for either the introduction of more flexible exchange rates internationally, or, alternatively, for an American delinking of the dollar from gold, which would allow the currency to float unilaterally.[142]

These efforts were not in vain, for in the second half of the 1960s neoliberals increasingly won support from industrialists in their campaign to liberalise financial markets. Up to this point, industry had been rather content with the Bretton Woods compromise.[143] But once far-reaching capital controls were introduced in the mid-1960s and could no longer be considered a temporary measure, industrialists and financiers grew concerned with their ability to carry on profitably in international business and found themselves searching for new ways to combine free movement of capital with free trade. Influential neoliberals in the MPS, as official advisers to governments, in their posts at influential think tanks and as counsellors to central lobby groups, recommended floating exchange rates as the ideal market-liberal exit from this impasse.

In the late 1960s, Machlup once again attempted to jumpstart meetings with bankers along the lines of the successful Bellagio conferences. He wrote to Friedman on 11 October 1968 that he was about to found another group, as 'the time has come, we think, to make a more aggressive push towards greater flexibility of exchange rates'. He also strategically restricted his advocacy to limited flexibility of exchange rates. As he put it to Friedman, 'I know, this is a compromise, but it is probably the only strategy towards recognition of the of the advantages of flexible rates.'[144] Only a few months later, Machlup opened the Bürgenstock conferences with a concrete proposal on these lines.

---

141 Quoted in Helleiner, *States and the Reemergence of Global Finance*, 120.
142 Machlup, *Remaking the International Monetary System*, esp. 118–21; cf. Christoph Scherrer, *Globalisierung wider Willen: Die Durchsetzung liberaler Außenwirtschaftspolitik in den USA*, Berlin: Edition Sigma, 2000, 9.
143 Helleiner, *States and the Reemergence of Global Finance*, 119.
144 Quoted in Leeson, *Ideology and the International Economy*, 63–4. Friedman replied on 23 October 1968 that he was pleased with Machlup's initiative: 'You may be right that the "band proposal" is the only effective strategy. It probably is at a time when you do not have a crisis. I am still of the opinion that the way flexible exchange rates will in fact be most likely to be adopted is as a result of a widespread international liquidity crisis which leaves that as the only alternative open to authorities.'

Financed by the Rockefeller Foundation and beginning in January 1969, this five-part international series of conferences was held in New York and Bürgenstock, Switzerland, and featured roughly equal numbers of internationally prominent economists and bankers. The meetings were considered important enough that leading central banks and governments dispatched their own observers.[145] A published conference volume, brought out after the second session, captures the profiles of those in attendance: of a total of thirty-four who presented papers, nine were MPS members who favoured flexible exchange rates, making up the clear majority of economists.[146] Other participants included high-ranking representatives of international private banks and large corporations, as well as four additional economists, two drawn from the Brookings Institution and one from the National Security Council.[147] Besides George Halm, an economist at Tufts University close to the MPS, Friedman in particular worked effectively to organise the subject matter.[148]

145   George N. Halm, preface to George N. Halm, ed., *Approaches to Greater Flexibility of Exchange Rates: The Bürgenstock Papers*, Princeton, NJ: Princeton University Press, 1970, vii. The conference was announced in 'Scholars to Debate Exchange Rates', *NYT*, 25 December 1968, 57. The meetings took place in January 1969 (Oyster Bay, New York), June 1969 (Bürgenstock, Switzerland), October 1969 (Washington, DC), January 1970 (Arden House, New York), February 1971 (Tarrytown House, New York). See Hoover Institution Archives, 'Register of the Fritz Machlup Papers', 2008.

146   Participating MPS economists were Milton Friedman, Fritz Machlup, Harry Johnson, Friedrich Lutz, Wolfgang Kasper, Erik Lundberg, Gottfried Haberler, Egon Sohmen and William Fellner. It is uncertain whether Herbert Giersch was an MPS member at the time. Two other economists belonged to the inner circle of the MPS, Thomas D. Willett (he worked very closely with Haberler; cf. Haberler and Willett, *U.S. Balance-of-Payments Policies and International Monetary Reform*, Haberler and Willett, *Presidential Measures on Balance of Payments Control*; Haberler and Willett, *Strategy for U.S. Balance of Payments Policy*) and George N. Halm (later MPS member).

147   Fourteen presidents, vice-presidents or chief economists represented the following banks from the US, Holland, Japan, Switzerland, England, Sweden and Canada: Westminster Bank Ltd., Morgan Guaranty Trust Company, First National City Bank of New York, De Nederlandsche Bank, the Mitsui Bank Ltd., Eidgenössische Bank, J. Henry Schroder Banking Corporation, Skandinaviska Banken, Royal Bank of Canada, Swiss Bank Corporation, Bank of America, Brown Brothers Harriman and Company. Corporate representatives from IBM and Fiat were present. Cf. Halm, *Approaches to Greater Flexibility of Exchange Rates*, 427.

148   Halm, preface to *Approaches to Greater Flexibility of Exchange Rates*. On Halm's closeness to the MPS, see his contribution in Erich Streissler et al., eds, *Roads to Freedom: Essays in Honour of Friedrich A. von Hayek*, London: Routledge & Kegan Paul,

Pragmatically, the conference was not concerned with pushing for a total adoption of exchange rate flexibility, a goal most in the MPS considered at the time to be unachievable, and which would have in any case found little support among bankers.[149] As mentioned, the priority was rather to introduce to bankers the prospect of a limited variant of flexibilisation.[150] As was typical of such MPS-affiliated meetings of the time, the series kicked off with a presentation making the case for flexible exchange rates.[151] Machlup introduced the topic by laying out a common terminology, a list of possible reforms and a framework for subsequent discussions of the Bürgenstock Group. He categorically ruled out any 'discussion of the orthodox gold standard' as a 'waste of time', and so cut down the topic to three alternatives: 'jumping', 'gliding' or 'no parities'.[152] Fixed exchange rates were excluded from the outset, narrowing the question to whether sliding or completely free flexibility of exchange rates were preferable to large jumps in parities.

Machlup furthermore took care to restrain his more outspoken MPS colleagues, with a view to most effectively marketing their shared ideas. Was it best accomplished through an aggressive sales strategy or gentler methods? He described this as the 'dilemma of advocacy: hard-sell or modesty', which meant that the 'uncompromising, and, therefore, unsuccessful advocate' might remain true to his principles by advocating the complete abolition of parities, but potentially at the cost of failing to influence his audience. Yet 'believers' in flexible exchange rates

---

1969. Halm had already supported limited exchange rate flexibility for years (George N. Halm, *The 'Ban' Proposal: The Limits of Permissible Exchange Rate Variations*, Princeton, NJ: Princeton University Press, 1965).

149   Machlup et al., 'Round Table on Exchange Rate Policy', 368; Hinshaw, *Monetary Reform and the Price of Gold*, 12.

150   The aims of the conference were 'intensive study of the various proposals for limited flexibility; and a confrontation between academic economists and practitioners from the banking and business world'. See Halm, *Approaches to Greater Flexibility of Exchange Rates*, v.

151   See Robert V. Friedenberg, 'Patterns and Trends in National Political Debates: 1960–1988', in Robert V. Friedenberg, ed., *Rhetorical Studies of National Political Debates, 1960–1988*, New York: Praeger, 1990, 198, 203. Friedenberg has shown that in relation to political debates the use of opening and closing speeches in debates is a powerful instrument for directing discussions from the outset.

152   Fritz Machlup, 'On Terms, Concepts, Theories, and Strategies in the Discussion of Greater Flexibility of Exchange Rates', in Halm, *Approaches to Greater Flexibility of Exchange Rates*, 33.

who promoted an insufficient system in order to broaden their appeal understood the risk that the balance of payments would not improve, thus discrediting the very idea. As a compromise, Machlup proposed exactly what MPS members had already demanded in 1966: advocates of floating exchange rates should at least push for a parity bandwidth 'of no less than 5 per cent', fluctuating by 2 per cent annually.[153]

Along with MPS-linked presentations of the standard arguments for flexible exchange rates set off by counter-arguments (delivered by private bankers from Switzerland and Japan – respectively, Max Ikle and Tadashi Iino),[154] there followed audience-friendly contributions devoted to pressing matters of finance: Donald Marsh, chief economist of the Royal Bank of Canada, assured the participants – as he had already done in the pages of *Ordo* – that Canada's experience with floating exchange rates was positive from the bankers' perspective; David Grove, chief economist at IBM, argued for floating exchange rates from the vantage of private foreign investment bankers; Herbert Giersch discussed business risks under floating exchange rates; while Machlup and Sohmen evaluated the possibility of hedging exchange rate risks through futures markets (an entire discussion cluster was devoted to the topic).[155]

These and other contributions debunked concerns that flexibilisation might shrink profit margins. Another top bankers' concern was serially 'attacked', as noted by a reporter who objected to the 'frequent repetition' of objections that relied on identical reasoning: in at least five

---

153   Ibid., 45, 47. See also Fellner, 'Rules of the Game, Vintage 1965'. Fellner recommended such limited flexibility as a realistic alternative in his 1970 article 'A "Realistic" Note on Threefold Limited Flexibility of Exchange Rates'.

154   Gottfried Haberler, 'The International Monetary System: Some Recent Developments'; George N. Halm, 'Fixed Exchange Rates and the Market Mechanism'; Herbert Giersch, 'Entrepreneurial Risk under Flexible Exchange Rates'; Fellner, 'A "Realistic" Note on Threefold Limited Flexibility of Exchange Rates', all in Halm, *Approaches to Greater Flexibility of Exchange Rates*. See also Harry G. Johnson, 'The Case for Flexible Exchange Rates, 1969', *Review* (Federal Reserve Bank of St. Louis), June 1969, which was reprinted in this volume.

155   Donald Marsh, 'Canada's Experience with a Floating Rate, 1950–1962' (cf. the very similar article in German in *Ordo*, 'Kanadas Erfahrungen mit beweglichen Wechselkursen', *Ordo* 19 [1968]); David Grove, 'The Wider Band and Foreign Direct Investment'; Giersch, 'Entrepreneurial Risk under Flexible Exchange Rates'; Fritz Machlup, 'The Forward-Exchange Market: Misunderstandings Between Practitioners and Economists'; Egon Sohmen, 'Exchange Risk and Forward Coverage in Different Monetary Systems', all in Halm, *Approaches to Greater Flexibility of Exchange Rates*.

instances it was claimed that falling exchange rates exert a stronger discipline on governments than do falling reserves.[156]

These efforts were evidently fruitful. In contrast to the economists' rather pessimistic expectations about reaching common ground, the 'first concerted effort to discuss' flexible exchange rates between practitioners and theorists of finance culminated in the bankers' unmistakable conversion. A survey at the conclusion of the first conference showed that 'a large majority of the participants in the Bürgenstock conference favoured greater flexibility in exchange rates'. Interestingly, most bankers advocated exactly the compromise proposal that Machlup had discussed in his introductory lecture, while some academics stuck to the more thoroughgoing demand for totally free exchange rates.[157]

One of the bankers in question recounted to the historian John Odell that 'at the outset, only one banker or businessman was favorable to a more flexible regime, and by the end only one remained firmly opposed'.[158] This may be an exaggeration, but it reflects the general tendency of the milieu. The conferences ultimately did play a significant role in convincing the business and banking world that flexible exchange rates were in their interest.[159] In this respect, the argument developed by the MPS at its meetings, which set up the opposition between capital controls and greater flexibility in exchange rates – the latter was presented as the only means for preventing the former given political constraints – was especially effective.[160]

Shortly after the first conference, major American banks (Bank of America, Chase Manhattan, First National of Chicago, etc.) came out in

---

156   John Williamson, 'Review of *Approaches to Greater Flexibility of Exchange Rates*', *Economica* 38, no. 149 (February 1971), 113. For a positive review, see Anne O. Krueger in *Journal of Finance* 26, no. 1 (1971).

157   Halm, preface to *Approaches to Greater Flexibility of Exchange Rates*, vi. Of thirty-four respondents, only three were in favour of no change, six cautious practitioners from banks and business argued for a wider band (2.5 per cent) and a large majority of eighteen respondents were in favour of a combination of a wider band (±3 per cent) and floating parity (2.5 per cent per year). Seven academics, most probably the core of the MPS members involved around Friedman and Haberler, stuck to their radical demand of 'freely floating rates'.

158   Odell, *U.S. International Monetary Policy*, 182.

159   This is also the assessment of Scherrer, *Globalisierung wider Willen*, 194; cf. George N. Halm, 'Floating and Flexibility', in Dreyer, *Breadth and Depth in Economics*.

160   Halm, preface to *Approaches to Greater Flexibility of Exchange Rates*, viii.

favour of limited flexibility.[161] After the second meeting, in June 1969, the participants published their joint conclusions in favour of increased flexibility in a press release: 'A majority favored both widening the range (or "band") within which exchange rates may respond to market forces, and permitting a more continuous and gradual adjustment of parities.'[162] The *New York Times* ran the story under the headline 'Wide Flexibility in Rates Favored: Businessmen and Bankers from 10 Countries Back Elasticity in Exchange' and reported extensively on the findings of the conference.[163] Out of these conferences there developed 'a growing transnational debate', in which neoliberal economists participated alongside major commercial banks, and where the demand for greater flexibility in exchange rates increasingly predominated. A contemporary growth in parallel academic and practical conferences of this type illustrate the development well.[164]

The influence of academic economists over the increasingly urgent demands from prominent bankers (especially in the US) for greater

---

161   Robert Metz, 'Market Place: Big Banks Call for Flexibility', *NYT*, 27 May 1969, 62. The arguments of the newly converted Bank of America were very similar to the arguments that had been put forward by MPS members for years and presented at the Bürgenstock conferences.

162   Halm, preface to *Approaches to Greater Flexibility of Exchange Rates*, vii.

163   Edwin Dale, 'Wide Flexibility in Rates Favored', *NYT*, 30 June 1969, 53: 'A group of 38 bankers, businessmen and academic economists from 10 countries, including several former high Government officials, announced today they favored, in one form or another, more flexibility in exchange rates among currencies.' The editors of the *NYT* and the *WSJ* had already swung in favour of floating exchange rates in late 1968 and early 1969 (see also Odell, *U.S. International Monetary Policy*, 182).

164   Odell, *U.S. International Monetary Policy*, 181. Friedman and Paul McCracken also popularised their monetary policy ideas with similar arguments, strategies and demands at a symposium of the First National Bank of Chicago in 1966 (see Milton Friedman et al., *What Should Monetary and Fiscal Policy Be in the Present Situation: A Symposium*, Chicago: First National Bank of Chicago, 1966), various MPS members at a conference in Madrid in 1970 (Harry G. Johnson and Alexander Swoboda, eds, *The Economics of Common Currencies: Proceedings of the Madrid Conference on Optimum Currency Areas*, London: Allen & Unwin, 1973); see Friedman and Haberler's comments at a conference of the Federal Reserve Bank of Boston in 1970, Machlup's at the 24th International Banking Summer School in Rome in 1971 (see Fritz Machlup, 'Changes in the International Monetary System and the Effects on Banks', in *Banking in a Changing World, Lectures and Proceedings at the 24th International Banking Summer School*, Rome: Associazione Bancaria Italiana, 1971, esp. 174). See also Milton Friedman and Rose D. Friedman, *Two Lucky People*, Chicago: University of Chicago Press, 1998, 220; Hoover Institution Archives, 2008.

flexibility in exchange rates and the abolition of all capital controls was perhaps not as clear-cut as it had been within academic economics, but it was nevertheless considerable. This striking metamorphosis in the banking world was also most certainly a reaction to the severe government restrictions placed on international capital movements. But the nearly universal approval of flexible exchange rates by the early 1970s was also 'a concession to the intellectual argument', as Herbert Stein put it.[165]

Neoliberal advocates of floating exchange rates and the Nixon administration

Historical scholarship has stressed the responsibility of neoliberal economists for the drastic monetary policy changes which took place under the Nixon administration. Often neglected, however, is the conspicuous number of MPS members and others in the same orbit who served as advisers and high-ranking members of government during this period. Neoliberal economists came to exert a particularly strong influence over monetary questions in the Nixon administration for two principal reasons. Ideologically, Nixon mainly recruited advisers with a decidedly pro-market liberal outlook. And because he paid little attention to matters of foreign trade, room opened up for new approaches in the field.[166] In this context, the AEI, close to the MPS in terms of personnel as well as ideology, 'served as a research and recruitment base for the Nixon Administration'.[167] Members of the epistemic expert community therefore acted as 'brokers' to introduce previously rejected theories and

---

165 Stein, *Presidential Economics*, 165.
166 Odell, *U.S. International Monetary Policy*, 187: 'In selecting his advisors and administrators, Nixon repeatedly turned to men with notably strict laissez-faire views, such as George Shultz, Herbert Stein and William Simon.' In contrast to other presidents, Nixon was, according to A. W. Coats, 'bored by economic discussion'. See Coats, 'Economic Ideas and Economists in Government', in Colander and Coats, *The Spread of Economic Ideas*, 115. This was also the judgement of his two CEA chairmen McCracken (see Paul McCracken, 'The Council of Economic Advisers under Chairman Paul W. McCracken, 1969–1971', in Erwin Hargrove and Samuel Morley, eds, *The President and the Council of Economic Advisers: Interviews with CEA Chairmen*, London: Westview Press, 1984, 327), and Stein (*Presidential Economics*, 365).
167 Joseph Peschek, *Policy-Planning Organizations, Elite Agendas, and America's Rightward Turn*, Philadelphia: Temple University Press, 1987, 168.

strategies.[168] Friedman and Haberler were particularly active as close advisers to Nixon, as were McCracken, Stein and Fellner, economists in the CEA.

As early as 1962, Allan Wallis (MPS member and a close friend and student of Friedman) had introduced Nixon to Friedman and organised a long meeting between the two.[169] Friedman sustained many informal contacts in Washington, which he used to advance the flexible exchange rate position along with other policy ideas.[170] In 1968, with the help of MPS member Arthur Burns, Friedman was brought into Nixon's Advisory Group on the Economy along with McCracken and future Federal Reserve Chairman Alan Greenspan, among others.[171] One of Friedman's most consequential moves was to introduce Nixon to his Chicago colleague George Shultz, himself a convinced advocate of flexibilisation, who would oversee their implementation as secretary of the treasury from 1972 to 1974.[172]

Friedman did not limit himself to the official channels available to him as a member of 'Nixon's economic inner circle'; he also engaged the president personally.[173] In October 1968, he drafted a confidential memorandum for Nixon, presented in person after the election (it was later published in an anthology of the American Coalition for Flexible Exchange Rates).[174] Entitled 'A Proposal for Resolving US Balance of

---

168 Excepting, as discussed, the SVR in West Germany and Canada. See Haas, 'Epistemic Communities', 31, for a general description of this process.
169 Leeson, *Ideology and the International Economy*, 99, 163.
170 Ibid., 117–24. Friedman was particularly influential with the reactionary and right-wing conservative senator and Republican presidential candidate for the 1964 election, Barry Goldwater, whom Friedman was able to convince to favour free exchange rates.
171 Friedman tried unsuccessfully to win Greenspan over to the MPS in 1974. See ibid., 163.
172 Friedman and Friedman, *Two Lucky People*, 375. The contacts between Shultz and Friedman were very close and personal – for example, Friedman invited Shultz to visit the Friedmans' beachfront apartment in Hawaii. Leeson, *Ideology and the International Economy*, 145.
173 Richard F. Janssen, 'Questions Involving Balance of Payments Pose Tough Decisions for New President', *WSJ*, 7 November 1968, 2; see for further detail on Friedman's role in the Nixon administration *Die Zeit*, 9 May 1969, 32, 54, 62, where it is stated that Friedman 'is considered President Nixon's unofficial economic adviser. The new American government attaches great importance to his voice.'
174 Friedman and Friedman, *Two Lucky People*, 376; the 1968 memorandum was not published until 1988 (Milton Friedman, 'A Proposal for Resolving U.S. Balance of Payments Problems', in Leo Melamed, ed., *The Merits of Flexible Exchange Rates: An*

Payments Problems', Friedman's argument appealed to Nixon's desire for both re-election and a stable monetary order, and extolled the benefits of free exchange rates with these ends in mind. Friedman wrote:

> There is probably no other economic measure that the new administration will have the power to take that can contribute anything like so much simultaneously to greater freedom of U.S. citizens from government control, increased economic prosperity, liberalization of international trade, and the freedom of maneuver of the U.S. government in foreign affairs.[175]

Friedman offered detailed proposals for action: he drafted a speech in which Nixon was to announce the end of Bretton Woods and back a floating dollar on television only weeks after the inauguration.[176] The Republican Ripon Society came out in support of Friedman's proposal in November 1968.[177] Although Nixon did not follow it immediately, his administration was nevertheless understood to be strongly influenced by the Chicago School's monetary policy concepts, a recurrent theme in the press.[178]

That same year, Haberler, who worked as an adviser to the Treasury Department, chaired the Task Force on US Balance of Payments Policies of the President Elect.[179] According to those involved, the corresponding report, which Haberler modelled closely after Friedman's ideas, carried

---

Anthology, Fairfax, VA: George Mason University Press, 1988). Haberler, Machlup and Johnson also published articles in the anthology.

175   Friedman, 'A Proposal for Resolving U.S. Balance of Payments Problems'.

176   Ibid., 430–1. The content of the memorandum was, at points, even identical word for word to a comment Friedman had made at a 1967 AEI-organised debate. See Friedman and Roosa, *The Balance of Payments*, 114.

177   The Ripon Society, like Friedman, demanded 'that Mr Nixon announce such a policy switch [to floating exchange rates] in his inaugural address' (Janssen, 'Questions Involving Balance of Payments').

178   In 1969, for example, the *WSJ* ran the front-page headline 'Policy Makers Try Out Milton Friedman's Ideas', with floating exchange rates as a central theme (Alfred L. Malabre, *WSJ*, 4 November 1969, 1f.; see also Hobart Rowen, 'Nixon Supports $35 Gold Price', *WP*, 25 October 1968, D7; Janssen, 'Questions involving Balance of Payments').

179   Other members were, among others, Fellner, Houthakker and Wallich. See 'Task Force on U.S. Balance of Payments Policies', Nixon Library, available at nixonlibrary.gov. See also Joanne Gowa, *Closing the Gold Window: Domestic Politics and the End of Bretton Woods*, Ithaca, NY: Cornell University Press, 1983, 99.

great strategic weight.[180] Above all, it called for the abolition of capital controls and the recently introduced controls on foreign direct investment, as well as more flexible exchange rates.[181] Drawing on years of preparatory research, Haberler's report also backed a strategy of passive neglect of the American balance-of-payments deficit (or what was referred to as 'benign neglect'). In this scenario, the US would passively accept a deterioration of its balance of payments, since – according to an analysis going back to the MPS conferences of the early 1960s – it was always in a position to abandon the gold exchange guarantee in the event of attacks on the dollar.[182] Against the backdrop of this threat, often invoked by Friedman, greater flexibility could then be obtained through international negotiations:[183]

> If for any reason . . . a 'gold rush' develops, the United States should suspend gold convertibility before our gold stock declines very much below its present level . . . In a period of transition during

---

180   Leeson, *Ideology and the International Economy*, 69; Odell, *U.S. International Monetary Policy*, 186; Scherrer, *Globalisierung wider Willen*, 196f; Gowa, *Closing the Gold Window*, 99; Conybeare, *United States Foreign Economic Policy and the International Capital Markets*, 248; Paul A. Volcker and Toyoo Gyohten, *Changing Fortunes: The World's Money and the Threat to American Leadership*, New York: Times Books, 1992, 65.

181   A summary of the report was published in 2001 as a source edition ('Task Force on U.S. Balance of Payments Policies', in *Foreign Relations of the United States, 1969–1976*, vol. 3, *Foreign Economic Policy; International Monetary Policy, 1969–1972*, Washington, DC: United States Government Printing Office, 1969, available at history. state.gov. According to Paul Volcker, the report was kept under lock and key for a time so as not to alarm currency speculators (cited in Scherrer, *Globalisierung wider Willen*, 196). See also Solomon, *International Monetary System, 1945–76*, 169.

182   Haberler, *Money in the International Economy*; Gottfried Haberler and Thomas D. Willett, *Presidential Measures on Balance of Payments Control*, Washington, DC: American Enterprise Institute, 1968. On the policy of 'benign neglect' in the task force report, cf. approvingly Thomas D. Willett, 'Gottfried Haberler on Inflation, Unemployment, and International Monetary Economics: An Appreciation', *Quarterly Journal of Economics* 97, no. 1 (1982), 166; critical with regard to radical American unilateralism William Fellner, 'The Dollar's Place in the International System: Suggested Criteria for the Appraisal of Emerging Views', *Journal of Economic Literature* 10, no. 3 (1972), 754.

183   Albert Kraus, 'A Dollar Standard? If U.S. Severs Its Gold Ties, Europe Must Accept the Fact or Go It Alone', *NYT*, 21 May 1969, 59f., for example, interpreted a corresponding speech by Friedman in Genoa as the unofficial threat of the American government (the stick), which was intended to support Nixon's official offer of negotiations (the carrot).

which convertibility was suspended, negotiations aimed at introducing new flexibility into the international monetary mechanism could proceed.[184]

In addition to a long-overdue adjustment of exchange rates, a system of limited flexibility similar to that aired at the Bürgenstock conferences and in the 1966 declaration of twenty-seven economists was an initial demand.[185]

Interestingly, the great MPS debates over the relative merits of floating exchange rates versus the gold standard also informed monetary policy in the first years of the Nixon presidency. With Friedman and Haberler, who explicitly argued against a gold price increase, another monetary specialist in Nixon's closest circle, Burns, took the opposite line in 1968. Burns was appointed Federal Reserve chairman in 1969 and remained one of the harshest critics of his MPS colleagues in the administration when it came to monetary questions – indeed, his close friendship with Friedman broke down partly as a result.[186]

In early 1969, when an increase in the price of gold and a policy of exchange rate flexibility were both still considered live possibilities, the flexibilisation camp gained the upper hand with Nixon's appointment of three outspoken advocates to his Council of Economic Advisers (CEA), the three-member panel of experts advising the US government.[187] Among them were McCracken (as chair) and – on Friedman's suggestion – the Chicago economist, industrial lobbyist and 'ideological floater' Herbert Stein, who was associated closely with many in the MPS.

---

184 'Task Force on U.S. Balance of Payments Policies', 1969.

185 'To provide continuing flexibility in the international monetary mechanism, this one-time realignment should be accompanied by: (1) The establishment of wider permissible trading bands for currencies under IMF rules (with fluctuations on either side of par to range up to 2 per cent or 3 per cent, instead of the present 1 per cent maximum). (2) The provision for automatic adjustments in parities by small amounts in instances where a currency remained at the upper or lower end of its band for some specified time period.' (Ibid.)

186 Rowen, 'Nixon Supports $35 Gold Price'; Janssen, 'Questions Involving Balance of Payments'; Leeson, *Ideology and the International Economy*, 157.

187 MPS members were previously active in the CEA, especially under Eisenhower (and Vice President Nixon) 1953–61. During this period, four out of eight CEA members were MPS members or later MPS members: Arthur F. Burns (chairman) 1953–56, McCracken 1956–59, Karl Brandt 1958–61 and Henry Wallich (later MPS member) 1959–61. For an introduction to the CEA, see Hargrove and Morley, *The President and the Council of Economic Advisers*.

A third CEA member, conservative economist Hendrik Houthakker, had already co-signed the declaration in support of flexible exchange rates initiated by the MPS in 1966.[188] Under Nixon, William Fellner of Chicago, himself a backer of flexible exchange rates along with Ezra Solomon, among others, also joined the council. From 1969 to 1974, three out of seven members of the CEA (and its chairs) were also in the MPS.[189]

As is the norm for such expert bodies, consensus was achieved quickly.[190] One of the three central 'maxims' that guided McCracken from the beginning in his tenure as chairman was the conviction 'we were going to have to move toward a floating exchange rate system'.[191] Stein recalls that while almost all members of the CEA were ideological 'free traders' who opposed inflation and subscribed to deregulation, the 'McCracken–Houthakker–Stein team' was particularly extreme. Guided by Friedman's theories, they supported Haberler's strategy of 'benign neglect', radically opposed controls and 'supported the floating exchange rate system that began in early 1973'.[192] The CEA, through its advisory activities, gave

---

188   Stein was suggested to Nixon by Friedman. See Michael M. Weinstein, 'Herbert Stein, Nixon Adviser and Economist, Is Dead at 83', *NYT*, September 9, 1999. Stein told Odell in an interview the following: 'Shultz, Flanigan, and I were ideological floaters.' See Odell, *U.S. International Monetary Policy*, 309. Peter Flanigan was executive director of the Council on International Economic Policy under Nixon. Stein, like Flanigan, was an adviser to Nixon in the working group initiated by Shultz, which prepared the US proposal for greater flexibility for the 1972 IMF conference (Odell, *U.S. International Monetary Policy*, 307).

189   The chairs were McCracken (January 1969 to December 1971) and Stein (from January 1972 until shortly after Nixon's resignation in August 1974). The other CEA members were Gary Seevers (economist and financial market specialist, from the late 1970s head of the futures brokerage department at Goldman Sachs & Co.), Marina Whitman (professor in Pittsburgh and later director at General Motors and other multinational corporations). Ezra Solomon was educated in Chicago and received his doctorate there. He is regarded as a conservative financial specialist, taught at Stanford in the early 1970s and was a close friend of George Shultz. Solomon had already caused a public stir before joining the CEA by openly declaring: 'I am not against letting the dollar float.' ('Proposed Member of Economic Panel Flexible on Parity', *NYT*, 17 June 1971, 59).

190   Herbert Stein, 'A Successful Accident: Recollections and Speculations about the CEA', *Journal of Economic Perspectives* 10, no. 3 (1996), 9.

191   McCracken, 'The Council of Economic Advisers under Chairman Paul W. McCracken', 323, 346. McCracken described himself in an interview in the late 1960s as 'Friedmanesque' (quoted in Stein, *Presidential Economics*, 139, cf. also Kraus, 'A Dollar Standard?').

192   Stein, 'A Successful Accident', 15f., 16, 19.

'cautious and conditional support' to both the strategic gambit formulated by Haberler's working committee and the floating band proposal.[193] Yet another leading neoliberal economist, Haberler's colleague Thomas Willett, served as chief economist of the CEA and then as a senior adviser and director of the Monetary Policy Research Division at the Treasury.[194] The ideological and personal affinities between the Nixon administration and the Chicago School provoked Marylin Bender of the *NYT* to describe the relationship – in reference to Friedman, Stein, Shultz and Ezra Solomon – as a 'love affair'.[195]

Nothing like a monetary, intellectual or political consensus prevailed within the administration at large, and during its first years the decisions that ultimately led to the collapse of Bretton Woods evolved slowly by way of arduous negotiations.[196] But the fact that 'some of the prominent economists who assumed government posts' were willing to 'challenge the basic elements of the Bretton Woods system' also allowed for new strategies to emerge.[197] While the government did not explicitly pursue Haberler's plan, according to Harold James's authoritative work, 'the United States adopted an extreme version of the policy politely referred to as "benign neglect"' which 'eventually undermined the Bretton Woods system'.[198] The task force recommendations managed simultaneously to address the widespread opposition to capital controls among bankers and within the Nixon administration and to combine it with an interest in autonomous economic policy, indispensable given

---

193   'Changes Backed in Money Parity', *NYT*, 31 January 1970, 45 and 'Outlines for "Crawling Peg" Given Qualified Approval by President's Advisers', *NYT*, 31 January 1970, 59.
194   Willett had already worked closely with Haberler since the 1960s and propagated floating exchange rates in joint publications. He had also worked closely with the AEI. See Haberler and Willett, *US Balance-of-Payments Policies and International Monetary Reform*; Haberler and Willett, *Presidential Measures on Balance of Payments Control*; Haberler and Willett, *A Strategy for U.S. Balance of Payments Policy*; see also Officer and Willett, *The International Monetary System*.
195   Bender, 'Chicago School Goes to the Head of the Class'. Similarly, Helleiner *States and the Reemergence of Global Finance*, 115. Odell, *U.S. International Monetary Policy*, 309: 'The ascendancy of the Triffin school in Washington during the 1960s was giving way to the Friedman school in the 1970s.'
196   These are described in detail by Paul Volcker, then Treasury undersecretary for monetary affairs (see Volcker and Gyohten, *Changing Fortunes*, 61–90).
197   Ibid., 61.
198   James, *International Monetary Cooperation since Bretton Woods*, 210–11.

the administration's geopolitical and military ambitions – goals which, given the momentum of financial markets as Haberler understood them, were bound to lead to floating exchange rates in the long run.[199] Nixon was passive with regard to the balance of payments, which only slowly deteriorated at first, but he opted to abolish capital controls in part as early as April 1969. With this 'step in the direction advocated by the task force'[200] he made a notable concession to the American business lobby as pledged on the campaign trail.[201] Major American banks – finance was a vital reservoir of support for the candidate – also began to call for liberalised capital movements in the late 1960s and, following the views of prominent neoliberal economists, held that an extension of exchange rate flexibility was the best way to bring it about.

When the US balance of payments deteriorated more drastically at the beginning of the 1970s, triggering an enormous outflow of gold, the administration's relatively restrictive monetary policy appeared to jeopardise the US's own economic growth and with it Nixon's re-election prospects. The government was left with only two options, as political scientist Christoph Scherrer put it: 'Either return to the monetary activism of the previous administration and seek a Keynesian-inspired reform of the world monetary system through negotiations, or try the neoliberal solution of flexible exchange rates.'[202]

The historian John S. Odell's *U.S. International Monetary Policy*, which weighs the causes of the collapse of Bretton Woods, concurs in attributing it primarily to the ideological influence of advisers inside the administration. That is, the end of Bretton Woods is to be explained primarily by the power of economic ideas. According to Odell, a

---

199 According to the analysis by Scherrer, *Globalisierung wider Willen*, 20–3.

200 Solomon, *International Monetary System, 1945–76*, 169. According to a close adviser to Nixon, Nixon was 'ideologically' motivated in abolishing controls (quoted in Odell, *U.S. International Monetary Policy*, 187).

201 See Conybeare, *United States Foreign Economic Policy and the International Capital Markets*, 245; Scherrer, *Globalisierung wider Willen*, 321. Even though in 1969 and 1970 important people such as Treasury Secretary Paul Kennedy and Secretary of State for Monetary Affairs Paul Volcker were in favour of adhering to Bretton Woods, they shared the neoliberal preference for free capital markets – and therefore, according to Scherrer, 'hardly consciously followed Haberler's script', but nevertheless 'executed it largely according to plan'. See Scherrer, *Globalisierung wider Willen*, 196. The inherent dynamics of the financial markets mentioned here could also be analysed using the fundamental policy trilemma introduced above.

202 Scherrer, *Globalisierung wider Willen*, 322.

'preference for purer *laissez-faire* policies and free-floating exchange rates' was at the forefront.[203] Eric Helleiner, for his part, likewise cites the role of neoliberal intellectuals, in addition to the interests of the US, which sought to consolidate its declining share of the world economy by establishing the most lucrative and liberal capital market.[204]

This crisis of the world monetary system had deep and systemic causes which originated in the failure to institutionalise a long-term, sustainable monetary system at the original Bretton Woods negotiations. The resulting instability invited alternative solutions in the early 1970s: an intensification of Keynesian-orientated reforms might have been possible, combining the effective regulation of capital movement and the expansion of the special drawing rights (SDR) into a real international world money, accompanied by mechanisms to reduce trade and payment imbalances. But Nixon rejected this path and opted instead for a new regime of floating exchange rates and liberalised capital markets. With this decision the significance of the concepts elaborated and propagated by MPS members comes into full view, for they were pivotal in determining which course ultimately prevailed.

On 15 August 1971, as part of his New Economic Policy (NEP), Nixon announced the abandonment of the dollar's convertibility into gold without consulting the IMF, effectively ending the Bretton Woods era.[205] The previous month, Nixon had met with McCracken, who suggested that he close the gold window and float the dollar in response to the dramatic fall in the value of gold. In McCracken's telling, Nixon responded enthusiastically and summoned Treasury Secretary John Connally to a meeting with the CEA chairman. McCracken was thereby able to persuade Connally, who called the decisive conference at Camp David; by the time it took place, the decision to abandon Bretton Woods was a foregone conclusion.[206]

---

203 Odell, *U.S. International Monetary Policy*, 342.
204 Helleiner, *States and the Reemergence of Global Finance*, 115. Leeson has taken this interpretation the furthest, notwithstanding its focus on one figure, Friedman. See Leeson, *Ideology and the International Economy*.
205 Eichengreen, *Globalizing Capital*, 128–34; Leeson, *Ideology and the International Economy*, 63–90; in detail Gowa, *Closing the Gold Window*, who focuses on the contradiction between national autonomy and the costs of international cooperation.
206 Odell, *U.S. International Monetary Policy*, 254; James, *International Monetary Cooperation since Bretton Woods*, 218f. Richard M. Nixon, *The Memoirs of Richard*

At this point, however, it must be emphasised that Nixon did not pursue a neoliberal economic policy, strictly speaking – the administration was in fact more ambivalent. Herbert Stein describes a condition of 'general schizophrenia', and Nixon's speechwriter William Safire summed up the viewpoint aptly as follows: 'His heart was on the right and his head was, with FDR, "slightly left of the centre".'[207] Confronted with the onset of the crisis of growth in the 1970s together with persistent inflation, the government relied on Keynesian measures to stimulate the domestic economy. The NEP, which Nixon pursued from August 1971, aimed at full employment and boosting growth. But this expansionary, US-centric approach only exacerbated flight from the dollar and other difficulties, such as inflation, as a 1973 presidential report makes plain:

> The combination of problems created a dilemma for economic policy. A rate of expansion and a level of unemployment less favorable than policy had projected could have been remedied by more expansive fiscal and monetary measures. But this remedy would have made the other problems worse. It would have stimulated the still lively expectations of continuing or even accelerating inflation and it would have speeded the flight from the dollar ... The problems had to be dealt with simultaneously.[208]

The abandonment of dollar–gold parity in 1971 can be understood only in the context of this dilemma. That flexible exchange rates, the dissolution of Bretton Woods and the liberalisation of capital movements were

---

Nixon, New York: Grosset & Dunlap, 1978, 343. Nixon recalls in his memoirs 'those [present at the Camp David conference] who had the best grasp of the difficult complex of economic relationships: John Connally, Arthur Burns, George Shultz, Paul McCracken, and Herbert Stein – all members of my Economic Council – as well as Peter Peterson, head of the Council for International Economic Policy, and Paul Volcker, the Treasury Undersecretary in charge of monetary affairs'. Three of the seven economic policymakers who advised Nixon on the decision were MPS members, and another, Shultz, was very close to Friedman. Before the decision in August 1971, Nixon commissioned George Shultz to obtain Friedman's approval for the NEP – but the letter arrived too late (Leeson, *Ideology and the International Economy*, 75).

207 Stein, *Presidential Economics*, 135; Safire cited in Robert M. Collins, *More: The Politics of Economic Growth in Postwar America*, Oxford: Oxford University Press, 2000, 103.

208 US Presidents, *Economic Report of the President, 1972*, Washington, DC, 22, cited in Collins, *More*, 118.

considered at all, must be credited to neoliberal advisers inspired by the debates of the 1960s.

Nixon rejected attempts to preserve the foundations of Bretton Woods – especially fixed exchange rates and capital controls – through a new arrangement, set out in the Smithsonian Agreement of 1972.[209] Against the majority of the capitalist world, he worked to establish a regime of floating exchange rates with the dollar as the undisputed reserve currency mediated by global liberalised financial markets.[210] Treasury Secretary Shultz was uniquely committed to the project.[211] To make good on it, he consulted with Friedman and the MPS-dominated CEA under Herbert Stein.[212] Indeed, Friedman wrote Shultz's decisive 1972 IMF conference speech, the first official statement of the new US position.[213] William E. Simon, Shultz's successor at the Treasury, was

---

209 On the reform efforts, see Helleiner, *States and the Reemergence of Global Finance*, 99–122; Eichengreen, *Globalizing Capital*, 132–4.

210 Helleiner has demonstrated this convincingly as has Odell. See Helleiner, *States and the Reemergence of Global Finance*, 106–21, Odell, *U.S. International Monetary Policy*, 292–343. Even in 1973, there was still extremely strong opposition to free exchange rates and the need for capital controls. A committee of the C-20 group that dealt with 'disequilibrating capital flows' was blocked by the US; many countries had demanded, according to a Federal Reserve memo, that the IMF should have the authority to force countries to impose capital controls. Another memo noted that 'the United States is isolated in its opposition to controls' (both quoted in Helleiner, *States and the Reemergence of Global Finance*, 108f.). The US abolished the capital controls introduced in the 1960s as early as 1974.

211 'With Shultz and his colleagues, a "purer" laissez-faire strain in American thinking came into its own, along with a salient belief in the theory of freely floating exchange rates.' (Odell, *U.S. International Monetary Policy*, 306). The chairman of the CEA Stein recalls: '[Shultz] was a close friend, admirer and disciple of Milton Friedman. His thinking was devotedly monetarist.' Stein, *Presidential Economics*, 145. Shultz's activities and his close ties to Friedman are documented in detail in Leeson, *Ideology and the International Economy*, 141–4, 167–80; Odell, *U.S. International Monetary Policy*, 305–26.

212 Herbert Stein noted how the CEA, in close cooperation with Treasury Secretary Shultz, 'influenced policy in a way that Stein would describe as successful'; he emphasised as the most important success that the CEA had propagated a 'floating of the dollar' from the outset. The abolition of capital controls was particularly promoted by Stein and Shultz. Stein, 'A Successful Accident', 19.

213 See Helleiner, *States and the Reemergence of Global Finance*, 115. In a speech on Friedman's ninetieth birthday, Shultz described in detail the extent to which he propagated Friedman's ideas during the IMF negotiations. George P. Shultz, speech at the University of Chicago's belated celebration of Milton Friedman's ninetieth birthday, 7 November 2002, available at freetochoosenetwork.org.

also a committed partisan of free capital movements and flexible exchange rates. In 1975, he proved instrumental in ensuring that the 'Declaration of Rambouillet' not only legitimised and institutionalised flexible exchange rates, now codified in the IMF Articles of Agreement, but so firmly cemented the principle that any return to fixed exchange rates would be possible only with US assent.[214] Simon, too, joined the MPS in the 1970s.

Of course, the importance of neoliberal ideas and their exponents in the demise of Bretton Woods does not diminish the causative significance of other structural and political factors, such as the lack of flexibility of the monetary system, an expansive and unworkable American monetary policy, and destabilising foreign exchange and gold speculation.[215] But these facts did not in themselves force political decisions, which were shaped by neoliberal monetary experts according to a specific school of thought.[216] Odell formulates this as follows:

> An alternative leadership group less willing to rely on market forces to reshape the monetary system would have been more likely to press for early reform negotiations among states than was the Nixon

214 Simons compared this agreement with the original Bretton Woods agreements and called it 'one of the most significant and beneficial international developments of the present decade' (quoted in Otmar Emminger, *On the Way to a New International Monetary Order*, Washington, DC: American Enterprise Institute, 1976, 21). Since the introduction of fixed exchange rates within the IMF requires a majority of 85 per cent, the US has an effective veto. Shultz recalls that this was set up intentionally (cf. Leeson, *Ideology and the International Economy*, 183).

215 These are the most important causes according to James, *International Monetary Cooperation since Bretton Woods*, 205. The importance of speculation is also emphasised by Maurice Obstfeld and Alan Taylor, *Global Capital Markets: Integration, Crisis, and Growth*, Cambridge: Cambridge University Press, 2004, and Peter M. Garber, 'The Collapse of the Bretton Woods Fixed Exchange Rate System', in Michael D. Bordo and Barry Eichengreen, eds, *A Retrospective of the Bretton Woods System*, Chicago: University of Chicago Press, 1993, 461–94.

216 Cf. Leeson, *Ideology and the International Economy*, 8. CEA Chairman Stein recalls: '[Nixon] believed in free trade and came to believe in floating exchange rates and thought that was a great thing that had been done. But he was also very nationalistic, rather inclined to believe that others were out to exploit us economically, and there was, I suppose, a struggle for his soul between the Connally forces [John Connally was US Treasury Secretary 1971–72] and the University of Chicago forces about the matter.' Herbert Stein, 'The Council of Economic Advisers under Chairman Herbert Stein, 1972–1974', in Hargrove and Morley, *The President and the Council of Economic Advisers*, 366.

administration: A school of thought more inclined toward active management . . . would have been likely to infer from the same mixed 1973 facts that currency markets were calling for firmer management [and] would have been less eager to dismantle price controls and capital controls.[217]

Neoliberal theories developed primarily within the MPS clearly inspired the strategies, demands and convictions of key members of the Nixon administration, even if the boundaries between the Society and its wider milieu were always porous.[218]

217 Odell, *U.S. International Monetary Policy*, 342.
218 Friedman also played a decisive role in the founding of the first exchange for futures transactions at the Chicago Mercantile Exchange (CME), itself led by Friedman's close friend Leo Melamed. Only with Friedman's academic credibility was it possible to obtain the necessary political support and approval of private businessmen. See Leo Melamed, 'The Birth and Development of Financial Futures', paper presented at the China Futures Seminar, Shen Zhen, Guangdong Province, 25 April 1996; Leo Melamed, 'The International Monetary Market', in Melamed, *The Merits of Flexible Exchange Rates*, 421; Milton Friedman, *The Futures Market in Foreign Currencies*, Chicago: International Monetary Market of the Chicago Mercantile Exchange, 1971; Friedman and Friedman, *Two Lucky People*, 351; Robert Hershey, 'Currency Futures Due', *NYT*, 14 May 1972, F2.

Conclusion

In his autobiography *Two Lucky People*, written with his wife, Rose, Milton Friedman articulates the process through which economists and their ideas may change the course of events: they 'exert influence by keeping options available when something has to be done at a time of crisis'. He illustrates this central dictum with the collapse of fixed exchange rates: 'Such a crisis arose in 1971. If the alternative of floating exchange rates had not been fully explored in the academic literature . . . it is not clear what solution would have been adopted.'[1]

Friedman's chosen example is the subject of the present study, which has undertaken to analyse the dynamic by which 'keeping' economic theories 'available' played out concretely in the case of floating exchange rates. Rather than confine the study to their most prominent advocate, Friedman himself, it was necessary to survey the evolution of this idea

---

1   Milton Friedman and Rose D. Friedman, *Two Lucky People*, Chicago: University of Chicago Press, 1998, 220. Friedman had already argued during the Bretton Woods era that floating exchange rates would prevail in a crisis if the relevant theories had become widespread (e.g., Milton Friedman's contribution to American Enterprise Institute, *International Payments Problems: A Symposium Sponsored by the American Enterprise Institute for Public Policy Research*, Washington, DC: American Enterprise Institute, 1966, 90, and in a letter to Machlup of 23 October 1968, cited in Robert Leeson, *Ideology and the International Economy: The Decline and Fall of Bretton Woods*, New York: Palgrave Macmillan, 2003, 63–4). His MPS colleague Alan Meltzer argued along similar lines. See Alan Meltzer, 'An Appreciation: Milton Friedman, 1912–2006', aei.org.

across a transnational network of neoliberal advocates, at once an epistemic community and political pressure group, organised around the Mont Pèlerin Society.

Upon its founding in 1947, the goal of the Society was the establishment of an international monetary and trade order that would enable the free international movement of goods and capital, and also block democratic monetary policy by replacing it with an automatic, market-driven mechanism. This project, however, ran up against serious difficulties during the 1950s and 1960s. Not only had the Bretton Woods system institutionalised Keynesian economic policy internationally and imposed far-reaching controls on international capital movements, a fact which various MPS members interpreted as the greatest danger of the time, but internal consensus-building within the neoliberal movement was particularly rebarbative when it came to determining the correct strategy for monetary reform.

Despite their shared norms and principles, a heated controversy erupted between two epistemic communities within the MPS. Fault lines separated the mostly older advocates of the classical liberal gold standard from the younger partisans of a *neo*liberal monetary system based on flexible exchange rates. In the early 1950s, the overwhelming majority of MPS members supported the gold standard, but this disposition was already slowly changing. The decisive factors in the transformation did not only lie in the distortions of the global trade and currency system, which had come under increasing pressure and began to show signs of breakdown. Just as important was the repeated, insistent presentation of arguments for flexible exchange rates delivered at the annual MPS conferences (especially in the 1950s), and the intense internal disputes with advocates of the gold standard (especially in the first half of the 1960s); each current interpreted economic developments in its own manner, and this also had an effect. With some frequency, to the result was the 'conversion' of influential members of the Society to floating exchange rates. By the end of the 1960s, these had achieved a certain predominance, though they remained controversial. Yet the gold standard was ultimately understood to be infeasible, while floating exchange rates came to represent a workable neoliberal concept that could appeal to political and social elites – precisely those actors who might help to establish liberalised capital markets.

Through the MPS conferences, the theory and attendant political strategies underwent extensive elaboration, in process helping to solidify a transnational epistemic expert community of neoliberal advocates. This network was not content to explore the 'alternative of floating exchange rates in the academic literature' (as Friedman somewhat innocuously put it); rather, MPS members were active in their attempts to influence monetary policy debates at the highest levels. They achieved this through publications, the organisation of events and the domination of academic institutes, activities often closely coordinated with MPS-affiliated think tanks. The work carried out in this meeting place of 'capitalists from all countries' (as it was described by the MPS member Schmölders) was itself tied to specific economic interests at a global level and extended well beyond the usual scope of scientific research.[2]

Overall, it is striking that MPS members acted as a relatively coherent network both in terms of content and organisation: *substantively*, the debates at the MPS conferences were particularly significant. The arguments, perspectives and strategies developed therein, as well as the busy networking of MPS members in general, led to tighter coordination in their arguments for flexibilisation, both in publications and in meetings with academics, politicians and bankers. These arguments remained more or less unchanged from their genesis in the 1950s, for which Friedman was primarily responsible (Haberler also admitted this during a discussion at the 1969 AEA).[3] The powerful uniformity of content and argumentation within this transnational network was particularly evident in the construction of the intellectual problem to be answered (priority was given to the adjustment problem and to inflexibility of prices and wages); the definition of certain central concepts (floating exchange rates, adjustment, the division of proposals for reform) and the causal links between them; the argumentative strategies adopted

---

2 Günter Schmölders, *Gut durchgekommen? Lebenserinnerungen*, Berlin: Duncker und Humboldt, 1988, 123. This study suggests that the MPS network is an exception to the following thesis by John S. Odell, *U.S. International Monetary Policy: Markets, Power and Ideas as Sources of Change*, Princeton, NJ: Princeton University Press, 1982, 126: 'Despite the supposed interests of various economic groups with respect to international monetary questions, the 1960s and 1970s saw virtually no campaigning by organised groups on these issues. This is one of the most striking findings of this study.'

3 Fritz Machlup et al., 'Round Table on Exchange Rate Policy', *American Economic Review* 59, no. 2 (1969), 357.

(unrealistic assumptions, the threat of controls, imported inflation); the way technical counter-arguments were dispelled (stabilising speculation, discipline of falling exchange rates, superfluity of international reserves); and the internal coordination of concrete proposals for reform (unilateral abandonment of the gold exchange guarantee, limited flexibility).

In contrast to these zones of fundamental agreement, internal differences persisted regarding the radical nature of certain positions. While some economists around Friedman advocated a completely market-determined system of floating exchange rates, excluding all state intervention, others (most notably William Fellner) considered such a demand to be utopian and far too risky, instead pleading, at least for a time, for a regime of limited flexibility. These more cautious positions, however, did not indicate principled disagreement, but were based primarily on divergent *strategic* considerations and represented a compromise that was judged to be more realistic and acceptable. In the process, a kind of informal 'division of labour' emerged between the strategic-conceptual advancement of the argument by radical advocates and the pragmatic-political incorporation of other positions by their more accommodating colleagues.[4]

Beyond their basic agreement on matters of substance, MPS members also cooperated at an organisational level to achieve the hegemony of floating exchange rates. Machlup in particular, used his extensive contacts among economists, central and private bankers as well as his biographically conditioned mediator role as an 'American-Austrian' in setting up conference series to which he invited a disproportionately large number of MPS economists.[5] The Society loomed large over this

---

[4] See the expert discussion of the AEA in 1969, discussed in chapter 3 (Machlup et al., 'Round Table on Exchange Rate Policy'). Yet even the most radical advocates of free-floating exchange rates in the MPS were repeatedly able to persuade themselves to publicly support compromise proposals – for example, in the declaration of the twenty-seven economists of 1966, cf. Fritz Machlup et al., 'Vorschlag für eine Reform der internationalen Währungsordnung', *Ordo* 17 (1966); Friedman, contribution to American Enterprise Institute, *International Payments Problems*, 90; Milton Friedman and Robert Roosa, *The Balance of Payments: Free versus Fixed Exchange Rates*, Washington, DC: American Enterprise Institute, 1967, 127; Machlup et al., 'Round Table on Exchange Rate Policy', 358; Marylin Bender, 'Chicago School Goes to the Head of the Class', *NYT*, 23 May 1971, F3.

[5] Fritz Machlup, 'Nationalism, Provincialism, Fixed Exchange Rates and Monetary Union', in Wolfgang Schmitz, ed., *Convertibility, Multilateralism and Freedom: World Economic Policy in the Seventies. Essays in Honour of Reinhard Kamitz*, Vienna: Springer, 1972, 265.

transnational pool of experts, and it drew from an already networked epistemic community of economists who shared common normative, principled and causal presuppositions. These conferences might be presented as 'neutral' and 'independent', but neoliberal perspectives invariably predominated. Such a dynamic indicates unambiguously that, as Peter Haas has put it, epistemic communities of experts exert influence through the 'creation and maintenance of social institutions that guide international behavior'.[6]

The meetings made a significant contribution to popularising flexible exchange rates and liberalised capital markets among economists and bankers. MPS members were the most frequent participants in the most consequential conferences on monetary questions over the course of the 1960s, which helps to explain how the pro-flexibilisation camp grew from 'a meagre platoon to an army'.[7]

Even though their efforts met with success among economists and private bankers, to an extent, their desired reforms – especially the repeated proposals for the introduction of limited flexibility – did not immediately gain traction, due to the ideological and institutional inertia of Bretton Woods.[8] But along with the hegemonisation of the underlying theory – retrospectively, it is to be understood as a necessary precondition – historical events did their bit. When a currency crisis of particular concern to the US broke out at the start of the 1970s, MPS advocates of floating exchange rates, with the help of an associated think tank, managed to place their interpretations, causal explanations and strategies before high-ranking advisers within the Nixon

---

[6] Peter M. Haas, 'Introduction: Epistemic Communities and International Policy Coordination', in *International Organization* 46, no. 1 (1992), 4.

[7] Friedman, cited in Leeson, *Ideology and the International Economy*, 63. The only economists who took part in the three most important monetary policy conference series of the 1960s were five MPS members: Machlup, Haberler, Fellner, Johnson and Lutz. See also chapter 3, above. Centring on the MPS also makes it possible to focus on central figures such as Fellner, Haberler, Machlup and Lutz and their networks, which are given too little attention in analyses that concentrate particularly on the Chicago School. For example, in Anthony M. Endres, *Great Architects of International Finance: The Bretton Woods Era*, London: Routledge, 2005; Odell, *U.S. International Monetary Policy*.

[8] See Robert Triffin, 'The Impact of the Bellagio Group on International Reform', in Jacob S. Dreyer, ed., *Breadth and Depth in Economics: Fritz Machlup – The Man and His Ideas*, Lexington: Lexington Books, 1978, 153; Leeson, *Ideology and the International Economy*, 29–40.

administration, and to present flexibilisation and liberalisation of capital markets as a sensible way out of the impasse. In fact, MPS members seemed to have hoped for crises to occur, as windows of opportunity for market-radical transformations. In the foreword to his columns in an anthology published in 1968, Friedman wrote: 'The story is not yet over. A dollar crisis is still to come, and hopefully, like the gold crisis, will turn out to be a blessing by forcing us to free the dollar.'[9]

An analogy can be drawn to Hayek's insight into the influence of Keynesian ideas during the collapse of the 1932 gold standard. In the neoliberal case, by the early 1970s, the US and other governments began to deviate from the rules of monetary policy as laid down in Bretton Woods, in part because of the influence of new monetary policy ideas promoted by the network of neoliberal economists who had started developing them a decade earlier.[10]

Outside of the European Monetary Community, floating exchange rates came to be the globally dominant currency system over the long term.[11] At the same time, real experience with flexibilisation has turned out to be rather different from its advocates' predictions in the 1950s and 1960s. Two points must be briefly highlighted here. Contrary to the central hypothesis that speculation and flexible rates would exert a stabilising influence, from the 1970s onwards rates in fact often fluctuated dramatically, driven by destabilising speculation and so-called

9   Milton Friedman, *Dollars and Deficits: Inflation, Monetary Policy and the Balance of Payments*, Englewood Cliffs, NJ: Prentice-Hall, 1968, 236, 245. Machlup explained to international bankers in 1971: 'While I do not like crises, I am not afraid of them either. The world has learned and gained from the crises of 1967, 1968 and 1969. These crises caused Governments to take actions they had far too long delayed.' Fritz Machlup, 'Changes in the International Monetary System and the Effects on Banks', in *Banking in a Changing World, Lectures and Proceedings at the 24th International Banking Summer School*, Rome: Associazione Bancaria Italiana, 1971, 183.

10   Hayek: 'The fact that the otherwise so conservative heads of central banks deviated relatively easily from the traditional rules of monetary policy can be attributed to the influence of new monetary policy ideas propagated by academics, which became widespread in the post-war years.' See Friedrich A. von Hayek, 'Was der Goldwährung geschehen ist', in *Was der Goldwährung geschehen ist. Ein Bericht aus dem Jahre 1932 mit zwei Ergänzungen*, Tübingen: J.C.B. Mohr, 1932, 7.

11   According to the IMF, 97 per cent of the member states still had fixed exchange rates in 1970; in 1980 this figure was only 39 per cent and in 1999 only 11 per cent (cited in Carmen Reinhardt, 'Mirage of Floating Exchange Rates', *American Economic Review* 90, no. 2 (2000), 65. In addition to the eurozone, various smaller economies have also pegged their currencies to one of the three leading currencies.

overshooting. Such fluctuations often had no relation whatsoever to real economic developments.[12] Global foreign exchange trading has exploded since the liberalisation of foreign exchange and financial markets in the 1970s, to an extent hardly imaginable at the time the policy was adopted. In 2010, currencies worth more than $3.2 trillion were traded daily – more than seventy times the daily trade in goods and services.[13] By 2022, the figure stood at $7.5 trillion. And foreign exchange trading has long since ceased only to finance international trade, but is now largely driven by speculation on changing rates and hedges against the same. Flexible exchange rates between major currencies and largely liberalised foreign exchange and capital movements have created an international market for speculative bets on future revaluations or devaluations of national currencies – a lucrative business with sometimes disastrous consequences, as the 1997–98 Asian financial crisis demonstrated.[14]

Floating exchange rate advocates, 'believing that international capital movements would be stabilising under such a system [of flexible exchange rates]', as Peter Isard summarises the lesson of the 1970s experience, 'committed the common error of comparing the perceived shortcomings of the prevailing exchange rate regime with an idealization of an alternative'.[15] Ronald McKinnon characterised these widespread notions of harmony and equilibrium among MPS members as a fantasy wrapped in 'the emperor's new clothes'.[16] The thesis that a country might

---

12 See Barry Eichengreen, *Globalizing Capital: A History of the International Monetary System*, Princeton, NJ: Princeton University Press, 1996, esp. 141; Eric Helleiner, *States and the Reemergence of Global Finance: From Bretton Woods to the 1990s*, Ithaca, NY: Cornell University Press, 1994, 123f. See also Charles Kindleberger, 'The Case for Fixed Exchange Rates, 1969', in Federal Reserve Bank of Boston, *The International Adjustment Mechanism: Proceedings of the Monetary Conference*, Boston: Federal Reserve Bank of Boston, 1970, 96.

13 BIS, *Triennial Central Bank Survey, December 2007: Foreign Exchange and Derivatives Market Activity in 2007*, Basel: BIS, 2007. Reliable figures have been available only since 1979, when the BIS began publishing corresponding surveys every three years.

14 Jörg Huffschmid, *Politische Ökonomie der Finanzmärkte*, Hamburg: VSA Verlag, 2001, 42–51; Joseph Stiglitz, *Globalization and Its Discontents*, New York: W.W. Norton, 2002, esp. chapters 4–7; Eichengreen, *Globalizing Capital*, 186–90.

15 Peter Isard, *Exchange Rate Economics*, Cambridge: Cambridge University Press, 1995, 191.

16 Ronald McKinnon, 'Floating Exchange Rates 1973–1974: The Emperor's New Clothes', *Carnegie-Rochester Conference Series on Public Policy* 3, 1976.

isolate itself from global monetary policy developments through flexible exchange rates and achieve a certain degree of monetary policy autonomy has also been refuted by real historical developments. Since the 1970s, new and more severe forms of discipline have emerged, and they have brought about the global enforcement of a monetarist, anti-inflationary monetary policy.[17]

In what is perhaps the most significant consequence of the dissolution of Bretton Woods, floating exchange rates were the main prerequisite for the rapid dismantling of nearly all capital controls, and thus the explosion of international financial markets, aptly described by Jörg Huffschmid as the 'lever of counter-reform'.[18] It is well known that members of the MPS were highly consequential in bringing about this neoliberal counter-reform, which confronted Keynesianism, the welfare state and state control of the economy from the 1970s onwards. That they also played an essential role in the much earlier propagation of floating exchange rates should be understood as a significant precondition for the rise of neoliberalism.

As Robert Leeson has observed, in the process of elaborating and popularising flexible exchange rate theory in the 1960s, 'academic economists behaved "as if" they were members of a coordinated coalition pressing for flexible exchange rates'.[19] An analysis of the MPS shows that key economists involved in the process of disseminating this idea were indeed members of a transnational neoliberal network and exchanged theories and strategies regularly. They worked closely in various ways to popularise and then realise in practice this process of flexibilisation and liberalisation.

---

17 See Helleiner, *States and the Reemergence of Global Finance*, 124.
18 Huffschmid, *Politische Ökonomie der Finanzmärkte*, 106–32. Maurice Obstfeld and Alan Taylor also note: 'Floating dollar exchange-rates have allowed the explosion in international financial markets experienced [in the last thirty years].' Maurice Obstfeld and Alan Taylor, *Global Capital Markets: Integration, Crisis, and Growth*, Cambridge: Cambridge University Press, 2004, 3.
19 Leeson, *Ideology and the International Economy*, 2, 46.

Appendix

Table 1: Presidents of the Mont Pèlerin Society, 1947 to 1972

Friedrich von Hayek	1947–61
Wilhelm Röpke	1961–62
John Jewkes	1962–64
Friedrich Lutz	1964–67
Daniel Villey	1967–68
Friedrich Lutz	1968–70
Milton Friedman	1970–72

Table 2: Presentations on the topic of international electoral order at the General Meetings of the MPS, 1947 to 1970
Compiled from the texts of the MPS conferences at the Liberaal Archief in Ghent, Belgium.

Legend:
✓: Presented an essay on the topic of international monetary order and the essay is available in the LA.
×: Presented an essay on the topic of international monetary order but the essay is not available in the LA.
Grey: Advocates the reintroduction of some kind of gold standard.
White: Advocates floating exchange rates.
* Maurice Allais and Heinrich Irmler did not take a clear position.

	1947	50	53	57	60	61	64	65	68	70
Allais, Maurice*								✓		
Friedman, Milton	✓	✓				✓		✓	✓	
Graham, Frank	✓									
Haberler, Gottfried				×			✓	✓	✓	✓
Hahn, Albert				✓	✓	×		×		
Hazlitt, Henry						✓				
Heilperin, Michael					×	✓		✓		
Hutt, William H.									✓	
Ilau, Hans						×				
Irmler, Heinrich*										✓
Kemp, Arthur						✓				
Lutz, Friedrich		✓	×			×				
Machlup, Fritz						✓	×			
Powell, Enoch									✓	
Röpke, Wilhelm	✓									
Rueff, Jacques				×		✓		×		
Sennholz, Hans						✓				
Sohmen, Egon								✓		
Veit, Otto					✓					

Appendix

Table 3: Participation in key monetary conferences during the 1960s

Legend:
O: Organizer
P: Participant
Bold: Members of the Mont Pèlerin Society
Italic: Economists closely associated with the MPS or future members
Grey: The three central monetary policy conference series of the 1960s
* Conferences where only those economists who also participated in other conferences are listed – all other conferences have all participants listed

	1963 Zürich (Hunold, ed., 1963)	1963 Group of 32 economists (Machlup/Malkiel 1964)	1965 Washington AEI (AEI, ed., 1966)	1965 New York NICB (NICB 1966)*	1966 Core Group of Bellagio Conference	1966 Declaration of 27 economists (Machlup et al. 1966)	1966 Chicago (Shultz/Aliber, ed., 1966)*	1966 Chicago (Mundell/Swoboda, ed.,1969)*	1967 1. Bologna-Claremont (Hinshaw, ed. 1967)*	1968 Genoa Resolution on gold standard*	1969 2. Bologna-Claremont (Hinshaw, ed., 1971)*	1969 Bürgenstock (Halm, ed., 1970)	1970 Madrid (Johnson/Swoboda, ed., 1973)*	1971 AEI (Machlup/Gutowski/Lutz, ed., 1972)*
Adams, Robert		P												
Allais, Maurice								P	O					
Baroody, William														P
Bauer, Wilhelm					P									
Bernstein, Edward		P	P					P			P			P
Bloomfield, Arthur	P							P						

	1963 Zürich	1963 Group of 32 economists	1965 Washington AEI	1965 New York NICB *	1966 Core Group of Bellagio Conference	1966 Declaration of 27 economists	1966 Chicago (Shultz/Aliber, ed., 1966) *	1966 Chicago (Mundell/Swoboda, ed.,1969) *	1967 1. Bologna-Claremont *	1968 Genoa Resolution on gold standard *	1969 2. Bologna-Claremont *	1969 Bürgenstock	1970 Madrid *	1971 AEI *
Brandt, Karl		P												
Burns, Arthur														P
Caves, Richard						P								
Chandler, Lester	P													
Cooper, Richard N.												P	P	P	P
Cortney, Philip			O				P	O	P					
Day, Alan	P					P								
D'Estaing, Giscard							P							
Dieterlen, Pierre	P													
Dupriez, Léon	P													
Ellis, Howard											P			
Exter, John			P							P	P			
Fellner, William	O	P		O	O							P	P	P
Ferrari, Alberto	P													
Ferrero, Rómulo		P												
Friedman, Milton		P			P	P					P		P	
Giersch, Herbert					P						*P*		*P*	
Grubel, Herbert G.							P					*P*		
Gudin, Eugênio		P												
Gutowski, Armin														O
Haberler, Gottfried	P	P	P	P	O		P			P	P	P	P
Hahn, Albert	P				P									
Halm, George N.	*P*				*P*						*P*			
Hansen, Alvin					P					P				
Harberger, Arnold					P	P						P		
Harrod, Roy	P	P	P					P	P		P			

Appendix

	1963 Zürich	1963 Group of 32 economists	1965 Washington AEI	1965 New York NICB *	1966 Core Group of Bellagio Conference	1966 Declaration of 27 economists	1966 Chicago (Shultz/Aliber, ed., 1966) *	1966 Chicago (Mundell/Swoboda, ed.,1969) *	1967 1. Bologna-Claremont *	1968 Genoa Resolution on gold standard *	1969 2. Bologna-Claremont *	1969 Bürgenstock	1970 Madrid *	1971 AEI *
Hazlitt, Henry									P					
Heilperin, Michael	P	P		P							P			
Hinshaw, Randall									O		O		P	
Hirsch, Fred		P												
Houthakker, Hendrik						P								P
Hunold, Albert	O													
Johnson, Harry G.		P			P	P	P	O				P	O	P
Johnson, Thomas			P											
Jong, Frits de		P												
Jouvenel, Bertrand						P								
Kasper, Wolfgang												P		P
Kenen, Peter B.		P		P	P									P
Kindleberger, Ch.		P	P											
Kojima, Kiyoshi		P												
Krause, Lawrence												P		
Lamfallussy, A.		P			P									
Lundberg, Erik												P		P
Lutz, Friedrich	P	P	P		P	P						P		O
Machlup, Fritz		O	P		O	O		P			O	P	P	O
Malkiel, Burton		P												
Marris, Stephen												P		
McCracken, Paul		P												P
McLeod, Alex		P												
Meade, James					P			P						
Meiselman, David														P
Meltzer, Alan			P		P	P								

	1963 Zürich	1963 Group of 32 economists	1965 Washington AEI	1965 New York NICB *	1966 Core Group of Bellagio Conference	1966 Declaration of 27 economists	1966 Chicago (Shultz/Aliber, ed., 1966) *	1966 Chicago (Mundell/Swoboda, ed.,1969) *	1967 1. Bologna-Claremont *	1968 Genoa Resolution Goldstandard *	1969 2. Bologna-Claremont *	1969 Bürgenstock	1970 Madrid *	1971 AEI *
Tower, Edward												P		
Triffin, Robert	P	O	P	O				P						P
Uri, Pierre		P												
Vanek, Jaroslav					P									
Viner, Jacob			P											
Walker, Charls			P											
Wallich, Henry C.			P								P		P	P
West, Robert L.					P									
Willett, Thomas D.												P		P
Woitrin, Michel						P								
Yeager, Leland B.								P						

The table was compiled from the lists of participants in the respective anthologies. For the three most important conference series, all participating economists were included, whereas for others, only those participating in other meetings were. For further discussion, see chapter 3.

Biographical Glossary of Important Members of the Mont Pèlerin Society

Burns, Arthur (1904–1987). Columbia University economist who emigrated to the US at an early age from what is now Ukraine, director of the NBER, chairman of the CEA 1953–56, chairman of the US Federal Reserve 1970–78. He had close contacts with Friedman at an early age, whose macroeconomic analyses he strongly influenced.

Cortney, Philip (1895–1971). Businessman born in present-day Romania, educated in France, emigrated to the US in the 1940s. President of Coty Inc., a leading French cosmetics firm. In 1957, he became chairman of the American Council of the International Chamber of Commerce (ICC), and later president of the industrial lobbying association NICB. He was a close friend of his intellectual teacher von Mises and one of the most important American advocates of a return to the gold standard.

Fellner, William J. (1905–1983). Studied in Budapest, Zurich and Berlin, emigrated to the US in 1938 after a few years in a family business in Budapest. Worked as a professor in Berkeley and from 1952 until his appointment in 1973 as Sterling Professor of Economics at Yale. He co-founded the Bellagio Group and was a member of the CEA under Nixon from October 1973 to February 1975. He worked closely with AEI from 1970 and became AEI's second resident scholar from 1975. Fellner became close friends with Haberler and Lutz in the 1950s and called for floating exchange rates from the early 1960s.

Ferrero, Rómulo A. (1907–1975), trained agricultural engineer, minister of finance and agriculture in Peru (1945 and 1948 respectively), adviser to the Peruvian Foreign Ministry and the Peruvian Central Bank and professor at the Catholic University of Peru. As one of the leading Latin American neoliberals, he joined the MPS as early as 1956. He published widely on economic topics and called for flexible exchange rates for developing countries at a very early stage.

Friedman, Milton (1912–2006). Next to Keynes the most influential economist of the twentieth century. Studied economics in New Jersey and Chicago (with Jacob Viner, Frank Knight and Henry Simons) and wrote his dissertation at Columbia University. In Chicago he met his wife Rose (sister of MPS member Aaron Director) and began lifelong friendships with George Stigler and Allan Wallis. He taught at the University of Chicago from 1946 to 1976, where he played a major role in shaping the so-called Chicago School of Economics. After his retirement, he worked at the Hoover Institution in Stanford until his death. Friedman held countless academic positions and was awarded the Nobel Prize for Economics in 1976. His economic works range from the foundation of the theory of floating exchange rates and monetarism to contributions to economic history, statistics and international financial markets. He was an adviser to the Chilean dictator Pinochet, the American presidential candidate Barry Goldwater and American presidents Richard Nixon and Ronald Reagan, and he was a member of Reagan's Economic Advisory Board. Friedman was also known as an influential intellectual: with popular bestsellers such as *Capitalism and Freedom* (1962) and *Free to Choose* (1980), as a regular columnist for *Newsweek* (1964–83) and in a ten-part television series *Free to Choose* (broadcast in 1980), he popularised his justification of neoliberal capitalism and his attacks against Keynesianism and the welfare state. Friedman was one of the most active MPS members and president of the MPS from 1970 to 1972.

Graham, Frank D. (1890–1949). Princeton economist, one of the most important critics of the gold standard and advocate of a commodity reserve standard. In recent research he is regarded as the earliest liberal advocate of flexible exchange rates. His contributions in the 1930s revolutionised international trade and equilibrium theory.

Giersch, Herbert (born 1921). German economist at the University of Münster, in London and Saarbrücken, member of the Scientific Advisory Board of various ministries, founding member of the SVR (1964–70), director of the influential Kiel Institute for the World Economy (1969–89). Giersch joined the MPS in the late 1960s or early 1970s and was MPS president 1986–88.

Gudin, Eugênio (1886–1986). Brazilian delegate to the IMF board from 1951 to 1956, minister of the economy 1954–55 and director of Brazilian Telegraph and Railway Companies. He was a member of the MPS from 1954, was vice-president of the IEA in 1959 and is considered one of the most important Brazilian neoliberals.

Haberler, Gottfried (1900–1995). Studied with Hayek and Machlup under Ludwig von Mises in Vienna in the 1920s and then attended various US and British universities on a Rockefeller Foundation scholarship. He taught in Vienna from 1928 to 1936 and then at Harvard University until his retirement in 1971. From 1971 to 1995 he was senior resident scholar at the AEI. Haberler worked as a financial expert at the League of Nations from 1934 to 1936 and was economic adviser to the Board of Governors of the Federal Reserve System from 1943 to 1947. He served as an adviser to the Treasury Department in the 1960s and 1970s, and in 1968 chaired future President Nixon's influential Task Force on US Balance of Payments Policies. He was also president (1950–51) and from 1953 honorary president of the IEA, president of the NBER (1955) and president of the AEA (1963). His most important contributions to economics are in the fields of business cycle theory, international trade and international financial markets. He joined the MPS in 1949 and was one of its most active members.

Hahn, Ludwig Albert (1889–1968). German economist, stock market speculator and banker. Hahn had held Keynesian positions in the 1920s and 1930s but became a staunch opponent of Keynes in the 1940s. Hahn was one of the most influential international stock market specialists and bankers who, in addition to his private-sector successes, also made a name for himself as an economist in Frankfurt. He remained one of the harshest critics of the American expansionary monetary policy until his old age and proposed flexible exchange rates for hard currency countries as a solution.

Hayek, Friedrich August von (1899–1992). One of the most influential economists of the twentieth century and, along with von Mises, the most important member of the Austrian School. Hayek studied law and economics in Vienna, attended von Mises's private seminar with Machlup and Haberler, with whom he also directed the Austrian Institute for Business Cycle Research. From 1931 he taught at the London School of Economics, from 1950 at the University of Chicago and in 1962 accepted a professorship at the University of Freiburg. Hayek founded the MPS in 1947 and was its president until 1961. In 1974 he was awarded the Nobel Prize for Economics.

Hazlitt, Henry (1894–1993). American economist, journalist and philosopher. Hazlitt popularised the economic ideas of the Austrian School in his widely read books and articles for *WSJ*, *NYT* and *Newsweek*. In 1946 he was vice-president at the founding of the FEE and editor of the *Freeman*. A close friend of Mises and Hayek, he played an important role in linking European neoliberals with American economists.

Heilperin, Michael (1909–?). Polish economist, member of the Austrian School, participant in the Colloque Walter Lippmann, from 1935 to 1964 professor at the neoliberal and Rockefeller Foundation–funded Graduate Institute of International Studies in Geneva.

Hutt, William Harold (1899–1988). Neoliberal economist who distinguished himself above all with work on the critique of trade union 'collective bargaining' and Keynesianism. Hutt studied at the London School of Economics, was a professor at the University of Cape Town, South Africa, from 1928 until the 1970s, then emigrated to the US. He was a founding member of the MPS.

Ilau, Hans (1901–1974). Member of the Hessian parliament in the first election period for the LPD, managing director of the Chamber of Industry and Commerce (IHK) and co-founder of the Aktionsgemeinschaft Soziale Marktwirtschaft (together with MPS members Rüstow, Erhard and Röpke, among others). Ilau worked together with the WEI.

Johnson, Harry Gordon (1923–1977). Began his career as a Keynesian at Cambridge but distanced himself from it in the mid-1950s. After moving to the University of Chicago, he largely assimilated and became one of the most central proponents of the monetary approach of balance of payments and floating exchange rates.

Kemp, Arthur (1916–2002). Economics professor at Claremont Men's College in California 1953–81, research assistant to Herbert Hoover and president of the American Medical Association 1959–60. Kemp was treasurer of the MPS from 1969–79.

Kamitz, Reinhard (1907–1993). NSDAP member and candidate for the SS, student of Hayek in Vienna in the late 1940s and Austrian finance minister 1951–60. As a liberal and 'free market economy man' he worked to put Austria on a neoliberal path of development.

Lutz, Friedrich A. (1901–1975). Student and assistant to Walter Eucken in Freiburg, researched and taught at the International Finance Section in Princeton from 1939 to 1953 (where he worked closely with Loveday, Graham and Haberler) and as a professor in Zurich from 1953 to 1972. Lutz was already invited to the founding meeting of the MPS but was only able to attend MPS conferences from 1949 onwards and presided over the MPS as president from 1964 to 1967 and from 1968 to 1970. Lutz was married to Vera Lutz, a well-known economist and also a member of the MPS, who wrote a dissertation on free banks under Hayek. He was co-editor of the neoliberal journal *Ordo* from its foundation in 1948 until his death and sat on the advisory board of the Aktionsgemeinschaft Soziale Marktwirtschaft. Lutz advised the BIS in the second half of the 1950s, the SVR in the early 1960s and sat on the Scientific Advisory Board of the Federal Ministry of Economics in the FRG from 1965.

Machlup, Fritz (1902–1983). American Austrian economist, studied with Ludwig von Mises in Vienna in the 1920s together with Haberler and Hayek, was a successful entrepreneur of a cardboard box factory from 1922 to 1932 and emigrated to the US in 1933. There he taught at Buffalo from 1935 to 1947, then at Johns Hopkins University, and from 1960 to 1971 he was Walker Professor of International Finance and director at the International Finance Section of Princeton University. Machlup is a founding member of the MPS and was its treasurer from 1954 to 1959. His academic work, which he made known in countless publications, lies primarily in the areas of industrial organisation, information economics, international monetary order, exchange rates and international capital markets.

McCracken, Paul (1915–2012). American economist, earned his doctorate at Harvard and taught at the University of Michigan from 1948. He was a member of the CEA under Eisenhower (1956–59) and chairman of the CEA under Nixon (1969–71), chairman of the Council of Economic Advisers at the AEI and interim president of the AEI (1986). McCracken was a director of various multinational corporations such as Dow Chemical Co., Sara Lee and Texas Instruments.

Meltzer, Allan (1928–2017). American economist at Harvard University, University of Chicago and University of Pennsylvania, who has distinguished himself with work on monetarism and the history of the Federal Reserve. He worked for the CEA under Kennedy and Reagan, was a member of the Shadow Open Market Committee from 1973 and worked as a researcher at the AEI.

Meyer, Fritz (1907–1980). German economist, *Habilitation* (roughly equivalent to a second doctorate) in 1938 in Freiburg with Walther Eucken on the 'Equalisation of the Balance of Payments' and was professor of economics at the University of Bonn and president of the Rheinisch-Westfälisches Institut für Wirtschaftsforschung from 1947. He was one of the central figures of ordoliberalism and editor of its principal journal, *Ordo*, for many years. Meyer was a member of the SVR from January 1964 to February 1966 and advocated floating exchange rates within this framework.

Mises, Ludwig von (1881–1973). Economist and philosopher born in what is now Ukraine, together with von Hayek the most important member of the Austrian School. Von Mises studied under the Austrian economist Eugen von Boehm-Bawerk and taught from 1913 to 1934 as a private lecturer in Vienna, after his migration from 1934 to 1941 at the Graduate Institute of International Studies in Geneva and from 1945 to 1969 as a visiting professor at New York University.

Powell, Enoch (1912–1998). British politician, member of the British Parliament for the Conservative Party from 1950 to 1974 and for the Ulster Unionist Party from 1974 to 1987, minister of health 1960–63 and senior financial secretary to the treasury 1957–58, particularly known for his racist outbursts concerning British migration from the Commonwealth.

Rueff, Jacques (1896–1978). French economic and financial expert, political theorist and probably the most influential French liberal of the twentieth century. After serving as the French financial attaché in London (1930–36) and director of the Treasury Department in the Ministry of Finance during the Depression (1936–39), he was dismissed as director of the French Central Bank in 1941 because of his Jewish ancestry. Due to his strong anti-Keynesian stance, he was temporarily displaced from the national political stage to high international positions after the war (president of the Inter-Allied Reparations Agency, prime minister of Monaco, judge at the European Court of Justice). It was only under Charles de Gaulle in 1958 that Rueff regained strong influence in France. As chairman of a committee to stabilise the franc, he drafted the Rueff Plan, which created a new franc (the franc-Rueff) and laid the foundation for France's liberal market development in the 1960s. Rueff, a member of the Académie Française, was one of the most important critics of the dollar standard and the world's leading advocate of a return to the gold standard – his tireless publishing and advisory activities had a decisive influence on de Gaulle's attacks on the hegemony of the dollar in the 1960s.

Röpke, Wilhelm (1899–1966). German ordoliberal economist, is considered one of the most important fathers of the social market economy. He studied in Göttingen, Tübingen and Marburg, taught in Jena, the US (as a Rockefeller scholar), Marburg and Graz. In 1933 he fled to Turkey and taught at the University of Istanbul (with Rüstow). From 1937 to 1966 he was professor of international economics at the International Graduate Institute in Geneva (with von Mises and Heilperin). In over 800 writings, he established a theoretical tradition very close to the Freiburg School of Ordoliberalism, which had a lasting impact on German post-war history. His close cooperation with Erhard and Adenauer as well as his contacts with other European neoliberals make him one of the leading European liberals of the twentieth century, both as a theoretician and as a practitioner. Röpke was president of the MPS from 1961 to 1962.

Sennholz, Hans (1922–2007). German-born economist of the Austrian School. He studied with von Mises, emigrated to the US in the 1950s, taught at Grove City College in Pennsylvania 1956–92 and was president of the neoliberal FEE 1992–97. From 1957 to 1970 he was a member of the ENCMP and a director of Gold Lake Mines and Multinational Investments Inc.

Simon, William E. (1927–2000). American businessman, in 1973 deputy secretary of the treasury and head of the forerunner of today's Department of Energy and 1974–77 US secretary of the treasury. Simon was an outspoken advocate of laissez-faire capitalism and became a member of the MPS in the 1970s. Simon founded several private financial services companies, sat on the board of more than thirty transnational corporations (including Halliburton, Xerox and Citibank) and worked closely with conservative think tanks such as the Heritage Foundation and the Olin Foundation.

Sohmen, Egon (1930–1977). Economist who grew up in Austria, studied in Vienna, Kansas and Tübingen, obtained his doctorate at MIT in 1958 on 'Economics of Flexible Exchange Rates' (published in 1961 and again in 1969 at the University of Chicago). From 1958 to 1961 he taught (together with Fellner) at Yale, then at the University of Saarbrücken (with Herbert Giersch and Wolfgang Stützel) and from 1969 in Heidelberg.

Stein, Herbert (1916–1999). American economist, had received his PhD from Chicago in 1958 and had worked with Friedman, Machlup, Homer Jones, Lutz and Aaron Director since the 1940s. Stein worked for the think tank CED since the 1940s and was a member of the CEA in 1969–71 and chairman in 1972–74 under Nixon and Ford. He then became a senior scientist at AEI and a professor at the University of Virginia.

Veit, Otto (1898–1984). Economics professor in Frankfurt, president of the Hessian Landeszentralbank and member of the board of directors of the Bank deutscher Länder, which became the Bundesbank in 1957.

Yeager, Leland B. (1924–2018). American economist and founder of the neoliberal Virginia School of Political Economy (with James Buchanan and Ronald Coase), taught at Auburn University and worked as an associate scholar at the Cato Institute. MPS member since the 1950s. He formalised the theory of floating exchange rates in various textbooks.

Index

A
Adams, Robert, 163
Advocacy Coalition Framework (ACF), 8n21
AEI, 100–1, 104–5, 125, 130–2, 130n127, 140
Aktionsgemeinschaft Soziale Marktwirtschaft (ASM), 11
Aliber, Robert, 132
Allais, Maurice, 162, 163
American Bankers Association (ABA), 129
American Economic Association (AEA), 103, 110, 110n52, 114–15
American Finance Association (AFA), 132
Asia
   1997–98 financial crisis in, 159
   MPS members in, 17n11
Austrian School, 18, 35n90, 45, 45n23, 63, 88, 92–3

B
Baroody, William, 130, 163
basic policy trilemma, 24, 24n45

Bauer, Wilhelm, 123, 163
beggar-thy-neighbour policy, 27
Bellagio Group, 73, 79, 107–13, 112n61, 116, 118–19, 121
Bender, Marilyn, 146
benign neglect, 68, 84–5, 88, 143, 145–6
Bernstein, Edward, 126, 163
blockchain technology, xii
Bloomfield, Arthur, 163
Böhm, Franz, 46, 105
Bolkestein, Frits, 18
Brandt, Karl, 71, 130, 130n129, 164
Bretton Woods monetary system (1944–71), 2–3, 14–37, 40
   abolishment of, xiv
   benign neglect and, 146
   Canada and, 54
   dissolution of, 149–50
   history of, 9
   provided for Keynesianism, 41–2
Brookings Institution, 100n9, 135
Buchanan, James, 17, 132n136
Bürgenstock Group, 136
Burns, Arthur, 141, 144, 164, 167

C

Canada
  Bretton Woods rules and, 54
  floating exchange rates and, 36, 128, 131
  full convertibility of currency in, 31–2
Capitalism and Freedom (Friedman), 40
capital markets, liberalisation of, 157–8
capital movements, liberalisation of, xiv, 149–50
'The Case for Flexible Exchange Rates' (Friedman), 55, 62–3
Cassel, Francis, 93–4
Caves, Richard, 164
central banks, policy and, 117–28
Chandler, Lester, 164
Chicago Mercantile Exchange (CME), 9n23, 152n218
Chicago School, 18, 45, 45n23, 92–3, 93n214, 93n216, 127, 142, 146
Coats, A. W., 140n166
  The Spread of Economic Ideas, 98n4
Colander, David C., *The Spread of Economic Ideas*, 98n4
Colloque Walter Lippmann (CWL), 15, 17
Committee for Economic Development (CED), 133
'Commodity-Reserve-Currency' (Friedman), 57–8
Connally, John, 148
Conybeare, John, 129n126
Cooper, Richard N., 164
Cortney, Philip, 73, 75, 85, 102–3n17, 133, 164, 167
Council of Economic Advisers (CEA), 106, 117, 144–6, 144n187, 150, 150n212
cryptocurrency, xii–xiii
currencies, xiii, 24, 31–2, 98–9n5. *See also* Bretton Woods monetary system (1944–71)
Currency Convertibility (Haberler), 64
currency crisis, 34, 116, 116n73
Curtis, Thomas, 126n115

D

Davenport, John, 38–9, 44–5
Day, Alan, 164
decentralised autonomous organisations (DAOs), xii
'Declaration of Rambouillet', 151
de Gaulle, Charles, 33, 33n81
Denord, François, 11
d'Estaing, Valéry Giscard, 122, 164
Dieterlen, Pierre, 164
dollar
  dollar crisis, 158
  as world reserve currency, xiii
  'dollar gap'/'dollar glut', 52n49
  The Dollar and the World Monetary System report, 133–4
Douglas, Paul, 86
Dupriez, Léon, 164
Dutch guilder, 32n75

E

economic crisis (2008), 5–6
'The Economic Consequences of Mr. Churchill' (Keynes), 20–1
Economists' National Committee on Monetary Policy (ENCMP), 75
Eichengreen, Barry, *Globalizing Capital*, 26, 26n53
Einaudi, Luigi, 18
Ellis, Howard, 164
embedded liberalism, 23
Emminger, Otmar, 2–3
empirical studies, 131n133, 131n134
Endres, Anthony, 9, 94–5, 94n220
epistemic expert community, 8, 94, 94n219
Erhard, Ludwig, 18, 122–3
Eucken, Walter, 46, 61, 105

Index

Europe, full convertibility of currency in, 31. *See also specific countries*
European Monetary Community, 158
European Payments Union, 62
expert advisory bodies, on policy, 106
Exter, John, 102–3n17, 164

F

fascism, rise of, 14–15
Fellner, William, 69, 69n123, 167
   Belaggio Group and, 73
   on central banks, 118–19
   on fixed exchange rates, 111
   on floating exchange rates, xvii, 111, 113, 156
   Friedman on, 127
   as a key actor, 102n16
   as member of CEA, 145
   as member of MPS, 9–10, 113–14n66, 114
   organised the Group of 32 Economists, 107
   participation in MPS conferences by, 100, 102, 164
   on policymakers, 119
   as president of AEA, 103
   rejection of gold standard, 112n61
   relationship with Nixon, 141
Ferrari, Alberto, 164
Ferrero, Rómulo, 103, 164, 168
finance, insurance and real estate (FIRE) sector, xiv
financial crisis (2008), vii
Fisher, Anthony, 105
fixed exchange rates, 22–37, 63, 63n96, 158n11
flexibalisation, 48, 59, 61–2, 65–6, 70, 75–8, 80–1, 83, 93–4, 103–4, 111, 124–6, 157–8
flexible exchange rates. *See* floating exchange rates
flexible exchange rate theory, hegemonisation of, 97–152
floating exchange rates, 35–6, 37n96, 45–6, 47n31, 48n34, 126n115, 127, 131, 131n134, 136–7, 156, 158
   in academic mainstream, 111
   advocacy of, 89–96
   in Canada, 128
   Friedman on, 38, 54–6, 54n55, 60, 101
   Haberler on, 120–1, 120n93
   Lutz on, 117
   Machlup on, 119–20
   neoliberal advocates of, 140–52
   popularisation of in private sector, 130
Ford Foundation, 107
foreign dollar reserves, growth of, 33
France
   monetary policy in, 81
   MPS members in, 17n11
   in 1960s, 33
'freedom fighters', 5, 45–8
free exchange rates. *See* floating exchange rates
'Free vs. Fixed Exchange Rates' (Friedman), 89–90, 89n202
Freiburg School of Ordoliberalism, 18, 46
French franc, 32n75
Friedman, Milton, 16, 17, 52n50, 168
   advocacy for floating exchange rates, x
   Capitalism and Freedom, 40
   'The Case for Flexible Exchange Rates', 55, 62–3
   Chicago Mercantile Exchange (CME) and, 152n218
   'Commodity-Reserve-Currency', 57–8
   on controls, 41, 63n97
   criticism of European Payments Union, 62

Friedman, Milton (*continued*)
  demands of, 125
  on dollar crisis, 158
  on exchange rate flexibility, 36–7n95
  on fixed exchange rates, 63, 63n96
  on flexibilisation, 61–2, 61n90, 75–7
  on floating dollar unilaterally, 126
  on floating exchange rates, xvii, 38, 54–6, 54n55, 60, 90–1, 101, 117, 126n115, 127, 131–2, 156
  'Free *vs.* Fixed Exchange Rates', 89–90, 89n202
  on gold price increase, 144
  on gold standard, 58, 58n7, 59n80, 74
  on Graham, 53–4
  as Group of 32 Economists and MPS member, 107–8n37
  letter to Davenport, 44–5
  letter to Haberler, 64
  as member of MPS, 9–10, 113–14n66, 114, 115, 130
  on monetarist rule, 59
  on MPS, 50
  on obstruction of democratic economic management, 61
  participation in MPS conferences by, 100, 102–3, 164–5
  presentations of, 162
  as president of American Economic Association (AEA), 103
  as president of MPS, 161
  on receiving letter from Machlup, 134n144
  relationship with Goldwater, 141n170
  relationship with Greenspan, 141n171
  relationship with Nixon, 141–2
  relationship with Shultz, 141n172, 148–9n206, 150
  on stabilising, 56
  turned down CEA post, 102–3n17
  Two Lucky People, 153
Friedman, Rose D., *Two Lucky People*, 153

G
Gandil, Christian, 12n33
General Arrangements to Borrow, 33
German Council of Economic Experts (SVR), 106, 122–4, 123n103, 123n106, 124n109
Germany
  capital controls in, 67
  German Council of Economic Experts (SVR), 106, 122–4, 123n103, 123n106, 124n109
  imported inflation, 46n27
  MPS members in, 17n11
  promotion of free-floating exchange rates in, 46
Giersch, Herbert, 113–14n66, 123, 137, 164, 169
Gilbert, Milton, 110, 110n52
Gilpin, Robert, 23
global foreign exchange trading, 159
Globalizing Capital (Eichengreen), 26, 26n53
gold currency standard, 26–7
gold reserves, shrinking of, 33
gold standard, xvii, 24–7, 25n47, 35–6, 43–6, 47n31, 53, 58–9, 59n80, 64–6, 68, 68n118, 74–5, 78, 82–3n176, 87–8, 94, 110, 110n49, 112, 112n61, 122, 158
Goldwater, Barry, 141n170
The Good Society (Lippmann), 15, 15n2
Gordon, Donald, 54
Graham, Frank D., 53, 57, 58n75, 104, 104n20, 162, 168
Gramsci, Antonio, xiii
Great Depression, vii–viii, 14–15
Great Society programme, 32
Greenspan, Alan, 141, 141n171

Index 179

Group of 32 Economists, 99
Group of Ten, 117
Grove, David, 137
Grubel, Herbert, 122n100, 164
Gudin, Eugênio, 103, 164, 169
Gutowski, Armin, 131n135, 164

H
Haas, Peter, 8, 96, 96n224, 109, 157
Haberler, Gottfried, 41, 46, 52n50,
    63, 67–9, 69n123, 80–1, 80n169,
    83n178, 91, 102n16, 125,
    146n194, 155, 169
  on benign neglect, 84–5, 143, 145
  as chair of Task Force on US
    Balance of Payments Policies of
    the President Elect, 142
  on conflicts of ideas, 81–2
  on controls, 88n197
  Currency Convertibility, 64
  on fixed exchange rates, 82
  on floating exchange rates, xvii, 9,
    113, 120–1, 120n93
  on gold price increase, 144
  on gold standard, 87–8
  as Group of 32 Economists and
    MPS member, 107
  'International Liquidity and
    Exchange Rates', 105
  on international money, 86
  as member of MPS, 9–10,
    113–14n66, 114, 115, 130
  *Money in the International
    Economy: A Study in Balance of
    Payments Adjustment,
    International Liquidity and
    Exchange Rates* (Haberler),
    82n175, 105
  participation in MPS conferences
    by, 100, 164
  presentations of, 162
  as president of American
    Economic Association (AEA),
    103
  promotion of neoliberal form of
    financial market liberalisation,
    133–4
  relationship with Nixon, 141
  The Theory of International Trade,
    63–4
  'U.S. Balance-of-Payments Policies
    and International Monetary
    Reform: A Critical Analysis',
    88n198
Hahn, Ludwig Albert, 52, 66–8,
    103n18, 124, 169
  as Group of 32 Economists and
    MPS member, 107
  as member of MPS, 113–14n66
  participation in key monetary
    conferences during 1960s, 164
  presentations of, 162
Hall, Peter, 93n217
Halm, George N., 113–14n66, 135,
    164
Hansen, Alvin, 95n221, 113–14n66,
    164
Harberger, Arnold, 103
  on floating exchange rates, 132
  as member of MPS, 113–14n66
  participation in key monetary
    conferences during 1960s, 164
  promotion of neoliberal form of
    financial market liberalisation,
    133–4
Harris, Ralph, 17
Harrod, Roy, 95n221, 102n16, 164
Hartwell, Ronald, 39, 49–50, 51n45,
    93n214, 97–8, 103
Hayek, Friedrich August von, 15–16,
    18, 170
  on distinction between 'original
    thinkers' and 'second-hand
    dealers in ideas', 49
  as founder of MPS, 4
  on gold standard, 58–59
  'The Intellectuals and Socialism', 20
  on Keynesian ideas, 20–1, 42–3

Hayek, Friedrich August von (*continued*)
  on liberalism and neoliberalism, 19
  as member of MPS, 9
  on monetary nationalism, 42
  'original thinkers', 22
  on power of ideas, 20n27
  as president of MPS, 161
  The Road to Serfdom, 41
  'second-hand dealers in ideas', 22, 22n36
  social-philosophical reflections of, 20
  study on gold standard, 21
Hazlitt, Henry, 162, 165, 170
hegemonisation, of flexible exchange rate theory, 97–152
hegemony, 20
Heilperin, Michael, 47, 52n50, 66–8, 74–5, 83, 102–3n17, 170
  on floating exchange rates, 84
  on gold standard, xvii, 58–9, 110n49, 112
  as Group of 32 Economists and MPS member, 9n23, 107
  participation in key monetary conferences during 1960s, 165
  presentations of, 162
Helleiner, Eric, 1–2, 9–10, 30, 148
  States and the Reemergence of Global Finance, xvii
Hesse, Jan-Otmar, 66
Hinshaw, Randall, 122n101, 165
Hirsch, Fred, 165
Houthakker, Hendrik, 113–14n66, 165
Huffschmid, Jörg, 160
Hunold, Albert, 15, 71, 106n28, 165
Hunold-Hayek crisis, 71
Hutt, William Harold, 82–3n176, 88, 162, 170

I
Iino, Tadashi, 137
Ikle, Max, 137

Ilau, Hans, 73–6, 162, 170
imported inflation, 46n27, 66–7, 66n112, 124
impossibility theorem, 24–5, 40
inflation
  capital controls and, 120
  in early 1920s, 47
  Friedman, on, 58
  gold price and, 75
  imported, 46n27, 66–7, 66n112, 124
  Keynesianism and, 42–3
  Machlup on, 79
  in 1970s, 149
  Powell on, 88
  Stein on, 145
  Vietnam War and, 32
'In Search of Guides for Policy' (Machlup), 119–20
Institute of Economic Affairs (IEA), 104–5
institutions, hegemonic possibilities and, 97–106
intellectual climate, of 1950s and 1960s, 35, 35n88
'The Intellectuals and Socialism' (Hayek), 20
international banking, growth of, 33–4
International Clearing Union, 31
'International Liquidity and Exchange Rates' (Haberler), 105
International Monetary Fund (IMF), 29–30, 33–5, 106–7, 111, 117, 128, 148, 151
International Monetary Policy (Odell), 147–8
international neoliberal advocacy network, 48–9
'The International Monetary System' panel, 72n133
Irmler, Heinrich, 162
Isard, Peter, 159

Index

J
James, Harold, 30
Japan
  on floating exchange rates, 137
  full convertibility of currency in, 31
  gold and, 25
  MPS members in, 17n11
Jewkes, John, 161
Johnson, Harry Gordon, xviii, 34, 51, 70–1, 91, 92n212, 102n16, 105, 121, 170–1
  on central bank, 127n120
  demands of, 125
  on floating dollar unilaterally, 126
  on floating exchange rates, 132
  Friedman on, 127
  as Group of 32 Economists and MPS member, 107
  as member of MPS, 113–14n66
  participation in MPS conferences by, 100, 165
  'The Role of Networks of Economists in International Monetary Reform' lecture, 101–2n15
Johnson, Lyndon B., 34
  Great Society programme, 32
Johnson, Thomas F., 103–4, 130, 130n129, 165
Jones, Homer, 127
Jong, Frits de, 165
Jouvenel, Bertrand de, 103, 113–14n66, 165

K
Kamitz, Reinhard, 128, 171
Kasper, Wolfgang, 103, 165
Kemmerer, Edwin, 104
Kemp, Arthur, 72–4, 162, 171
Kenen, Peter, 115n71, 165
Kennedy, John F., 34
Kennedy, Paul, 147n201
Keynes, John Maynard
  Bretton Woods and, 22
  demand management, 23
  'The Economic Consequences of Mr. Churchill', 20–1
  International Clearing Union, 31, 31n72
  Tract on Monetary Reform, 27n57
Kindleberger, Charles, 51, 69n124, 91–2, 99, 109, 165
Klaus, Václav, 18
Klein, Naomi, 101
Kojima, Kiyoshi, 165
Krause, Lawrence, 165

L
laissez-faire liberalism, 14–16, 150n211
Lamfalussy, Alexandre, 165
Leeson, Robert, 9, 9n22, 10, 160
Lindsay, Greg, 6
Lippmann, Walter, *The Good Society*, 15, 15n2
Lundberg, Erik, 107–8n37, 165
Lutz, Friedrich A., 46, 52, 52n50, 55–7, 60, 67, 69n123, 102n16, 105, 123, 131n135, 171

M
Machlup, Fritz, 41, 46, 50, 51n46, 52n50, 64–5, 69, 73, 75–6, 85–6, 86n187, 91–2, 171–2
  on adjustment of internal prices, 79–81
  attempting meetings with bankers, 134
  on Bellagio Group taxonomy, 116
  on central banks, 118, 119
  on controls, 120–1
  demands of, 125
  on fixed exchange rates, 111
  on floating dollar unilaterally, 126
  on floating exchange rates, xvii–xviii, 9, 76–7n155, 76–8, 101, 111, 113, 119–20, 134, 136, 137

Machlup, Fritz (*continued*)
   Friedman on, 127
   on gold standard, 65n105, 122
   influence on monetary policy by,
      108–9
   'In Search of Guides for Policy',
      119–20
   as member of MPS, 9, 113–14n66,
      114–15
   organised the Group of 32
      Economists, 107
   participation in MPS conferences
      by, 100, 102, 102n16, 165
   *Plans for Reform of the
      International Monetary System*,
      78–9
   presentations of, 162
   presented Bellagio findings to
      AEA, 112, 112n59
   as president of American Economic
      Association (AEA), 103
   at Princeton University, 104
   promotion of neoliberal form of
      financial market liberalisation,
      133–4
   on taxonomic differentiation,
      109–10
   testified at hearing of
      Congressional Monetary Policy
      Committee, 126
'Machlup-Fellner-Triffin schema', 109
Malkiel, Burton, 165
Marris, Stephen, 165
Marsh, Donald, 137
Marshall, James, 121
McCracken, Paul, 103, 144–5,
      145n189, 148, 172
   as member of MPS, 9–10, 130,
      130n129
   participation in key monetary
      conferences during 1960s, 165
   relationship with Nixon, 141
McKinnon, Ronald, 159
McLeod, Alex, 165

Meade, James, 60, 113–14n66, 165
Meiselman, David, 165
Meltzer, Allan, 103–4, 172
   on floating exchange rates, 132
   as member of MPS, 113–14n66
   participation in key monetary
      conferences during 1960s, 165
Metzler, Lloyd, 113–14n66
Meyer, Fritz W., 46, 67–8, 105,
      113–14n66, 123, 172
Mirowski, Phil, 11
Mises, Ludwig von, xvii, 41, 44, 46,
      58–9, 63, 85–6, 85n186, 172
Molsberger, Josef, 12
monetary nationalism, 42, 48, 48n34
monetary policy
   autonomous, 22–37
   as a political question, xi–xii
*Money in the International Economy:
   A Study in Balance of Payments
   Adjustment, International
   Liquidity and Exchange Rates*
   (Haberler), 82n175, 105
Mont Pèlerin Society (MPS), 14
   founding of, 4
   'freedom fighters', 5
   goal of, 154
   internal debates at conferences of,
      38–96
   membership of, 4n8, 5, 17n11, 18,
      18n19, 167–74
   patriarchal structure of, 2n4
   presentations of, 162
   presidents of, 161
   public relations initiatives, 99
   published mentions of, 98n3
   role of conferences and personal
      meetings, 51n48
   as a transnational neoliberal
      network, 14–22
   women in, 17–18n14
Morgenthau, Hans, 27–8
Morley, Felix, 130
MPS Newsletter, 100n11

Index

Müller-Armack, Alfred, 12
Mundell, Robert, 24n45, 60-1, 95n221, 102n16

N
Nash, John, 105
National Industrial Conference Board (NICB), 133
National Security Council, 135
nation-states, 32n77, 42
neoliberal advocacy, of floating exchange rates, 140-52
neoliberalism
  conceptualisation of freedom in, 41
  end of, xi
  monetary policy as a key problem for emerging, 38-45
  political project of, ix
  use of term, 18-19
neoliberal monetary policy
  contexts of, 14-37
  controversy of, 45-8
  floating exchange rate advocacy, 89-96
  functions of MPS conferences, 48-52
  as a key problem for emerging neoliberalism, 38-45
  1950s, 52-71
  1960s, 72-88
  origins of, 38-96
Neue Zürcher Zeitung (*NZZ*), 13, 55n59
New Economic Policy (NEP), 148-9n206
1950s, MPS conferences during, 52-71
1960s
  hegemonisation of flexible exchange rate theory during, 97-152
  MPS conferences during, 72-88
Nixon, Richard, x, 2, 34-7, 51-2, 68, 140-52, 140n166

non-fungible tokens (NFTs), xii
Nordmann, Jürgen, 11
Nurske, Ragnar, 28-9, 28n62
Nutter, Warren, 132n136

O
Odell, John S., 9-10, 33n82, 113n63, 138, 151-2
  International Monetary Policy, 147-8
Offelen, Jacques Van, 12n33
Ordo (journal), 12, 105, 112-13, 137
'original thinkers', 22, 49

P
Paish, Frank W., 103
paradigmatic formula, 80n169
pensée unique, 39, 39n4
persons, hegemonic possibilities and, 97-106
Plans for Reform of the International Monetary System (Machlup), 78-9
Plehwe, Dieter, xvii-xviii, 11, 20
Plickert, Philip, 11, 11n30
policy entrepreneurs, think tanks and journals as, 104
Polyani, Karl, 25-6
popularisation, interactivist model of, 7-8, 7n18
Powell, Enoch, 86-7, 105, 162, 172-3
private banks and economy, 128-40
Ptak, Ralf, 11

Q
quantitative easing (QE), xii-xiii

R
Ramonet, Ignacio, 39
Reagan, Ronald, 19-20
research brokers, think tanks and journals as, 104
Reuss, Henry S., 126
Ripon Society, 142, 142n177
The Road to Serfdom (Hayek), 41

Rockefeller, David, 129n126
Rockefeller Foundation, 107, 135
'The Role of Networks of Economists in International Monetary Reform' lecture, 101–2n15
Roosa, Robert V., 132
Röpke, Wilhelm, 9, 71–2, 105, 161–2, 173
Rothbard, Murray, 35
Rougier, Louis, 15
Rueff, Jacques, 43, 52n50, 71, 75, 81, 83, 122n101, 173
   on gold standard, xvii, 110n49, 112
   as Group of 32 Economists and MPS member, 107
   presentations of, 162
Ruggie, John, 23
Rüstow, Alexander, 71, 105

S
Safire, William, 149
Salant, Walter, 102n16
Scherrer, Christoph, 147
'schizophrenia', 76
Schoeck, Helmut, 65–6n107, 66
'scientisation of the social', 7, 7n16
Scitovsky, Tibor, 113
'second-hand dealers in ideas', 22, 22n36, 49
'secularised sect', 50
Seevers, Gary, 145n189
Sennholz, Hans, 58–9, 74, 162, 173–4
Shultz, George, 132, 141, 141n172, 148–9n206, 150, 150n212, 150n213
Simon, William E., 9, 150–1, 151n214, 174
Simons, Henry, 59–60
Skousen, Mark, 45, 92, 92n213
Smithsonian Agreement (1972), 150
Sohmen, Egon, 67, 69, 69n124, 83, 92, 102–3n17, 123, 123n106, 137, 174
   as Group of 32 Economists and MPS member, 107
   as member of MPS, 113–14n66
   presentations of, 162
Solomon, Ezra, 145, 145n189
Solomon, Robert, 117n78
Sowell, Tom, 17
special drawing rights (SDRs), 33, 33n82, 148
The Spread of Economic Ideas (Colander and Coats), 98n4
Starbatty, Joachim, 11–12
'Statement of Aims', 16–17n10
States and the Reemergence of Global Finance (Helleiner), xvii
Stein, Herbert, 103, 104, 129n124, 144, 145n188, 145n189, 149–50, 150n212, 151n216, 174
   on floating exchange rates, 132
   relationship with Nixon, 141
Stigler, George, 53, 103–4, 114n68, 132
   on floating exchange rates, 9, 132
   as member of MPS, 114
St. Louis Fed, 127
Stone, Diane, 104

T
Thatcher, Margaret, 19–20
The Theory of International Trade (Haberler), 63–4
think tanks, xviii, 22n36, 49, 97–8, 102, 104–5, 134, 155
Tooze, Adam, xiii
Tower, Edward, 166
Tract on Monetary Reform (Keynes), 27n57
trade unions, controversy over, 45n25
transnational elite network, 94, 94n219
transnational expert communities, 119
transnational neoliberal network, 14–22

Triffin, Robert, 32n78, 36, 79, 95n21, 102n16, 106, 111, 121
   on central banks, 118
   organised the Group of 32 Economists, 107
   participation in key monetary conferences during 1960s, 166
Two Lucky People (Friedman and Friedman), 153

U

United Kingdom (UK)
   abandonment of gold standard, 20–1
   adoption of Bretton Woods Monetary Agreement, 22–3
   Bank of England, 25, 31n72
   floating exchange rates in, 105
   MPS members in, 17n11
United Nations Conference on Trade and Development (UNCTAD), 5–6n11, 6
Uri, Pierre, 166
'U.S. Balance-of-Payments Policies and International Monetary Reform: A Critical Analysis' (Haberler and Willett), 88n198

V

Vanek, Jaroslav, 166

Veit, Otto, 52n50, 68, 162, 174
Villey, Daniel, 161
Viner, Jacob, 104n20, 166
Virginia School, 70
Volcker, Paul, 91, 147n201

W

Walker, Charles, 101, 166
Wallich, Henry C., 115n71, 116, 166
Wallis, Allan, 141
Walpen, Bernhard, 11, 20, 50
Walter Eucken Institute (WEI), 105
West, Robert L., 166
West German mark, 32n75
West German Sachsverständigenrat (German Council of Economic Experts, SVR), 106, 122–3, 123n103, 123n106, 124, 124n109
White, Harry Dexter, 22, 28
Whitman, Marina, 2, 145n189
Willett, Thomas D., 80n169, 88, 88n198, 135n146, 146, 146n194, 166
Woitrin, Michel, 166
women, in MPS, 17–18n14

Y

Yeager, Leland B., 70, 126, 166, 174